The real man smiles in trouble, gathers strength from distress, and grows brave by reflection.
—Thomas Paine

VAGABOND PILOT

A Journey of Discovery and Renewal

ROBERT J. YOUNG

RED SKY PRESENTS • NEW YORK

DEDICATION

To my Parents.

For Blanche Krosney Young, my dear Mother: You were filled with so much love, you taught me about giving one's self to make a difference for others.

For Sidney D. Young, my dear Dad: You went from working in a button factory to putting yourself through law school at night to become one of the most powerful and influential real estate lawyers in New York City. You blessed me with such abundance and opportunities, teaching me life's hard-learned lessons and inspiring me to be a Pilot.

You both always encouraged me to reach for the stars.

I hope I have made you proud.

RIP.

INTRODUCTION

---→

Life certainly does work in strange ways. I had always thought I would grow old and live out my days in my home in the cul de sac. Ocean views, my beloved Santa Monica Airport across the street, my plane awaiting trips about the west, swimming in the lap pool, comfortable, enjoying SoCal, the weather, the good life. No worries. *La Dolce Vita.*

Ha!

Not to be so. The Universe does what it must. Like when I had rented a home nearby for over sixteen years and a fire interrupted my entire life. Time to move on, I thought. Wouldn't you? In came a new love and a new house I'd always wanted, right up in the Mar Vista Hills, overlooking the Pacific, a view of SMO, my lap pool. Dreams do come true.

Crash.

Then to my shock, my beloved older brother with whom I worked for years, suddenly died. He, unbeknownst to me, had left so much legal baggage behind that my entire life was upended. No more house. No more cushion. Déjà vu all over again.

In 1972, rather than travel to Europe as then was the craze, I decided to see America and find out if what I had read and learned

about this vast land from "sea to shining sea" held up to my scru-
tiny. It was heady times. Men were exploring the moon. America
was booming. Oh, and there was some scuttlebutt going on about
a break-in into the Democratic Party's headquarters by Republican
Party operatives at a place called Watergate.

I had been convinced before I went away to college that we
Americans were all we were cracked up to be. But hearing others,
questioning a war as I came into adulthood amongst new lessons
learned with smarter and wiser college and law school friends, put
fissures into my blind patriotic fervor. I was keenly aware of the
hypocrisy of our leaders. So disappointed by my government. No,
Uncle Sam, say it isn't so!

An endless war in Viet Nam, deceit amongst our leaders. Attempts by our adults and our leaders to crush us adolescents, us
Boomers, with our new ideas. I needed some fresh air. A new perspective. Something to hold on to, something to give me direction.
Law school wasn't doing it for me. It was filled with soon-to-be-
lawyers, most of whom I would never call my friends, and whose
burgeoning arrogance and self-righteousness I came to detest. So
I decided I would see the USA. Me and my dog, Bozo. Camp out.
Explore.

Maybe even find Me.

I knew I couldn't go back to New York and work for my Dad
after graduating law school. We hadn't talked much in the last
few years. His disdainful observation in those days was inevita-
bly, "When are you getting a haircut?" At least, that's what I recall.
Anyway, my brother was already there. That shadow of sibling
rivalry had shaped me, ruled me all my life. I desperately needed
to find *Me*.

I was pained, heartbroken from the end of a serious first live-in love romance, and I didn't have a clue. California beckoned. Once Willie Mays had left New York when I was ten, all I ever dreamed about was the sunshine, California girls, and following my beloved Giants westward.

And so I did.

It is funny, isn't it, that once again, here I am, set to embark on another cross-country sojourn. This time, fulfilling a lifetime passion ever since I became a pilot, to fly across America in my own plane.

Years ago, upon graduating college, I couldn't become an airline pilot as I had long dreamed. I wrote to all the major airlines requesting an application for employment. To find contact information, I had to go to the library at my college to get a copy of the New York City phone book—couldn't just look it up on my phone or ask Siri. Back in those days, I had to turn all those pages the old-fashioned way. I had to actually read a book. And what a book that telephone directory was! A five-inch-thick treasure trove of information.

But all those airlines required perfect vision. So, what then was this blind-as-a-bat boy to do?

"Why don't you go to law school?" asked my dear Dad.

I had been enamored by his profession, loved picking him up at the train station where he would come down the stairs, leather brief case in hand, nattily dressed. He would take out his work at home and place it carefully on his desk, and it all seemed so important and so special. The onion skin copies of contracts, blue-backed documents, the order in which he placed them, the precision with which he reviewed them, were fascinating to me. And he was helping people. I saw how much his clients needed him when they arrived at our home. I was intrigued and impressed, as any child might be by my bigger-than-life father.

But in college, after I found a stint of Pre-Med not to my liking, I was turned on by political science, government, and how things worked. I fell in love with Constitutional Law as laid out by Professor Edward Beiser at Brown, but I still wanted to fly. Or be a sportscaster. Pursue my passions. But a lawyer?

"I don't want to go to law school," I told Dad. "I want to get a job and make money."

"You don't have to be a lawyer. Law school will give you a healthy background to do anything. You will know how the law works and effects business and just how much you can push the envelope."

I pondered his words.

"If you ever need a job, you won't have to depend on anyone else. You can always hang out your shingle and earn a living as a lawyer."

I pondered some more.

"And I'll pay for it!" Sidney Young did not get to represent the biggest builders and developers in New York City by not being a shrewd and wise negotiator.

"Sold!" I exclaimed.

And so it was.

I traveled about America with Bozo that last summer before the end of law school. Eleven weeks. KOA (Kamp Grounds of America) campgrounds. Driving out I-40. Wow! This place is huge. And then, meeting the Rocky Mountains. The Grand Canyon. California. It shaped me. The West beckoned. The Universe had spoken. Yes, this was where I would live. A job in LA clinched the deal.

I don't know what I will find out there all these years later. My eyes see things differently. I am not a child of twenty-four, but now a man nearing the end of his life journey. I am as excited as that naïve young law student was, going to see the USA in his F-85, 3-on-the-tree Oldsmobile. *Travels with Bozo* will now be *Travels with Two Niner Lima*. Different vehicle. Different perspective.

I am filled with questions about the future, life.

What's it all about, Alfie?

Moments.

But now, it is different. Even if the news is the same. Man is still as nuts and crazy as he was in 1972. Still waging wars. Israel and the Palestinians are still at it. Russia is still causing problems, trying still to be relevant. China, as always, the enigma. It is all beyond me now.

Receding like white noise.

I am a free soul. No more boundaries. No more future job, needing to be whoever I'm told to be. No, I surrender. I stand in awe at the years gone by, the life experiences I've had, the adventures that shaped me. Now, total and absolute surrender to the Universe. My guide, wherever it may take me, to whatever it might show me. No expectations. Just for me to be, to accept the delivery of its manifestations without doubts but only with the excitement to explore whatever that may be, along with my evolution from its instructions, these presents, its gifts.

I am experiencing for the first time of my existence in this incarnation a liberation from expectation and demand. I don't know what awaits me out there. Maybe it is all the same and it is just the years gone by that have taught me the lessons and shaped who I have become.

I have not a clue. But, I suspect fun awaits in the midst of discovery. Discovery of so much more.

And so many more miles to go before I sleep.

GLOSSARY OF AVIATION TERMINOLOGY

————————————————————————→

Air Traffic Control (ATC) *An elite group of more than 14,000 specialists who provide a vital public service to guide pilots, their planes, and 2.7 million daily passengers from taxi to takeoff, through the air and back safely on the ground.*

Annual Inspection *The inspection is performed at least each 12 calendar months by authorized persons to provide a complete and comprehensive inspection of the aircraft. The inspection determines the condition of the aircraft and the maintenance required to return the aircraft to an Airworthy condition.*

Automated Terminal Information Service (ATIS) *A continuous broadcast of recorded aeronautical information in busier terminal areas, including airports and their immediate surroundings.*

Automated Weather Observation Service (AWOS) *A fully configurable airport weather system that provides continuous, real time information and reports on airport weather conditions, operated, maintained and controlled by aviation service providers.*

Center of Gravity (CG) *Is the point over which the aircraft would balance. Its position is calculated after supporting the aircraft on at least two sets of weighing scales or load cells and noting the weight on each set of scales or load cells. It affects the stability of the aircraft. To ensure that the aircraft is safe to fly, the center of gravity must fall within specified limits established by the aircraft manufacturer.*

Commercial Airman Certificate *One of the FAA-issued pilot certificates as evidence that the individual is duly authorized to exercise certain piloting privileges. A commercial airman is one who may act as pilot- in-command of an aircraft for compensation or hire, as well as carry persons or property for compensation or hire. Training for the certificate focuses on a better understanding of aircraft systems and a higher standard of airmanship.*

Cruise Speed *Is the speed of the aircraft that is maintained in the cruise phase of flight. It is denoted as Vc in aeronautics.*

Debriefing *Is a report of a mission or project or the information so obtained. It is a structured process following an exercise or event that reviews the actions taken.*

Directional Gyro (DG) *Is a flight instrument used in an aircraft to inform the pilot of the aircraft's heading. It is sometimes referred to as the Direction Indicator or by its more modern term as the Heading Indicator.*

Dorsal Fin *Is an extension to the vertical stabilizer, or tail, of an aircraft. Its main purpose is to improve directional stability.*

Emergency Locator Transmitter (ELT) *Is an emergency position-indicating radiobeacon, used in emergencies to locate airplanes, vessels, and persons in distress and in need of immediate rescue.*

Federal Aviation Administration (FAA) *A governmental body of the United States of America with powers to regulate all aspects of civil aviation in that nation as well as over its surrounding international waters.*

Federal Aviation Regulations (FARs) *Rules prescribed by the FAA governing all aviation activities in the United States.*

Fixed Base Operator (FBO) *Is an organization granted the right by an airport to operate at the airport and provide aeronautical services such as fueling, hangaring, tie-down and parking, aircraft rental, aircraft maintenance, flight instruction, and similar services.*

Flight Service Station (FSS) *An air traffic facility that provides information and services to aircraft pilots before, during, and after flights, but unlike Air Traffic Control, is not responsible for giving instructions or clearances or providing separation.*

Foreflight *Is an integrated flight app on iPad, iPhone and the web which provides flight planning, aviation weather, maps and charts for pilots and aircraft.*

Gross Weight (GW) *Is the sum of the weights of the aircraft, fuel, crew, passengers, and cargo.*

Ground Control *Is the controller, usually situated in the Tower, who controls all ground traffic and movement at the airport and on its runways and taxiways.*

XVI		R O B E R T J. Y O U N G

High Pressure *Is when the air has higher pressure which results in dry weather with mostly clear skies with larger diurnal temperature changes due to greater radiation at night and greater sunshine during the day.*

Hypoxia *Is a condition in which the body or a region of the body is deprived of an adequate oxygen supply at the tissue level. It generally occurs in healthy people when they ascend to high altitude, where it causes altitude sickness leading to potentially fatal complications: high altitude pulmonary edema (HAPE) and high altitude cerebral edema (HACE). At altitude, the symptoms develop gradually and can include fatigue, numbness/tingling of extremeties, confusion/disorientation, reduced level of breathlessness, and loss of pallor.*

Instrument Flight Rules (IFR) *A set of regulations that dictate how aircraft are to be operated when the pilot is unable to navigate using visual references under visual flight rules.*

Instrument Rating *Refers to the qualifications that a pilot must have in order to fly under instrument flight rules. In order to obtain this rating, a pilot must have logged at least 50 hours of cross-country flight time as pilot in command, with a total of 40 hours of actual or simulated instrument time on the areas of operation to be tested.*

Instrument Currency *To maintain an instrument rating, the pilot must maintain his/her instrument currency, which requires that a pilot must have performed and logged six (6) instrument approaches, holding procedures and tasks, and show capability to intercept and track courses through the use of navigational electronic systems.*

Lift *Lift is the force that directly opposes the weight of an airplane and holds the airplane in the air. It is mostly generated by the wings of an aircraft due to the shape of the wings.*

Low Pressure *Is when the air has lower pressure and usually brings stormy weather and has counterclockwise winds.*

Lycoming Engine *Lycoming Engines is a major American manufacturers of aircraft engines. With a factory in Williamsport, Pennsylvania, it produces a line of horizontally opposed, air-cooled, four, six and eight-cylinder engines.*

Magnetic Compass *Is an instrument that has a magnetic needle that can turn freely upon a pivot and align itself with the Earth's magnetic field, and indicate the direction of the magnetic north of the planet's magnetosphere.*

May Day Code *Is an international distress call used in voice communications advising that the plane is in danger of crashing to the ground. The specific squawk code for the transponder indicating this status as an all-out emergency is 7700.*

Military Operations Area (MOA) *Is an airspace established to separate or segregage certain nonhazardous military activities from IFR traffic and to identify for VFR traffic where these activities are conducted.*

Pitch *Is the up or down movement of the nose of the aircraft along the transverse axis of the aircraft.*

Private Airman's Certificate *One of the FAA-issued pilot certificates that allows the holder to act as pilot in command of an aircraft privately, not for remuneration. Different types of private licenses are issued for the major categories of aircraft, including lighter than air aircraft, rotorcraft, fixed wing aircraft, glider aircraft, powered lift aircraft, powered parachute, and weight-shift control aircraft.*

Roll *Is the up and down movement of the wings of the aircraft, caused by a deflection of the ailerons, along the longitudinal axis of the aircraft.*

Sectional Map *Is an aeronautical chart, or map, designed to assist in the navigation of the aircraft. Sectional charts typically cover a total area of 340 x 340 miles, printed on both sides of the map. Using these charts, pilots are able to determine their position, safe altitude, best route to a destination, navigation aids along the way, alternative landing areas in case of an in-flight emergency, and other useful information such as radio frequencies and airspace boundaries.*

Special Flight Rules Corridor *Is a special flight rules area in which the normal regulations of flight do not apply in whole or in part, especially concerning airspace classification, altitude, course, and speed restrictions. The Los Angeles Special Flight Rules Corridor provides two routes, one for southeast-bound traffic and one for northwest- bound traffic, at 3,500 feet and 4,500 feet, respectively, following the Santa Monica VOR 132 degrees radial between the Santa Monica Airport and the intersection of Interstate 405 and Imperial Highway.*

Surface Area of Wing *Is the area of the wing, calculated from a top-down view and measuring the area of the wing. It is an important value when calculating the performance of an airplane.*

Tower *Usually a tall, windowed structure located on the airport grounds, it is responsible for airport operations including flight data, clearance delivery, ground control, and local control (usually within five miles of the airport).*

Trainer *Is a class of aircraft designed specifically to facilitate flight training of pilots and aircrews.*

Transponder *Is an electronic device that produces a response when it receives a radio-frequency interrogation to assist in identifying the aircraft on air traffic control radar. Air traffic control units use the term "Squawk" when they are assigning a transponder code.*

True Air Speed *Is the speed of an aircraft relative to the airmass in which it is flying.*

Two Niner Lima *Is the Air Traffic Control name and lingo for the subject aircraft in this Journey, N9329L.*

Vertical Stabilizer *Is the fin of the aircraft, or its tail, typically found on the aft end of the fuselage body, intended to reduce aerodynamic side slip and provide directional stability to keep it flying straight.*

Visual Flight Rules (VFR) *A set of regulations under which a pilot operates an aircraft in weather conditions clear enough to allow the pilot to see where the aircraft is going.*

VOR *A Very High Frequency (VHF) Omni-Directional Range (VOR) is a type of short-range radio navigation system for aircraft, enabling aircraft with a receiving unit to determine its position and stay on course by receiving radio signals transmitted by a network of fixed ground radio beacons.*

Wingspan *Is the distance from one wingtip to the other wingtip of the airplane.*

Yaw *Is the side to side movement of the nose of an aircraft caused by the deflection of the rudder of the aircraft, a hinged section at the rear of the vertical stabilizer.*

CHAPTER 1

———————————————————————→

PREPARATION AND PRE-FLIGHT PLANNING

PAVE
PILOT
AIRCRAFT
ENVIRONMENT
EMOTION

THE PILOT:

I'M SAFE

Illness – Do I have any symptoms? All doctors visited and signed off.

Medication – Have I been taking prescription or over-the-counter drugs? Yes, but none that effect performance.

Stress – Am I under psychological pressure from the job? Worried about financial matters, health problems, or family discord?

See below. Acceptable levels not too extreme to interfere or effect Pilot performance.

Alcohol – Have I been drinking within 8 hours? 24 hours?
   No.
Fatigue – Am I tired and not adequately rested?
   No. Ready to go!
Eating – Am I adequately nourished?
   Will be prepared for each leg and in-flight snacks will be carried. Water. Other snacks.

Planning and preparing for my Journey across America adventure was not like just hopping into my plane to head up the coast to Camarillo, a twenty-minute jaunt I have done countless times since I learned to fly at Santa Monica Airport back in 1979. No, there was lots more to consider, plan, and prepare.

One of most remarkable things that has changed for me since I have been a pilot was how my flying lessons and skills have incorporated themselves into my everyday life. Getting ready for this sojourn would require every bit of that.

To begin, I wanted my friends to know I would be visiting now that life and the Universe were bringing me changes, and I would be able to accomplish a dream I have had for so many years. Time was squeezing into precious moments and, like most, I, too, had my bucket list. This trip was one item that first beckoned. So, I put this post out on Facebook:

✈ ✈ ✈

Robert Young
March 27 · Many of you have known me for years and know

me well. Some of you do not and might not understand. But now, a new chapter and many new adventures begin.

I have been doing the same thing since after I was a boy in college and learned that I couldn't be an airline pilot due to my poor vision (which in those days had to be 20-20). It had been my life-long dream, but my father said go to law school, and so I did.

As I gained more life perspective, had some knocks, and re-evaluated what was important to me, decades of lawyering (mainly as a litigator, always fighting), lost its appeal. Being in service to others for so long has come with the inevitable stress that accompanied career and familial responsibilities. So, now, it is time for *me*, and to see what life still has to offer. The discipline of getting to the desk every day and dealing with, and doing for, others is being re-configured. Now, do for those as I choose, no set routine, no expectations, no plans. Just bring it on, Universe!

Compelled to sell Dewey, the home I finally owned, closing it was not as bad as I had imagined. After I had sorted all my belongings and decided what treasures to keep, I watched it all taken away to be put into storage.

I had the remainder hauled away, and the house was not my home anymore. Just a house.

I am hanging out in Camarillo with my dear friends, Bruce and Dolly, and planning my first adventure, one which I have wanted to do for years after doing it twice by car. This time I will fly across the USA in my beloved Two Niner Lima and hope to stop and see many of you this late spring and summer. Want to stop and smell the flowers—no rush, no schedule. Further, to see as many air museums as well as you all. Departure is roughly planned for some time in early May and the journey will last through the summer. Then, back to LA to see what's next, or where, or whatever.

Look for *The Adventures of Capt. Bob and Two-Nine Lima* and the *Walk Our Talk Tour* on fb pages coming soon.

Love to you all.

✈ ✈ ✈

I had said a lot but honestly, most of it wasn't exactly all true. Things were a lot worse.

What had been happening to me the past decade, after answering my older brother's call for help back in 2009, was nothing short of stress, difficulties, and the awful discovery of dark family secrets filled with deceit and avarice. What I had believed in was all gone. Mistakes and misjudgments were made. Our parents and my older brother were now deceased. All of them, gone. Those who I had always lived for, sought their approval, desperate for their love, all gone.

Everything they left behind fell upon me. Family businesses and responsibilities. And all their bad stuff as well. I still have not recovered.

When I answered my brother's call to take over the family law practice in which I had for years wanted to be a part, little did I know who my older brother was, what he had become, and how he dealt with his family, friends, and clients. Despite my antennae registering something on the radar, he vowed to me before he died, or disappeared—which is a whole other story—that he was telling me the whole truth. But dishonesty and compartmentalization of his life were his norm, and to my dismay, the darkness in which he lived found me after his demise.

Seemed he stole or misappropriated, or whatever he did, millions of dollars from clients, or so my attorney calculated from remnants of the few documents and files he forgot and left behind. And while no one complained to me, a few had complained to someone before his end. One went to the District Attorney about which my brother told me, but no charges would be brought, or so he said. Some purported Mafia guys threatened him, and he confessed to me he was scared for his life and safety, especially from one individual. Other clients sued his estate and included me and the firm. There was no malpractice insurance to cover his misdeeds. I spent so much money on defense, and I need not tell you the inordinate amount of stress that accumulated over the years and ate at me.

Without him, business began to dwindle. I had to spend more money on attorneys, some good, some awful. Usually the ones I chose because of their loyalty as a friend proved to be worse than most.

But throughout it all, I felt I would succeed. I always did. Still do. The athlete in me always thinks I can win. Like when I played soccer in college, I would walk on the field on game day, certain I would score a few goals. Usually, I did. I was young, fast, nimble and quick like a fox, pouncing on opportunities. The moniker stuck and my college friends still, to this day, call me Fox. But the speed went, my business agility was not as keen as I thought I was, and financial losses were compounded by a major judgment in excess of three million dollars assessed against me because of my brother's wrongdoing into which I was dragged.

I was forced into bankruptcy when I could not sell my home at a price sufficient to pay off this client-judgment creditor of my brother's, who was now hell-bent-on-wheels to get even with me and his former attorney, my dear departed brother, who he claimed had swindled him out of his life savings.

"Me?" I protested. "I am not my brother's keeper. I had nothing to do with it. I lived in California."

Didn't matter. My name was the same.

My brother's family did nothing to make reparations for his misdeeds, despite my request after discovery of all of this after his death. And nary a word I heard from his children or his widow anymore.

Well, then, gosh, I thought. *Bankruptcy might not be so bad.* I had too many creditors from my minor league baseball venture days, the house was getting too expensive for me, and my love for the law was fading. A break-in at my house while I was sleeping was the message from the Universe. Time to move on.

By a Chapter 7, at least, I could clear up my debts and receive my Senior Homeowner's Exemption of one hundred seventy-five thousand bucks. That would be a nice chunk of change to begin anew.

Little did I realize what would happen. When the house was sold at a price even way below the last offer I got (before I had to file my petition) no Senior Homeowner's Exemption was granted. I was now facing the prospect of nowhere to go because I had not bothered to save any money. All I had was the equity in my home. I had to move out, now homeless, crippled financially, and having no idea what was next. I was in despair and was feeling, *wow!*

This is the end? Now what?

Throw in heart issues that have befallen me, and, well, it wasn't so pleasant. I knew I had to be well enough to take this journey, so I visited all my physicians and got their approval. Yes, it sure made sense to check off all the ailments and doctors and make sure the pilot was good to go. Cardiologist? Check. Prostate? Check. GP, annual exam? Check. Eye doctor? Check.

I am a tough old mule, stubborn, and still have that athlete in me. *Things will get better*, I thought. *I will survive. I always do. As long as I am healthy and able, that is what counts.* So having those last-minute check-ups and okays to go was an important item on my checklist.

Now I measured my riches, not in dollars and accumulations, but by the friends I have, and the precious commodity of time not to be wasted. I was becoming real Zen. Or rationalizing so skillfully to hold onto my sanity.

Bruce and Dolly, my dearest friends, remembered how I took care of them when they first moved to California, when they were virtually penniless after a business failure and bankruptcy. I cashed in my chips and found refuge in their beautiful home up in Camarillo, where they welcomed me and nourished me with their friendship and support.

Flying across America and seeing my friends and getting the love and nourishment I needed would be an answer. For now. I had no choice but to allow the Universe to show me what would be next. I didn't want to crawl into a hole and give up.

Oh, I thought. *I can be very good at wallowing. But time grows short. Stents in my heart to correct the same malady that befell my dear brother tick every day. Silently, yes, but the end is nearer.* Even though in some strange way death seemed so inviting—after all, no more worries and concerns about being penniless and homeless—but that surely was no solution.

I was scared. Of what, I didn't know. Perhaps, it wasn't fear and anxiety. But the obvious change was beginning; more evolution was in the air and I had no idea what it was, where I was going, or who I would be. Far cry from when I chose, or was compelled to choose, to go to law school. Then, I knew the goal. At this point, I didn't know where the goal line was, never mind what the goal was supposed to be.

But isn't that what must be for all of us, at some time—that which supplies our forward motion, to keep going, keep moving? The basic survival instinct? Like the shark who has to keep moving or die. A fear that wells up and almost overcomes us, so we power back, keep our wings level, and fly through the turbulence. And, hopefully, come out the other side.

I will get into Two Niner Lima and fly, I resolved, certainly to tomorrow, to new adventures, new locales, new sites. I will see, feel, and taste America again. Find a new home. Find a new beginning.

Really, find *Me*? Or so I thought I might.

Life was too precious to dawdle. Mortality had its firm grip on me, and it was quickly approaching. It was time. Capt. Bob was okay to go.

CHAPTER 2

-->

PAVE

<u>P</u>ILOT
<u>A</u>IRCRAFT
<u>E</u>NVIRONMENT
<u>E</u>MOTION

THE AIRCRAFT
N9329L
AA-1x/150 h.p.

American Aviation, a company based in Cleveland, Ohio, built my plane in 1971. Jim Bede designed this novel aircraft, which didn't use rivets on its wings, but a special bonding glue.

Its formal aircraft type number is AA-1A, as this is the second, up-graded model made by American Aviation. It was the 39th AA-1A manufactured and its serial number, 0039, is embossed on a metal identification tag attached on the rear of the fuselage.

It is not the same as the AA-1, which had a bad reputation for a trainer, as it was too hot and too fast, built with a small wing. Less surface area requires more speed to compensate for the reduced lift generated by the smaller wing. Novice pilots weren't doing too well flying them, so American Aviation modified the wing to make the plane a bit more docile for beginning pilots, as it was the first of its models, or the trainer, a two-seat version.

Its formal registration with the Federal Aviation Administration, who is master over all flying in the USA, is N9329L. Or, in pilot lingo, Niner Three Two Niner Lima. When Grumman American took over the failing American Aviation, these planes became known as Grummans, so my true call sign when contacting Air Traffic Control (ATC) is "Grumman Two Niner Lima."

She is not too big. She has two seats and, thus, can only carry two people, the pilot and passenger. She has an empty weight of 1,062 pounds and, with thirty-two gallons of fuel, baggage, and crew, she cannot exceed 1675 pounds, or her legally allowed gross weight.

Her cabin is forty-one inches wide and forty-five inches high. She is 19.24 feet from the tip of her nose (the spinner on the propeller) to the tail. Her wing span is 24.46 feet. She stands 6.80 feet tall.

To step into her I have to first climb up on the wing-walk on her left wing adjacent to the fuselage, and then slip into the pilot's seat, like a Mercury astronaut getting into his crammed space capsule. Picture a small MGB or Triumph Spitfire as about her size, but with wings.

Yes, I refer to my aircraft as a female. I have not christened her with a name, per se. I call her My Girl, or Baby, when I really need her. I talk to her before we take off and gratefully pat her on the nose after every trip.

She has treated me well.

This type aircraft was originally designed for a 108 horsepower, four-cylinder Lycoming engine. When I bought the plane for $13,900 in 1994, after the Northridge Earthquake scared the bejee-zus out of me, I realized I better do the one thing I love the most more often.

I flew the plane for nine years before I needed to replace the engine. Aircraft engines are different than car engines. Their effectiveness is measured by their compression capacity in each cylinder, as well as the time in service.

So, in 2003, when the engine could not meet its power standards, it was time for a new one. Now, aircraft engines are not cheap. Plus, I was not happy with the performance of the 108 h.p. engine. Although it sipped relatively little fuel (six or seven gallons per hour) and could even use automobile gas (which I used many times, lugging my ten-gallon, red plastic fuel tanks back and forth to the 76 Station across the street from the Santa Monica Airport), I always felt the plane under-powered and struggling, especially if I had a passenger.

I looked into adding a bigger engine and did so, employing the services of Ken Blackman and Northwest Mods, based up in Washington near Spokane. Ken was the Grumman Guru and one of the nicest souls I have come across in the flying world. He had a modification to add a 160 h.p. engine, de-rated to 150 h.p., by Lycon Engines, with auxillary fuel tanks to handle the higher fuel burn rate, plus a dorsal fin to diminish any yaw tendencies because of the added power.

What a difference it has made.

Two Niner Lima is like a rocket ship now, with just me on board. Add a passenger and there is no problem for the aircraft. Trust me when I tell you, but every pilot wants that extra power in his right hand when he pushes in the throttle. Having that capacity in Two

Niner Lima has made me grateful to have kept the machine for all these years. New avionics completed the overhaul.

Because of the modification, or the Blackman Conversion, the plane's formal identifier is AA-1x (150 h.p.), but it really is a 160 h.p. engine. If you need that extra ten horsepower, it is still there. I still don't understand why it was "de-rated" but I surmise that when Ken was obtaining the Supplemental Type Certificate from the FAA, showing the government why they should allow this modification, the issue came up and hence only up to 150 h.p. was allowed.

Reconfigured with a new engine, the aircraft now burns approximately ten to eleven gallons per hour and cruises at 130 knots true (its speed through still air). Of course, we pilots ride the winds, so going eastbound I knew I would be the beneficiary of tail winds a good portion of the time. Flight planning sets up 130 knots as my cruise speed and that specific fuel burn in planning each leg, which cannot encroach over three hours before I only have half an hour left in the tanks equal to my required reserve. On my trip to Phoenix and Tucson in December to see if my journey was doable, I had almost a thirty-knot tail wind, seeing a ground speed at 157 knots, or 172 miles per hour. Not too shabby!

Every year, a pilot's plane must be certified as airworthy. At that point, Two Niner Lima's last annual was done in October, 2018, so by the end of November, 2019, I would then need to have my mechanics at Bill's Air Center at Santa Monica Airport put Two Niner Lima through its annual inspection.

I really didn't need that now as I had been flying frequently, but I did need a good check-up, change the oil and tighten the nuts and bolts, so to speak.

I had no other complaints, or squawks, as we pilots say, for

Andre, Dennis and the crew at Bill's Air to deal with, except for the Emergency Locator Transmitter (ELT), which was inoperative, awaiting a new battery. An ELT will go off in a crash, or you can self-activate it, and it will broadcast a May Day Morse Code on the radio, along with your aircraft identifier, over an assigned radio frequency at 122.5 Mhz. Flight Service Stations throughout America, which handle weather and other services for pilots (including opening and closing flight plans) will pick up any such signal and report its location to the authorities. An immediate search and rescue mission will then be launched and directed by the FAA to look for the downed aircraft. I had to replace the ELT on Two Niner Lima when the battery was going, and it was broadcasting the distress signal when I was parked at the airport. I got a call from the Airport Administration alerting me to the problem. So, I had a new ELT, fresh oil and a new sunshade installed. Two Niner Lima was ready to go.

In addition, I added some cameras and a recording device to capture the trip. Now, don't get too excited—I was just learning how to use the Go Pro, as well as how to hook up the iPhone camera and video and tie it into the communications console where I plugged in my headsets. I knew that once I did, *voila!* The video would play back my voice speaking to the camera as well as ATC communications to Two Niner Lima. The iPhone camera had been mounted on the right front window over the glare shield. The Go Pro was positioned behind me on the speaker console, and if I get it just right, the viewer would see the back of my head, the instrument panel, and the view of the flight forward. I planned to experiment in video, timed photos, and bursts as the Go Pro is quite the little capable device, which I had barely mastered, barely able to turn it on and get it set up. As to editing into movies, well, I knew we'd have to see about that, but I hoped enough to be able to post the passage of my journey across America and share it with my friends as I went.

Because I have flown predominantly out of Santa Monica for my entire flying career, having first started in 1979, and obtaining my Private Certificate, Single-engine land aircraft, on Leap Year Day, February 29, 1980, I have flown in very stable weather. Southern California is known for its moderate weather, mainly because high pressure usually sits off the coast and warms us. It does us a bigger favor forcing any low pressure-based rain and storms careening down from the north, emanating out of the Gulf of Alaska, up and over the ridge of the high pressure. That's why we have so little rain in SoCal, which made this pilot the beneficiary of flying mainly in benign, stable weather in the Southwest.

Now weather is more of a concern. The Midwest and East do not have the good weather California enjoys. Not being on a schedule would be good, I thought, as it would allow me to fly only in good weather conditions. One never wants to be flying in a light, single engine aircraft in inclement conditions. Although I am instrument-rated, certified to fly single-engine land and multi-engine land aircraft in instrument meteorological conditions under Instrument Flight Rules (IFR), I am not current. Currency is self-policed and requires a certain number of approaches and holds every six months, to which I did not adhere. If push came to shove, however, and knowing my airplane, I could do it, but I did not want to get current and even consider that. It puts undue pressure on the pilot and machine. This was a trip where I wanted none of that.

But, stuff does happen. And a good pilot has to be prepared and analyze and weigh risk. We do that all the time when we are required to get a weather briefing from Flight Service before departure. Well, no, it is no longer Flight Service who provides the weather briefings for pilots. The FAA terminated that function and sold it to a private bidder. Now, it is Lockheed Flight Service but I still call the same 800 number: 1-800-WXBRIEF.

To be more aware of the weather, I have now gone digital. Yes, I know, sometimes it is so difficult to be dragged into the modern age. I have resisted it for a while even with flying, but to give myself more information, I purchased a new iPad and a yoke mount where I would be able to have synthetic vision and current weather on my screen. Foreflight is an incredible application, so now it is on both my iPhone and iPad and I will be using it as well. I have always done my flight planning and flying using a paper sectional map of the area and a good pen and pencil to draw my route but now, with Foreflight (as any modern device), it sure makes things easier. Foreflight would show the current weather along my route of flight. Rain, winds, anything on my route, all programmed ahead of departure. The more I do to feel prepared, the more confident I am, and the outcome I seek — a safe journey — is more assured.

Lastly, I had heard from many of my friends about this trip and how scared and worried they were for me. Of course, the love and support was touching, and as a pilot of thirty-nine years, I most certainly am aware of the measured risk I take every time I fly. But, I was seeing this trip, as it would be, as a series of short trips, which I have been doing about the southwest for years.

After all, that is what flying cross-country in a small plane means. I have only thirty-one usable gallons of fuel on board, and burn that fuel at a rate of ten to eleven gallons per hour. That puts me up against three hours flying time. I plan for three hours maximum anyway, since that would give me the legal requirement of half an hour of fuel remaining. That's the required reserve necessary when flying under Visual Flight Rules (VFR). However, sitting in a small aircraft for that amount of time, or at least in Two Niner Lima, my bladder has taught me that three hours is time enough, despite having a Porta Johnny on board for those emergencies when you just got to go.

Two Niner Lima is good to go.

CHAPTER III

————————————————————————✈

PAVE

PILOT
AIRCRAFT
ENVIRONMENT
EMOTION

EMOTION

When I was so depressed after a divorce, I thought I could just take the plane up and fly and feel better. I was terribly wrong. Divorce, and my reaction to it, was something I couldn't escape. When I tried it, I started crying as soon as I was up in the air, after only a few moments of exhilaration when the wheels left the runway, before the pain jumped out again, still too great.

That was my first experience of how emotional context can affect the pilot in command. I quickly returned to Santa Monica Airport and didn't fly again until I was long past the debilitating emotional pain to risk my welfare and safety. It's not like driving a car where you can just get in, and almost go on autopilot, regardless of any emotions present. Flying is a different story. The pilot

in command has to be in good mental and emotional states before
he or she takes to the air.

Thus, for my journey across America, I am extra vigilant on
how I am feeling under my present circumstances. I have been
through personal hell financially, as well as emotionally, these past
few years, losing my home, and basically now, homeless and penniless. Well, I do have a few pennies in the bank, enough to get going, and with social security and a few passive income receipts, as
well as work I am doing here and there as a lawyer, there is enough
to keep the coffers filled and buy enough gas along the journey to
make it so.

But really, I am not so sure I am in the best emotional condition. Not enough to deter me, as the pain has receded a bit. I have
my bearings, I am excited by the challenge, and I have been up in
Two Niner Lima getting ready, with no ill effects. But, in a broader
sense, I have been wondering about what, exactly, is going on with
my life journey and I wonder if this is just more defeat, the last hur-
rah, the end. Or, perhaps, just perhaps, the Universe is bringing me
to new adventures and new beginnings.

What I am trying to share with you is that I have admitted to
myself, this athlete who could score a goal anytime and succeed,
no matter what the obstacles, that I have lost hope about a better tomorrow and a better future. I have been so beaten down by
happenings that sometimes lately I cannot muster the strength
and fortitude to keep it all together and keep on going. I have
caught myself forcing a smile. I have caught my mind aimlessly
wandering.

I wonder about death. No more worrying about whether I will
have a roof over my head, and enough to eat, to continue to sustain
myself. I wouldn't have to worry about where I would be living or

what I might be able to afford. And so I think, well, maybe this is the end, and this trip could very well be it. *No mas. Finis.* Lights out. Is the Universe that cruel? Or, dare I even think, so wise?

Oh, now don't get me wrong. I am not looking to "buy the farm" or do anything rash but why, oh why—and how—did I manage to lose my home, my dear Dewey, the house I had fitted to my every dream and desire? I'd had it all, and then it was gone. I didn't do a good job, of course, and can't rail against what happened, since I do believe in taking responsibility for everything.

But it was like, well, really? I have to go? To where? I had just found my cousin, his wife and precious baby daughter, a home around the corner. Family was in the neighborhood. So, now I have to leave? Not see him raise his family? Off to where? No longer comfortable, forced into "begging" friends for a place to stay. I have fallen so far from the life I lived that I feel pretty shitty, to put it mildly. Beaten up. Ouch! I never knew such despair. Nor could I admit it before.

But I want to know. I want a reason. I always want to understand what is happening to me. That's the pilot in me. Trouble shoot the problem. Examine the parameters of the aircraft. What is it doing? What am I doing?

Now, I do not know. And in a few days, off I will go, hoping for an answer, for some direction, some glimmer to make me believe, make me feel that life, even with the years running out, is still so worth it, to enjoy and revel in being alive. I want to shake the pain, shake this morass I am slogging through. Wallowing in question serves no purpose.

So, off I must go. I have created a challenge and hope the stimulation and nourishment from friends helps me find Me again.

The excitement of the upcoming adventure far outweighs the emotional turmoil I have gone through. The Pilot has reviewed his emotional state and placed it in its proper perspective and context. Captain Bob is good to go.

CHAPTER IV

————————————————————————————————→

LEG ONE

May 24, 2019
SMO – AVQ with fuel stop at NYL
Santa Monica Airport, Santa Monica, CA, to Marana Regional
Airport, Tucson, AZ, with fuel stop at Yuma, AZ.
Distance: 398 nm
Route: SMO-OCN-JLI-IPL-NYL-AVQ
Start time (SMO): 9:12 a.m
Shut Down time (NYL): 11:28a.m. Start time (NYL): 12:10 p.m.
Shut down time (AVQ): 1:48 p.m.

Log Entry: SMO-NY: 2.4 hrs. Good flight. Bumpy on descent.
Slow ground speed down coast to OCN. Climb up to 9,500' to
clear San Diego mountains. Unfamiliar at NYL Tower inop.
NYL-AVQ: 1.7 hrs. Ok flight. Climb to 9,500' for smooth air.
Avoided MOAs.
Good landing.

I hadn't slept well the night before. Restless, I finally got back to my friend's home to crash after a long day — a doctor appointment in the morning, a ton of errands, and packing up Two Niner Lima. I was beat and needed a good rest, but it was not to be.

I had it all planned out. Two Niner Lima could handle the additional cargo in its small baggage compartment behind its two seats. To get through the summer, I needed to take all my clothes and belongings not in my POD in storage. I secured my suitcase with the straps used to hold down the cargo in this aircraft. Into the new carboard box I got with the sleeping bag from Amazon, I placed the old box of supplies and my tool kit, along with the Windex and paper towels, duct tape, and some extra hats, and the new sleeping bag. Then I pushed the box against the rear bulkhead. In between the suitcase and this carboard box of supplies and sleeping bag, I put my backpack and another two small, carry-on small duffel-type bags filled with my sweat suit and other warm clothing items. I laid my nice shirts, sports coat and pants wrapped in a suit garment bag on top. The compartment was stuffed. I would do the camera set-up when I arrived at the airport in the morning.

Although the cargo compartment was full, I was not worried that Two Niner Lima couldn't handle the full load, as it only had the weight of one passenger and the full fuel — close to the gross weight limitations of 1,675 pounds Two Niner Lima could lawfully carry (if not a few pounds over). I was not concerned.

Ken Blackman of N.W. Airmods, the Grumman Guru whose modification of Two Niner Lima I had installed in 2003, had told me when he delivered my plane back to me that I had plenty of power in my right hand. I could fly the plane over the gross weight limitation and she would do just fine. Of course, he cautioned me, your aircraft then becomes an experimental one so use your good judgment with the weather and gusty winds, and keep the center of gravity as close to the front of the aircraft when loading the baggage compartment.

And, so I did, remembering Ken's admonition when he and I took Two Niner Lima for a test flight shortly after his arrival at Santa Monica Airport. This dedicated Guru was a super guy who passed away only a few months ago. It was a joy to read the many final salutes from the Grumman Gang, regaling all with stories of Ken and his commitment to our aircraft and, more so, of how he touched so many with his friendship and comradery amongst his Grumman brethren. Knowing they were so right about this man who made Two Niner Lima into the bird she is, I was touched. Ken and I shared a very special time, making her into my little rocket ship.

For my journey, I figured a sleeping bag might come in handy. Many airports have camping spaces set aside in case pilots needed to sleep there, so I was prepared. I had thought about buying one of those small, throw-in-the-air, pop-up tents, but decided that was too much. After all, my intention was to stay with friends, not camp out. I had done that once before, traveling cross-country for weeks in the summer of 1972 with Bozo. *Travels with Bozo* is what I called my diary and the dozens of slides I took. Bozo, while not the typical guard dog, was a terrifically smart dog, trained in the streets of Washington, D.C. without a leash.

Previously I had camped out in a tent and sleeping bag in Kampgrounds Of America® sites. Bozo was a big help, warding off anyone who dared come near. He was larger than most miniature poodles, but not cut like a poodle. He had long curly hair, like his owner, the hippie going to law school then.

Although he would certainly bark at any person approaching our tent, his licks of joyful welcome might kill them before they got to me. My hair in law school, an emblem of being a member of the cool generation then, coupled with my moustache, was long, down to my shoulders, and curly like Bozo's, then an oxymoron to many in the hallowed halls of GW Law. I kind of enjoyed that rebel streak as well as my motorcycle and finding *me*. No doubt the purchase of the sleeping bag brought back memories, cherished ones, of an adventure long ago and comparisons to this new journey of finding Me again, if that's what the Universe has in store this trip.

I got the airplane all ready. Cameras set up. Walk around done. It was time to go. As my Captain Bob lid for the journey, I chose my Brown Soccer hat, replacing my stand-by Fullerton Flyer's orange hat. Maybe people would be friendlier when I arrived, I thought. Maybe those who knew about Brown . . . or those who liked soccer. Or so I wanted to believe.

We were all set.

Two Niner Lima started up after a few turns of the prop, surprising me that she had no hesitation and was also ready to go. I could have sworn she smiled back at me when I patted her on the nose and talked to her when I was doing my walk-around.

"Here we go, girl!" I said. "You ready?" I imagined her smiling and nodding, like an airplane in a cartoon.

Yes, obviously she was—she turned right over.

I tuned in the ATIS (Automatic Terminal Information System) and found the weather. Winds were calm and I prepared to taxi for take-off. I had left my car in the rear of tie-down space 821 outside of Proteus Aviation, near the beginning of Runway 3.

All was go and it was time.

I called Ground Control for clearance to Runway 21. Now, taking a deep breath, a looked around Proteus (as I knew I wouldn't be back for months), and we slowly taxied out, down Taxiway Bravo to the run-up area.

Two Niner Lima was all set. Run-up was nominal. Engine checked, instruments set, I called Ground Control for clearance to Runway 21 for departure. Then, over to tower:

"Good morning, Tower. Grumman Two Niner Lima, ready to go 21. Request right 270 into the corridor."

The controller advised, "I have your request." I thought I would be waiting a bit, but just a few seconds later, she advised, "Grumman Two Niner Lima, Runway 21, cleared for take-off as requested. Winds calm."

I looked toward Century City, back west of the airport, then replied, "Grumman Two Niner Lima, Runway 21, cleared for take-off."

Lights on, transponder on, throttle forward, I taxied onto the runway, straightened out, verified that my Directional Gyro matched the Magnetic Compass of 211 degrees to confirm I was, indeed, on Runway 21. Smoothly then, I pushed the throttle forward. The airspeed indicator came alive, its pointer moving, and at seventy knots, carrying a bit more speed because of the extra weight I had packed into the baggage compartment, I slowly pulled the yoke back toward me to "slip the surly bonds of earth." Two Niner Lima rose, lifting off, jumping into the air. I could hear her excitement. We were off.

I climbed up to fifteen hundred feet and, at the shoreline, I began my 270 degree right climbing turn into the Los Angeles Special Flight Rules Corridor and headed southbound over LAX at thirty-five hundred feet. This designated corridor allows VFR (Visual Flight Rules) traffic to transit the airspace over LAX.

I left the corridor at the South Bay curve of the 405 Freeway, contacted Los Angeles Approach and asked for advisories (flight following for a VFR flight) to Yuma, requesting seventy-five hundred feet down to Oceanside where I would then cross the San Diego mountains at ninety-five hundred feet, into the low desert and on to Yuma. We had a decent head wind going south but as soon as I turned eastward after Oceanside, the wind got behind us and we were showing an increase in our ground speed to one hundred thirty-six knots.

The flight was smooth for most of the way, until I began my descent into Yuma. The tower was closed so I had to figure out which runway to land on amidst the multiple runways, the wind direction, and listening to traffic to avoid anyone else. I got down okay, checked in with another aircraft to find out how to taxi to the fuel pit, and shut down to get fuel after 2.4 hours (two hours and twenty-four minutes) of flying time, engine start to engine shut down.

During all the excitement, I wanted to make a conscious effort to record my thoughts. I had hooked up my iPhone camera and was talking to it a bit until the suction cup holding the clamp apparatus failed. The Go-Pro behind me was also recording, but without sound. I looked back and up, into the entire LA Basin to say good-bye, and paused for a moment of reflection. My home of forty-five years looked glorious.

I didn't know if I would be coming back to live. This trip was to be a trip of exploration and discovery. Of me. Of where I might live out my days. I did not know as we cruised along, and I looked back at where the Universe had once brought me. There was a bit of a haze layer, formed when the high-pressure system keeps the storms and winds away, the air stable as a result. From my vantage point, it was like a line in the sky, the haze separated at approximately four thousand feet, creating a distinct demarcation of the clear blue sky above.

I marveled at the mountains surrounding this huge, populated metropolis stretching to the horizon with over twenty million people crammed in and appreciating it as much as I have—enjoying the unique topography, imagining the force of nature that formed all this beauty. I was, and am, always humbled by the scenery, sitting in this left seat, as if in a chair in a bubble of the clear canopy enveloping me, watching the beautiful world below drift by.

While a call from ATC (Air Traffic Control) interrupted those thoughts, I smiled, thinking of all the new topography and places and people I was going to encounter on this adventure. Feeling uniquely special in this place and time, having such a point of view, I wished so many more could see and feel what I saw and felt going on my way in this machine up in the air. It was a glorious day.

I called my friends in Tucson to advise I had landed in Yuma. Exhausted, I got out of the plane, feeling the lack of sleep the night before taking its toll. I wondered what the heck I was doing. Was this journey really such a good idea? Doubt came over me. A bathroom break and a snack of vegetables and some fruit I had packed on board helped rejuvenate me. I took on 17.8 gallons of fuel, and now, with full tanks again, I hopped on board. I texted my friends so they would know approximately when I would arrive at Marana Regional Airport.

Two Niner Lima turned right over again, and I followed a Cessna out to Runway 17 for a left-downwind departure to head for Tucson. I had to avoid the MOAs (Military Operation Area) so I flew to the Gila Bend VOR (Very high frequency Omni-directional Range navigation aid) to the Stanfield VOR, banked right and followed the freeway another sixty miles or so to the airport. At twenty-five miles out, I began my descent from ninety-five hundred feet, again so high to avoid the rock and roll of the desert mid-day heat. I was now getting bumped about, dancing with the thermals, all the way down to pattern altitude at three thousand feet.

AVQ (Marana Regional Airport) was quiet, and I landed un-eventfully on Runway 12. The wheels kissed the ground and I taxied to the transient tie-down spaces and shut down. This time, when I got out of Two Niner Lima, I wasn't tired at all. A huge smile plastered on my face, I took some photos of Two Niner Lima at AVQ, first leg of the adventure in the logbook.

We had begun.

CHAPTER V

LEG ONE

FRIENDS

One of the purposes of my trip was to see many of my friends, probably for the last time in this incarnation. Oh, yes, I know, how maudlin that sounds, but at seventy-one, and with stents lodged precariously in my heart, who knows how much time I have left. It was impetus to stop work and make time for me to enjoy and see friends with whom I have shared life's journey.

I had always thought I would live forever, since my parents finally succumbed at ninety-six and ninety-five. But, after my brother's death by heart attack at sixty-eight, I checked myself out at the same age, six years later. Lo and behold, I was filled with plaque and needed to watch out. An angiogram clearly showed occlusions, but no intervention was needed until one night eight months later, when I thought I was having a heart attack.

My friend Terri and I were on the phone gabbing when I told her, "I think I am having a heart attack!"

Classic symptoms manifested: Intense pain in both mandibles, pain radiating down both arms in the triceps, and a hot burning under my breast plate.

"Hang up and call 911!" Terri instructed. "And don't lie down. Sit in a chair and leave the front door open."

As I got up to do so, I belched. All the symptoms vanished, just like turning off a light switch. *WTF*? The same thing happened the next few nights. Belch or cough, and the symptoms vanished. I was perplexed. And, stupid enough not to go to the doctor or emergency room knowing full well I had coronary artery disease. Somehow I convinced myself it was not my heart, but a digestive problem, like the esophageal ulcer I had many years ago, when I was thirty. The mind can be a persuasive and all too powerful deadly influence when you want it to convince you it hadn't sent the message you want to hear.

I called my doctor first thing Monday and went into his office. Dr. Daniel, a kind young man with whom I have a very positive physician-patient relationship, always took an interest in me and all my madness. He examined me and did the blood workup. There were no enzymes present to indicate I was having a heart attack and he, too, suspected a digestive issue. He put me on the latest and greatest new med for such problems, and I left feeling a bit upbeat, thinking maybe that was all it was. He also gave me nitroglycerine just in case and instructed that if I was having a heart attack, these magic pills would work. If not, I would get a headache from taking one.

But the symptoms persisted. And when I got them, a few times when awakened by the pains in the middle of the night, the nitroglycerine alleviated the symptoms. But, other times, I just a got a headache and they would disappear with a cough or a belch if I could manage it, being not very good bringing up that involuntary response. I was still walking my almost three miles up and down the hills of Mar Vista where I lived, every morning chugging along, swinging my five-pound hand weights, sweating, but no more tired than usual. I was getting seriously concerned that despite the digestive medication, no improvements were happening.

I called my cardiologist, Dr. Peter, who practiced up in Chico where I had gone for my angiogram to check out the severity of the plaque in me. Peter was the younger brother of one of my closest childhood friends, Andy. We had played sports together in high school and kept in touch here and there over the years.

When he heard my anxious voice reciting my concern that the symptoms had not abated, he said, "I don't like what I'm hearing. Come on up and we'll take another look. I'll set up the angiogram right away."

Two days later I was on a Southwest flight to Sacramento. I would have to rent a car and drive another hour and a half to make it to Chico. But I knew something was wrong. I parked my car just adjacent to the Southwest Terminal 1 at Park One, a convenient lot at madhouse LAX when you would be away for only a few days. It's a short walk of a few hundred yards to the terminal, no more. I had to stop even before I got there. I was panting. I was frightened and hoped I would at least make it up to Chico to have the angiogram and whatever else before the fatal heart attack would get me. It was, to say the least, a bit depressing.

When I arrived and met Peter for dinner, he still didn't think anything was that bad, as he had seen and inspected my heart from the inside a few months before. I was hoping he was right.

The nurse awakened me from the anesthesia back in my hospital room. Chico is this small, college town, and everyone is kind and friendly. When she told me Dr. Peter had placed three stents in my heart, I started to cry.

"But now I am sick, and sixty-nine," I railed.

She smiled and told me "No need to be sad. You now have a heart all fixed up and have another sixty-nine years. Count your blessings. No heart attack, no damage to that muscle. It will be just fine."

Well, sure, easy for her to say, but after the shock wore off and I realized I wasn't going to die at any moment—I have adjusted my lifestyle. I am on top of this, and believe it or not, I have become more fatalistic, determined to have a good day, every day. I have a new cardiologist a bit closer in LA, and every three months I have a check-up. Heart medicine is progressing. Who knows how much more time anyone has? Time to live.

And so that became my new mantra and commitment. Slowly but surely, I took steps to make it so. This trip would be a manifestation of a long-time dream and, with it, I committed to re- connect with many friends and learn more about them and me and what it may have been why we traveled together.

For some reason I keep thinking that seeing people with whom I have grown and been close would enable me to get a better handle on me. Who I was. Where I am now. What impact, if any, I have had on them. I had liked to believe that although I didn't score as many goals as I thought I needed to, or get enough hits to earn the love of my father and be somebody (at least in his eyes), it was me to whom people responded. Not the lawyer, not the apparently well-to-do kid, not the one who scored the winning goal or had the headlines. Me. Robert. Bob. Bobby. Fox. *Me.* That yearning to be loved has never seemed to stop, the ache in the heart so hard to fill. My losses shook me.

Maybe I do make a difference, I thought. *Maybe people do care.* When my dear pal Bruce talked to me before I left his home in Camarillo to go into the city to get Two Niner Lima ready to go, he started crying. He told me how much he loved me and was worried about me taking this trip. Tears welled up inside me. I have known Bruce for almost fifty years, having met him after moving to Washington, D.C., to go to law school. He is a brother. We are so alike. So alike it scares us both. We have shared our journey together, over the years, many times, but never seemed to get enough laughing, loving life in the big way we do. I was so moved by his intimacy and concern.

I went to Tucson first to spend time with the Henrici family. Paul Henrici is the older brother of my former girlfriend and fiancée, Phyllis Henrici, whom I'd met at a Brown University Reunion Weekend back in 2002. We hit it off and dated for a long time, spending a lot of time with Paul and his wife, Carol, and their daughter, Hillary, and sons, Evan and Charlie, up in Lakeville, Connecticut. Now, Paul and Carol had moved to Tucson, and I felt it would be a good place to begin my adventure across the USA. I was looking forward to spending time with familiar faces.

Phyllis flew out from Los Angeles and we had a pleasant six days together. I consider them family and my relationship with Phyllis has become a very close, deeply loving, and supportive friendship. She has been my best friend and confidante these past years. Not so easy to do with someone you almost married, but our affection and concern for one another has grown and nourished me greatly. I would hope she would agree that I did the same for her. She is a solid soul, brilliant, and always there to encourage me and be real when I need it the most.

I was even more touched by my first reunions with old friends

I hadn't seen in over fifty years. I last saw Carol when I was in law school and went home to visit my parents in Rockville Centre, New York, the small village on Long Island where I grew up. When away from home at school, it was always a joy to go back and revisit my idyllic childhood and to enjoy home cooking—and oh, how my mom could bake her favorite goodies for me—and see old friends. In those days, Carol hung out with my pal Jerry who had left college and was then working in New York City. So, to see her in Tucson was such a treat.

The amazing thing was that it was as if no time had gone by. I felt the same closeness and attachment to her as I did, and do, to my boyhood friends with whom I am still close. She looked just like the Carol I knew, even though we both were now seventy. She, too, was battling heart issues, having had quintuplet bypass surgery. But her spirits were upbeat and positive.

We spoke candidly about death, enjoyed the lunch, and it was obvious the love of friendship and history was present and strong. I was touched by her affection and was howling with laughter when she reminded me—I couldn't even remember—of stories long ago, and the crazy things I did as a young boy and burgeoning adult. I held her tightly when we said goodbye.

Who knows if we will ever see anyone again? That thought enveloped me. It's how I feel every morning when I get up, and every time I get in my plane. Honestly, it is perhaps too much of a fixation, and maybe it's because of my heart. I think it is more an age quotient. Reality divided by Chronological Age x Heart Issues. Or something like that. The warmth of our bonds from our youth resonated in me after Carol dropped me off back at Paul and Carol's home.

The next day was even more impactful. I spent lunch and the

afternoon with an old campmate and classmate, Stephen. The last time I saw him he was the President of the high school, a popular, jovial, bigger than life guy, a year older than me. We also went to Camp High Lake together and spent a few summers in the Poconos. I'd heard he had become a BMOC (Big Man On Campus) at ASU in Tucson. My old ninth-grade girlfriend, Ronnie, who had dated Steve in high school and now lives in Dallas, who I will see in a few more stops, kept in touch and arranged our get-together.

I hardly recognized Stephen, as I hadn't been that friendly with him in school. In camp, when we were thirteen to fifteen, he was a fierce athlete and competitor, protecting "little Bobby Young" as he fondly referred to me all afternoon. We had a most pleasant lunch at Claire's Café and went up to his Historic COD Ranch. But I heard a man still lost and searching. He was lamenting that he did not become a lawyer like me, and he seemed ashamed of his journey.

Here was a man who had pursued his dreams, protested against the Vietnam War, walked his talk by pursuing other adventures, travelled and lived all over Mexico, restored historic homes in Galveston, owned and operated a boutique historic ranch in Tucson, and just seemed to have lived a full life beyond beyond.

But he was forlorn.

"If only I would have gone to law school and been like you," he sadly said. "Or like Bobby (another mutual friend)."

I saw pain in his eyes, and regret. Or was he still searching and questioning like I am? It didn't add up. Bobby was a mutual friend who became a very big player in the State Department and an advisor to Hillary Clinton when she almost became President. Steven had hobnobbed with Bobby Kennedy, Dick Gregory, and other politicos before the University President turned on him for his anti-war protests and leadership, which pushed his life into a new and not planned journey.

I questioned his denigration of his life and what the Universe had provided.

"My friend, whatever are you talking about? It is I who wants to be like you! Look at the amazing adventures you have had! And what you have done. And how you are so loved! Me? I did what my parents told me to do. I had no idea what I wanted to do. I still don't. Look at you and all you've experienced!"

His heart was still as big as always. I could feel it. He was still the loving, powerful, wonderful man I had known from yesteryear, but apparently tinged with regret. He had been hiding away, and he knew it. He, too, was still searching.

Perhaps it's not so unusual. Or so I hear. We get older. The end becomes closer. We have our regrets. In law school I knew I didn't want to be a lawyer. But, afraid of the wrath of my father and mother, and dependent, I obeyed and did what they said, rather than go off and dream and fly and do whatever it was my heart yearned to do. I was afraid of them and not so confident in myself, unwilling to risk the adventures of the unknown. Like I want to do now.

Stephen shared his pain and regret with this stranger. I am not so certain I have too many regrets. I rationalize that I am here at this point on my journey because of what and where I was before. But, our visit made me pause and reflect. And think more and more. Our minds can be so powerful to rationalize and convince us of anything but to survive. Fear confronts us and we make, and I made, choices. Now, I want more. I have felt this ever since my parents and brother's demise and I was set free, sadly, by their leaving.

With these old friends, I see something. A powerful connection of fragile souls was and still is present. The love was there and maybe, just maybe, the Beatles are right: All you need is love.

Perhaps, just maybe, I had something to do with that.

CHAPTER VI

---→✈

LEG TWO

May 29, 2019 AVQ – CHD
Marana Regional Airport, Tucson, AZ to Chandler Municipal
Airport, Phoenix, Arizona Distance: 68 nm
Route: AVQ-TFD (Stanfield VOR) - CHD
Start Time (AVQ): 9:57 a.m.
Shut-Down time (CHD): 10: 52 a.m.

It was time to go. I was not pumped up and excited to be moving, but sad. I was leaving my dear friends, my family to which I had been welcomed so many years ago, and every time I leave, I think the same. Is this the last time I will see these dear folks?

Paul and Phyllis took me to Marana Regional Airport early in the morning. I wanted to make sure to get airborne early in the morning to beat the desert heat, even though Flight Service, with whom I spoke the night before, was not predicting any moderate to severe turbulence from the desert heat at the lower altitude I'd be flying until later in the afternoon

We arrived at Tucson Aero Services Center just before 9 a.m. It is an FBO, its moniker for its aviation purpose, a Fixed Based Operator. FBOs are businesses situated on airports to handle wayward travelers like Two Niner Lima and Captain Bob, and to provide fuel and flight planning, as well as engaging in flight instruction and charter services. They are the gamut of all of the aviation services offered to pilots and the public.

Most interesting is that each FBO is a peek into the disparate aviation world. Our flying fraternity is a family and every pilot, no matter what aircraft he flies or arrives in, is always treated first-class, with a friendly welcome and gracious hospitality. It is a different kind of business that caters to a unique clientele

Sharing that common interest as a member of the community makes all of us realize how special a thing we pilots do, and how few of there are who are allowed to pursue this avocation. There are approximately six hundred thirty thousand licensed pilots and approximately three hundred ten thousand instrument-rated pilots in America today. Being a part of this unique club always made me feel pretty darn special.

Hey, Dad, see? Not only can I fly but I can do it solely by reference to my instruments! Oh, he did one day see me bring a plane in, when I landed a Piper Archer at Bermuda Dunes (UDD), having flown out to visit with the folks in Palm Desert at the condominium I had out there.

"I can't believe you flew out here in that thing!"

Okay, not so bad, Sidney, huh?

But, I digress. The point is that flying is a special thing. Not everyone does it nor can do it. It requires a special skill set learned over years of lessons and practical experience. When I first started, my instructor said I would be able to pat my head and rub my tummy at the same time, over and over. He was making the point about what pilots really do.

Multitasking describes it well. Planning the flight, being a meteorologist, flying the aircraft, navigating the flight route, communicating with air traffic control, and acting as the final authority on board—all put together, every second, sitting in that left seat.

We pilots never stop learning. I continue to practice, to keep learning, to seek the perfect flight, the perfect landing, when the wheels "kiss" the ground marking your smooth and most excellent arrival. It has been that professionalism which excites me, the lure of the captain with his four stripes, the left seat, all the instruments, the dials and gauges and the busy place a cockpit is, and those who fly from it, Masters of the Sky, precisely controlling this heavier than air machine that miraculously flies. I was hooked when I got to visit the cockpit as a toddler, a small boy running up and down the aisles of Eastern Airlines' Super Constellations enroute to the grandparents in Florida.

Back in those days it wasn't unusual for the pilots to keep the cockpit door open for a portion of the flight, and even inviting a curious child inside to experience the wonder. I fell in love, in awe of those who were the Gods, sitting there amidst this marvel of engineering, doing such an amazing thing.

FBOs can be huge, modern glass terminals, where Two Niner Lima can taxi up amongst the largest of private jets. I have had the red carpet rolled out for Two Niner Lima at Ontario, CA, Signature FBO, and have been inside the smallest of FBOs at Little River Airport in Mendocino, CA, run by two of the nicest ladies who just love their flying and home town, operating their business out of a small wooden 20' x 20' wooden shack beside the runway, not an iota of pretension in them, just the love of aviation reposing deep in their bones.

But all the pilots, whether they stop at Millionaire or in Little

River, fly a small single- engine plane like Two Niner Lima or command a business jet, are all still pilots. Equal, because we all started from the same place, at some airport, learning the same skills, sharing the love of the magic seen from the eyes of that little boy or girl, now doing it as he or she dreamed. And it is all these people with whom I share this sacred and common bond—our love of flying and everything aviation. We are the few who possess this little secret.

I had requested Two Niner Lima be fueled, tanks topped off, so I paid the pleasant young lady at the counter and said my goodbyes. I held on tightly to Paul, then Phyllis, perhaps a bit longer than a quick goodbye hug. I noticed I didn't want to let go. I watched them exit and then turned to get my bags.

Victor, a young man who had seen me lugging my suitcase, backpack and flight bag from the far away transient parking tie-down spaces when I arrived six days before, miraculously appeared.

"Need a lift to your plane now?" he asked. After my required pre-flight bathroom stop, off we drove in his golf cart out to Two Niner Lima on the transient ramp.

I got out and thanked him with a few extra dollars. He politely refused but I insisted. I always think it appropriate to tip and acknowledge that kind help. I do not understand how people cannot be kind and generous, but each to his own. His smile as he drove away was my reward.

Now, I was left with my own thoughts. I put the bags on the wing walk on the left wing and as I walked around to undo the straps of her cover, I patted Two Niner Lima on the nose.

"Ready?" I asked her. I wasn't so sure the pilot was. *WTF am I doing?* I thought. *I am leaving my friends, going where I do not know.*

That this emotion would grab me now was unsettling. I was scared and apprehensive. One more stop and I would be in no-man's land, in places I had never flown. Into weather I had never experienced flying only in the benign southwest air.

I was alarmed. "Okay, enough," I told myself. "Get to it. Focus!"

I took off her cover, loaded up Two Niner Lima, did my walk-around, and slid into the left seat.

Checklist complete, I pushed the starter, "engaged" as the checklist directs, just as Captain Jean Luc Picard would demand. The prop turned over, I tweaked the throttle, the engine fired, and Two Niner Lima came alive. Radios on. The chatter of other pilots over the Unicom, the common frequency used by all at this non-towered airport, echoed in my headset as I listened to the ATIS (Automatic Terminal Information Service).

As I pushed the throttle forward, I began to relax. I announced my taxi intentions, trundling down Taxiway Alpha to Runway 30 for takeoff. No more anxious thoughts, no more concerns. I was in the left seat. When the wheels left the ground, climbing out, I smiled about my passing anxiety when I had questioned why I was even on this journey. Wasn't it obvious?

I contacted Tucson Departure for flight following advisories, climbed to six thousand five hundred feet and headed to the Stanfield VOR on a heading of 304 degrees. I cut the corner of this VOR when I could see all the way up to Chandler Airport, the cut in the desert floor, indicating an airport forty miles or so out on the desert floor. I headed direct, turning right to a heading of 04 degrees. I began a leisurely descent of five hundred feet per minute down to the pattern altitude of two thousand, two hundred feet from, about fifteen miles out. Entering a left downwind pattern for Runway 22, I was pleased by the flight, and smiled even more with a good final approach, right on the glide slope, constant at my target final approach speed of ninety knots, rewarded when the wheels kissed the ground.

I was smiling again.

The hugs from Tami and Gia, my little darling five-year-old friend, made me realize: *Ah, yes, of course. This is why Two Niner Lima and I are on our adventure.*

CHAPTER VII

———————————————————————————✈

LEG TWO

FRIENDS

Phoenix was a must stop because of Gia. Gia Marie. This five-year-old little darling of a girl (oops, as she said, "I am not yet five—next week, Ice Cream Bob.") stole my heart years ago and I had to see her again. I can't get enough of the love this sweet child is.

Never having had children was always a regret. Things just didn't work out. I tried in one of my marriages, but my wife couldn't conceive. Later on, I learned she had an issue, and subsequent pregnancies over the years ending in an abortion leaves me now pained and with regret. The purity of a child, the innocence and pure love that they have just being a child, not yet tainted by life's burdens and the influence of others, touches me deeply. My mother loved children so maybe I get it from her. But anyone who engages with a child, especially a little girl like Gia Marie, well, their hearts will sing.

Tami, Gia's Mom, and I are close friends. Never anything romantic but I was touched by her honesty and authenticity years ago when I owned and operated a minor league baseball team in Maui, Hawaii. They were called Na Koa Ikaika Maui, which means The Strong Warriors of Maui. Tami was one of our Victory Girls, our hostesses at the ballpark. Minor league baseball is a kick, and fun family entertainment was our mantra. For twenty-five dollars you could bring your family to the game, enjoy the budding stars show off their skills in pursuit of their dreams to make it to Major League Baseball, and feed your kids and yourself. Not like going to Dodgers Stadium and paying twenty-five dollars just to park your car, never mind hundreds for your seats, and then more for a hot dog and beer. These days, going to a Major League Baseball game, one has to contemplate mortgaging their first born to pay for it all.

Tami had come to me privately when she discovered one of our employees was stealing money. At the ballpark and at the concessions stands, a lot of cash passed through during the game, and in those days, without safeguards and computers and iPads monitoring all your inventory and what you should have left in the till at the end of the evening, was a concern. So I was grateful when our general manager watched a bit more carefully and disposed of this employee gone astray. I was forever in my debt to Tami for her honesty and concern.

Years later, after becoming friends on Facebook, I saw a post from Tami looking for a place to stay in Los Angeles. By now, I had learned she had a child and was a single mom. I messaged her and she and Gia and her nanny stayed at my home in Mar Vista for a few days. Gia was just a little baby then, but that visit led to more.

When Gia was just two, she and Tami were visiting again and I introduced Gia to ice cream by taking her to Carvel, my favorite place. Having owned and operated a Carvel Ice Cream store in Rancho Mirage, I was the proud graduate of Carvel College and hold that degree in the highest regard. Go ahead and laugh, but making that soft ice cream, putting it on a cone the correct way—yes, there really is a correct way. It's side to side, not in a circle, never mind the secret to keeping the ice cream on the cone when dipping it into the chocolate fudge to make a Brown Bonnet. It took skill and learned mastery of this world of desserts. Gia fell in love with the whole adventure, and loving sweets like any child, she can never stop eating her share of whatever ice cream there might be. I earned her moniker that day of "Ice Cream Bob" and have worn it proudly.

Tami and Gia have visited frequently over the years. Tami is a life coach now, engaged further in spiritual pursuits. She is honest as pure sunshine, so authentic. We have had a sweet friendship, and she has allowed me to parent Gia and take care of her when we are together. I especially have enjoyed the friendship with this woman. Not one iota of desire or lust or any of that stuff with women we guys can get crazy about. No, truly, real friends. Yes, despite what Harry and Sally said, I cherish these two like a sister and her child.

Gia is an old soul, for sure. Wise beyond her years, her imagination is on display with her vast number of dolls, each named by her, and, of course, with whom I have to play when Gia starts but another story about them. Whether it was with Sparkles, or Peppa Pig, I reveled in the adventures she created.

"Just you pretend, Ice Cream Bob, that you are hungry and Peppa and Sparkles and I will feed you."

I did what I was told and howled and laughed with the same joy and purity that Gia radiates. Just magical. This child brings out the little boy in me.

We would swim for hours in the pool even though Gia couldn't swim a lick. "Watch me, Ice Cream Bob. I'm swimming!"

Of course, this was in the jacuzzi, or holding on to the edge of the pool. In the eyes of this little one, she was swimming. After a few years she did overcome her fear of the water and is now getting the hang of it. I took her to a pool in Phoenix and watched her swim, with her floaties, which I put on her arms and buckled her up.

But as is her usual, she was more interested in talking to the woman floating on an air mattress nearby. Gia is uncanny with people and will talk to anyone. Like when Tami was in Mexico, and people on the street were calling out to Gia, astounding her startled Mom. All her fans had met their Queen before at the resort's pool.

I wish I would have had a bunch of these little people. Sweet, loving, just delicious. So I get my fill from dear Gia, and I had to see her once more on my Journey with Two Niner Lima.

We spent some nice days together. We went to an authentic Western town on the outskirts of Phoenix and even to the Arizona Commemorative Air Force Museum where we saw many warbirds, including Sentimental Journey, a polished aluminum monster B-17, being worked over in the maintenance hangar. Her mom was getting over a bad cold, so I also took the car a few times, ran some errands and played with Gia a bit.

It was a tender moment saying goodbye when they both got up early to take me to the airport. I kissed the little one adieu for now.

Due to the desert heat I was anxious to get started to Roswell so I wanted to fly early in the day. The night before, Tami said she would get up early (at five a.m.) and take me. Of course, I couldn't sleep, anxious about the next leg. I was up at four, showered and ready to go. Tami was still not up so I tiptoed into Gia's room where Tami was also sleeping in the bunk beds. She was way too kind to give up her bedroom to me in her small Phoenix apartment, and I told her I would take an Uber to the airport.

"No way," she said, and up she slowly rose. She wrapped a sleeping Gia in a blanket, picked her up and out we went.

The ride to the airport was pure Gia. After buckling Gia in her car seat in the back of Tami's Toyota Rave, we began to talk. Tami announced it was time for her to start cleaning up Gia's room—again—and dispose of some of her toys. I mean, the child's room was littered with so many toys, mainly little dolls and figurines, that you had to be careful where you stepped.

"I think I'll donate them to a local charity or school," Tami said. From the back of the car, the sleeping child was no more and cried out:

"No, you can't take my toys!"

She was sound asleep when Tammi had placed her into her car seat but when she heard the dastardly proposal, no way was she going to let it slide. She had turf to protect, her own little ones to watch out for, and as she always does, she piped up.

Her mom and I both started laughing and Tami assured her that it would be only the toys she doesn't play with anymore.

"Oh, well, then, that's okay." Gia in a nutshell.

CAPTAIN JORDAN

I also spent some time with a very nice young man, Jordan. Captain Jordan now. Enrolled further in the aviation fraternity, he is being trained by Jet Blue to be a future pilot. He started out as a boy when his father taught him to be a balloonist, and he holds a Lighter Than Air certificate from the FAA. I wanted to spend some alone time with this future pilot and see how he was faring.

Jordan is the boyfriend of Hillary, Phyllis' niece. I have known him for many years now, having visiting with him in Lakeville, Connecticut, whenever I would go back there. He and Hillary have been in relationship since high school. It survived the separation of attending different colleges when Hillary pursued her art talent and mastery at the University of Texas. Austin was a long way from the small college Jordan attended in New England. Jordan is a solid soul, unpretentious, and unaffected. A hard worker, he did not come from money, and put himself through college, working as much as he was studying. I suspected the relationship would not survive. So, it has been a joy to see the love of two high school sweethearts blossom and sustain and nourish them both as they grow up and pursue their dreams. I think they have a darn good shot of holding on to each other even with more separation and distance as Jordan becomes a First Officer, ensconced in Phoenix, until he meets all the requirements to fly for a major airline.

I had put the bug into Jordan's ear when he was a balloonist, that he should consider flying for a living. The demand for pilots is bordering on the desperate these days so the opportunity to be employed is real and obtainable. Besides, I wanted to live vicariously through his journey. He will begin his career at twenty-six when he gets into the right seat of an Airbus A-320, the airplane Jet Blue has already slotted him to fly. Not the smaller Embraer 175, which is more like a regional jet the carrier also flies. So, he would be on the main lines, getting his choice of good routes.

Through Jordan, I was hearing what it could almost have been for me. I had not given up my dream of being a pilot when, years ago in the 1990s, I became fast friends with the two gentlemen who were running Presidential Airlines. I represented their company and found them money from Hong Kong investors, despite the deal falling through. Presidential was a start-up carrier flying Airbus A-300s out of Long Beach to Houston and Atlanta. They were packing them in, and I had met the Head of Maintenance at Castle

Creek Inn, but another investment in which I got my family involved, in Escondido, California.

That serendipitous meeting led me to George Warde and Ron
Burke. George was the former President of American Airlines. In
those early days he had run American Overseas Airlines, their sub-
sidiary until called to New York and assumed the Presidency of
that domestic airline. In those days, before deregulation in 1978
let capitalism loose, and George was brought to New York by the
"suits," the Civil Aviation Board (CAB) made and controlled the
airlines. That's how George referred to the Board and Wall Street
money—as the "suits".

Ron had been a pilot for Eastern Airlines and the first pilot to
fly the Boeing 757 in commercial service with that carrier, moving up to be Chief Pilot. Ron was a gentle, quiet man, married to
a wonderful woman, Nel-Ann. I was smitten by their beautiful,
young daughter Claudia, a class act like her parents.

Well, one thing led to another and before I knew it, we were going to start a new airline out of Melbourne, Florida, and I was their
lawyer looking for money. And find it I did, when Executive Jet
Aviation, headquartered in Switzerland but with offices in Florida,
wanted to meet and discuss George's and Ron's vision.

Melbourne was to Orlando like Ontairo, California, was to
LAX—an outlying airport from a major city hub airport that had
been ignored. Worse, any passenger there would have to fly to a
major hub to go anywhere. In Melbourne, only serviced by Delta
Airlines, if you wanted to fly to New York, you would have to either drive to Orlando or take Delta to Atlanta and change planes.
George and Ron had the vision to service the space business centered in the area and nearby Cape Kennedy (Canaveral now) by
flying low cost Boeing 737s out of Melbourne non-stop to New

York and Boston as well as to Huntsville, Alabama, where many rocket contractors were centered.

I flew into Orlando and stayed overnight at the Burke's lovely home, as Ron insisted. It was there I met Claudia and Nel-Ann. We met up with George in Melbourne and the Cape Canaveral Port Authority treated us royally with a VIP tour of the new Disney Cruise Lines terminal before they launched that service. You could see Disney all over, even down to the inlaid tiles on the floor, comprising a huge, smiling Mickey Mouse. This was after an extensive tour of the airport facility, where our new carrier might be located, and extensive discussions with Executive Jet.

But the highlight was the VIP tour of Cape Kennedy. We walked through the Vehicle Assembly Building (VAB), a cavernous building, so big inside it creates its own weather. It was built years before to assemble the Saturn V rocket to take our astronauts to the moon.

We walked in and I gasped. There it stood. The Space Shuttle Discovery, standing upright, its booster solid-fuel rockets already attached. It was to be rolled out to Pad 39 in a few days for launch. I couldn't believe it. A little boy's dream. After all, I could recite the first few minutes of communications of John Glenn's historic flight in Friendship 7 from a record I had bought, so you darn know for sure, for this now grown-up space junkie, this was the ultimate fix. Aviation and space had its tender hooks in me. Looking up, seeing this feat of engineering standing so high stretching to the top of the VAB, wrapped in its gantry, workers buzzing around it, took my breath away.

Even more impressive was the trip up and onto Pad 39. I was awestruck again. After all, we only get to see that Pad from a distance of almost three miles. That's where the tv cameras were placed for the many moon launches and shuttle launches I had watched, on the other side of the Banana River. Now, I walked out on the very spot. I looked up at the gantry, towering over this mass of concrete, over three hundred feet high. The enormity of where I stood, the immense depth and strength of the mass of the concrete, still lingers in my memory even twenty years later.

I was a proud American that day, witnessing what the Space Race created with its innovation and the amazing capabilities of which our country is capable when we put our minds to it.

George and I then parted ways with Ron who lived in Orlando. I was flying out of Miami back to Los Angeles and George had a flight back to Oklahoma, I recall, where he lived. For almost four hours he regaled me with his life and stories and lessons to be learned in the airline business as he drove us south on I-95. The man was a genius.

He shared with me his difficulties bringing American Airlines into the jet age, his battles with his board about committing to the coming jet age, during which he was overruled and replaced by his successor, Bob Crandle, who then had the luxury of time at George's expense. He railed about Wall Street and their demands to always make a profit as investors when profit was hard to come by under the restraints by the CAB. Best, he outlined what was necessary to keep an airline going, explaining the economics and the costs involved.

I remember his favorite line: "Want to become a millionaire? Buy an airline for a billion dollars and lose it all. Then, you'll be a millionaire." His folksy, Oklahoma way of saying it ain't so easy, pal.

We all had another go-round after Executive Jet passed. George and Ron were running Casino Express, a junket operator flying two 737s out of Elko, Nevada. Ron asked if I wanted to fly for them, as I had shared with him my dream to be a pilot.

"Really?" I couldn't believe it.

"Go get your Commercial and Multi-Engine rating and we'll put you to work."

So I did, and I was then scheduled with their next class of pilots to be trained at Boeing up in Seattle. I was ecstatic. Got myself all cleaned up and off any marijuana, increased my exercise routine, and was flying more to keep myself sharp. I couldn't believe my lifelong dream was about to come true.

The call from Ron the Monday before I was to leave for Seattle late that week dashed my plans. Seems the owner wanted to sell the airline and both George and Ron wanted me up in Elko the coming weekend to help them negotiate the deal.

"We'll send you to the next class, Captain Bob," Ron advised.

We each affectionately addressed one another as Captain Ron and Captain Bob, pilots sharing the status of those lucky enough to be able to maneuver these amazing machines through the air.

He was far too kind, I always thought. After all, my friend had a long and distinguished career at Eastern Airlines, rising to become the first pilot in the airline and in America to fly the Boeing 757 aircraft when Eastern was the launch carrier for this new bird. Me? Well, I am the Captain of Two Niner Lima but nowhere was our pilot status on the same level. Captain Ron flew DC8s over the Andes, the wings flexing like a bird in the thunderstorms he encountered. He mastered and captained all the planes in the fleet of Boeing aircraft Eastern had, finally rising to Chief Pilot, a nod to his superior talents. You could see the deft touch he had when he took control of Two Niner Lima on one of our jaunts down to San Diego, taking him to visit Claudia who had moved to California.

As fate would have it, our negotiations broke down on payment terms. I went back to Los Angeles, awaiting their advice for the next class. The call was not what I expected. Their contract had been terminated, they were out running Casino Express, and we would talk when Captain Ron got back to Orlando.

Life sure does happen when you are busy making plans.

My seeing Jordan then was my way of experiencing the journey I missed. I wanted to know how he was faring, all about his training, and what was different about it from mine. Over dinner, he told me of flying in Arizona, dealing with the heat. Now a private pilot, he was working on getting his commercial certificate by building up his flight time to the required two hundred hours. He was also learning to fly solely by reference to instruments to procure his instrument rating.

I was able to share some pointers I had learned over the years. Learning to fly takes time. As you learn, you plateau out, fall back, and learn some more, until it all comes together and makes sense. Jordan was having some inconsistency in his landings. Landing, I tried to explain, is all about the final approach. A good landing is derived from a constant airspeed and a stabilized final approach, the touchdown point not moving in your windshield, steady as centered. Chasing your airspeed is an indication that your landing will not be so hot.

When you are next on an airline in line for landing, listen to the engines on descent and final approach. Steady, constant sound? Okay, this will be a good one. Loud and changing—uh-oh, carrier landing coming. You know that kind, like landing on a naval aircraft carrier. Your arrival isn't greased on, but boom! You know you have arrived, teeth rattling, down and rolling out a bit too fast. Often in windy conditions, or rain or snow, it is advisable to carry some additional speed other than your normal final approach speed, to counteract the winds. In Two Niner Lima, my final approach speed is eighty-five to ninety knots, and I slowly retard the throttle when passing over the threshold.

The other most important thing I shared with Jordan about landing was where to look when beginning the flare of the plane. When we flare the aircraft, we are breaking the descent and bringing up the nose just slightly so as not to touch down first on the nosewheel, a dangerous situation. It can result in the aircraft porpoising rapidly, even to the point of accident and nose wheel collapse if you do not break the cycle by a go-around or a slight increase in power to re-flare.

The pilot must transition his or her point of vision from the touch down point, which is obscured by raising the nose of the aircraft in the flare, to the end of the runway, adjusting for one's shifting perspective of the height of the aircraft above the ground. Out loud, I always remind myself, "Look at the end of the runway." And as I flare, I always hear dear Bill Beecher's kind firm voice instructing me to do so. I shared this tip with Jordan, which, of course he knew.

And that led me to my last point in helping this fledging pilot. When flying solo, or with an instructor, always talk out loud, whether it be reading the check list, making a turn to a certain heading, or changing a frequency. It was another small thing, I felt, that had made me a better pilot. Jordan was most gracious as we discussed these points over a hamburger at his favorite new burger joint in Phoenix, near Falcon Field where he is training.

I further explained to him the ups and downs of training to be a commercial pilot with an instrument rating. He would go further than I, obtaining his CFI (Certified Flight Instructor) rating as well as his required ATP (Air Transport Rating). He seemed in a rush and questioned staying in the Phoenix heat for another few years. I exhorted him to stay in the moment, and to enjoy the learning curve. His skills would improve immensely, I told him, as he got more time in the left seat and learned to control the aircraft even more adeptly.

He listened. He heard. A bright young man, eager to be the best in any endeavor he chose, he would soon be done with training and in the cockpit of a Jet Blue airliner. I had no doubt of that.

But the best was when Jordan helped me with my flight planning on the new Foreflight app I had downloaded. He keyed me into how to make it work and before we got up from the table, I had some semblance of an idea how to do my flight planning on Foreflight. This help would prove to be invaluable on my journey.

Captain Jordan dropped me off back at Tami's apartment. I was proud of him and felt privileged to be able to teach him a bit and share knowledge and wisdom gained over my years as a pilot, and an evolving soul. I felt myself smiling broadly. It was a joy to participate in his journey, so remarkably close to mine.

I was tickled walking up the stairs to the apartment, amused at how the Universe had opened a pathway to my own, with Two Niner Lima now flying across the USA.

CHAPTER VIII

—————————————————————————————✈

LEG THREE

June 3, 2019

CHD – ROW with fuel stop at DMN Chandler Municipal Airport, Phoenix, Arizona, to Roswell, New Mexico, with fuel stop at Deming, New Mexico

Distance: 223 nm CHD-DMN. 207 nm DMN – ROW.

Total: 430 nm. Route: CHD – DMN Direct.

DMN – Direct ELP

(avoiding restricted military areas)

direct ROW Start time (CHD): 6:24 a.m.

Shut Down time (DMN): 8:48 a.m.

Start time (DMN): 10:42 a.m. (local time)

Shut down time (ROW): 12:59 p.m.

Log Entry: CHD-DMO: 2.4 hrs. Up early. Engine start @ 6:24 a.m. Mostly smooth but some light chop. Nice FBO. Bert. Refueled 10 gals.

DMN-ROW: 2.3 hrs. Climbed fr. 9500' to 11,500' per con-

troller inquiry. Relatively smooth. Just beat thunder-
storm. Winds 140/13 gusting 25. Density altitude adjust-
ment @ take-off. Nice FBO. Av Flight. Mohammed.

I was anxious as one can be beginning a new adventure. I hadn't slept so well and the early start after Tami and Gia dropped me off found me in Two Niner Lima. The sun was just coming over the horizon, a big ball of bright yellow shining right into the cockpit as I was stowing my one small suitcase and two small carry-on duffel-shaped bags and backpack in the cargo compartment.

I got the Go-Pro hooked up in its holder clamped to the speaker box on the ceiling so it would be peering over my shoulder and out front and more with its wide-angle lens. Then I coordinated its blue tooth connection to the app on my phone, positioned my iPhone video in the RAM holder (suctioned to the right front window), and turned on my iPad (in another RAM holder on the pilot's yoke). The Stratus Receiver I had placed in its holder on the glare shield, and I turned that on. The Foreflight app came alive, and I focused my attention on coordinating all these aids and media before I began my checklist for engine start. At 6:24 a.m., Two Niner Lima was up and running.

Concerned about the desert heat and the thermals rising from the floor of the desert, over which I would be flying all day to Roswell, I wanted to get going very early. Maybe I could avoid the worst when the morning air would be cooler.

Despite the bad sleep, I was on top of things when I taxied out to Runway 22L for departure. Run-up was nominal. I adjusted for the already increase in density altitude, pulling out the mixture until full power was reached, which adjusted the mixture of air and fuel coming together in the carburetor to reach maximum power. In the heat and summertime, in deserts and mountain airports, a pilot has to be aware of his density altitude. Many have not and paid the price when the aircraft fails to perform at its full power setting because of the failure to take the change of density altitude into account. I was like a cat ready to pounce on this one item. Having briefed myself on the way to the airport and checked on ATIS, it was an issue, as it always would be in the mountains and desert, especially during the summertime.

Departure cleared me up to nine thousand, five hundred feet, and I threaded Two Niner Lima alongside a Military Restricted Areas to Deming, New Mexico. The air was relatively smooth, with only some light, intermittent chop. I landed uneventfully at this airport and taxied to the small terminal.

A fuel truck, an old one at that, pulled up in front of me as I was shutting Two Niner Lima down. The driver, a burly, middle-aged man with a moustache, wearing a flannel shirt and baseball cap, inquired if I needed fuel.

"Yes, please," I replied. "Top off all four tanks." The 2.4-hour flight (two hours, twenty-four minutes) had me transfer fuel from the auxiliary tanks to the main tanks during the trip and all tanks were down.

Two Niner Lima has two main tanks, right and left, which each hold ten gallons of fuel. She also has two auxiliary tanks, right and left, of which each hold five gallons of fuel. Because the aircraft is so small, a depletion in one side will cause imbalance, so I run each of the main tanks on and off for thirty minutes, until they're down to one-quarter fuel remaining. I verify this by looking at the fuel level, a clear plastic vertical tube mounted on each of the side panels of the cockpit just above the floor. It has a red plastic little

ball, or a float, sitting on top of the fuel reposing in the tank, des-
ignating the amount of fuel in that tank. After the fuel level reach-
es one-quarter remaining in both tanks, I then switch on the fuel
transfer pumps for each auxiliary tank (the five-gallon tanks), and
those ten gallons of fuel are transferred into the main tanks. All of
this is essential to keep the plane in balance. Every flight requires
this diligence about fuel transfer.

I walked into the small terminal at Deming, New Mexico. Fox
News was blaring on the large TV on the wall. It was an old building, its interior painted a robin's egg blue, where I found a couple
of old couches and the usual FBO information. I needed to go the
bathroom but before I did, I asked Bert (the lineman's name was
short for Robert) if there was any food.

"Vending machines in the back," he informed me, pointing to
the room adjacent to the Men's room door, where I could see a candy machine and a soda machine.

I was starving. I had taken a few carrots and cherry tomatoes
to munch on while I was at Tami's—my usual snacks—along with
a bottle of water. Not having had my morning jolt of caffeine, I felt
the onset of a headache. Without my coffee, well, I'm a goner until
I get some in me. I was hungry and thirsty, and on my way to the
bathroom I contemplated purchasing a Snicker's bar just to keep
me going.

"You like ham and cheese?" Bert inquired as I came out of the
bathroom.

"Why, yes," I replied. "Although I'm not a big fan of ham, I'll
eat anything now!"

There on the counter in front of me was this ham and cheese
sandwich wrapped in a plastic wrapper. Next to it was a Snickers
bar.

"Well, then, go into the kitchen—it's to the right in the back," said Bert. "Take that ham back and grab yourself a tuna sandwich out of the refrigerator."

I picked up the ham and cheese sandwich and the Snickers bar and walked into the kitchen as Bert instructed. Inside this old refrigerator was a box of sandwiches. They must have been for a vending machine, but there was no vending machine for sandwiches. I took a tuna sandwich out of the box and came back into the main room where Bert was hunched over behind the front desk, pecking away on a calculator.

"Thanks, Bert. What do I owe you for these?"

"You don't owe me anything."

"Really? That is so kind of you."

"It's what we do here. Our pleasure. Hope you enjoy it."

I sat down on one of the couches to eat. We began to talk. I was touched What? Something for free? Someone being so kind to this stranger in the middle of nowhere?

Bert had left Corpus Christi years ago and had come out here to work for Lockheed on a "rocket project." When I asked which one, he said, "Well, one of those space things that I can't talk much about." I didn't press him about it, after all, he was sworn to secrecy if he was working on those kinds of projects. I was heading to Roswell and Area 51, the beginning of it all—crashed saucers, aliens, and who knew what else.

We chatted for a bit. He offered to give me a loaner car and suggested I head into town for lunch. I thanked him so for his kindness, not only for that gesture but, again, for the food. I was still floored that someone was so nice. He also was a pilot and said he loved the quiet life out there. I could see the isolation all over as I flew over the desert into DMN. It did have a certain appeal. I mean, I was even experiencing that when staying with Bruce and Dolly in

Camarillo. Going into the city on every trip was jarring. I sensed the peace and quiet of this remote area.

My peaceful thoughts of solitude and bliss were interrupted when Bert said out loud, "Damn!" I looked up and saw him watching TV. Along the bottom of the screen crawled some message about the "Flood of Migrants" at the border, and Fox News was playing it up in their inimitable fashion.

"This is out of control!" Bert opined.

My chance to engage in a political discussion was here. *Careful, Bob, don't offend this nice, gracious man with any of your liberal rants.*

"It sure is a terrible problem," I said. "Whatever can we do about it? Why is this happening now. Bert? It is bad here also?

I got Bert started.

"It sure is. You see those three big hangars out there? The government is processing over two hundred to three hundred migrants a day. Trump is scaring them away now that we've got someone tough enough to do something about it. Obama and the Democrats just let them in. You'll see. All the helicopters keep coming and going and taking them away."

I was astounded. Those concentration camps were right out the window a few miles away on the side of Deming Municipal Airport? I stared at the hangars far away. Huge hangars. With the rounded roofs sloping down on each side. Like they used to have at Idlewild Airport, now JFK, that I remember so well when visiting as a kid those times I could convince my dear Mom to take me to the airport.

"What do you think is causing so many to come now, Bert?"

I wanted to draw Bert out into an exchange about causation, not symptoms. I wanted to hear what this New Mexican resident thought. Being from California, I am sympathetic to illegal immigration. Doesn't mean we shouldn't do something about it, but not this. California was dependent on it, I had lived within it for almost fifty years, and there are fixes and solutions. But not this inhumane, separating families stuff, like animals. Like the Nazis. No way.

I have known and worked with many Mexican people, and other Hispanic people, both who came here legally and illegally. All they really want is something better for their families, a job to earn money to send money back home, to support their families if they came here, a chance at a better life in America.

"Give me your tired, your poor, your hungry . . ."

I was born under the shadow of the Statue of Liberty. My great grandfather, after who I was named, emigrated from Odessa in Urkaine to New York in 1881 for a better life.

We should be utilizing our strengths to enroll these illegal residents into a fair plan along the road to citizenship so we can all benefit. Fine them, delay their path to citizenship, create worker's programs—anything but this horror that I'd read about and was now hearing about, just a few miles away.

I was sickened staring out at the possible crimes being committed in our names, right there, over there in those hangars.

Bert wasn't on the same page as I was.

"I don't know. Must be because Trump is finally getting tough and they're seeing no more chances to get in here. I am glad he is!"

"But I thought it was those gangs terrorizing Guatemala and Honduras that have these people running scared. Can't we help them in some way?"

"No chance. They shouldn't be coming here!"

"Yes, I know, Bert. Tough situation for all of us. No easy answers. We have the same problem in California." I had told Bert of my trip and where I'd started.

And now, I saw a middle-age man who had his opinion, his experience. I wasn't angry that it wasn't like mine. I saw the differences all around me. I respected him. I just don't think that's what America is about. Strong borders, yes. But compassion and respect for others—for sure, yes.

We are better than all this.

It was time to go.

I settled up the gas bill. Two Niner Lima took ten gallons. Fuel was slightly cheaper in Deming, close to five dollars per gallon, not the five-fifty plus I had been paying so far all over. Graciously I thanked him again for his kindness and courtesy, gave him a hug and solid handshake, and walked out to Two Niner Lima for the trip up to Roswell.

I was eager to get there before noon. Weather forecasts had a thunderstorm on its way. I buckled in and went through my pre-flight when, lo and behold, my dream plane taxied up next to me and shut down. I had heard it in my headset as the pilot of the Cirrus Vision Jet announced his intentions to land on a ten-mile final approach from the airport. And there it was, rolling right next to me for his fuel stop.

Every pilot dreams of flying bigger and faster aircraft. I am no exception. With the advent of sophisticated, single engine turbo-prop aircraft and light jets, single-pilot capable, well, I had dreamed and dreamed. I was so grateful for Two Niner Lima and being able to fly, but always daydreaming of winning the lottery and someday, yes, just someday, having enough money to own and operate that Vision Jet. Like looking at a Playboy centerfold, I have been ogling the future in either *Flying Magazine*, or *Plane and Pilot*. Someday, yes, someday, I would be in the left seat of that bird.

So, I just stared, listening to the turbine whine of the jet wind down and shut off, then watching the pilot open up the air stair door. He came down with his two little dogs on a leash, taking a break just like I did. *Not too shabby, my friend.*

I turned my attention back to Two Niner Lima and the task at hand.

My flight path to Roswell was a narrow path between restricted military air space direct from Deming to El Paso and a left turn north up to Roswell. Again, I adjusted for density altitude, took Runway 26 and all of its eight thousand feet for departure and lifted off. Two Niner Lima gathered its speed against the density altitude effects as it slowly climbed into cooler air.

We went up to nine thousand, five hundred feet again, following right on course on my Foreflight map. Thankfully the air was smooth. As I got to ELP, Albuquerque Center handed me off to El Paso Approach.

"El Paso Approach, Grumman Two Niner Lima, ninety-five hundred feet."

"Grumman Two Niner Lima. Roger. Are you familiar with the restricted areas and mountainous terrain?"

I was puzzled. I'd never heard such an inquiry, ever. The controller was terse, and I felt she was trying to tell me something. Like, "Little Plane, are you sure you want to go to Roswell?"

"Roger. Yes, ma'am. Familiar."

I heard nothing more. But I was puzzled. Did I not flight plan correctly? I looked at Foreflight and the map. No—our route of flight was correct. Altitude chosen was correct, as the MEA (Minimum Enroute Altitude) chart said eighty-eight hundred feet. That meant I would be close to seventeen hundred feet above any terrain, ample clearance. But maybe the Controller knew something I did not. Doubt creeped into my choice.

I saw El Paso before me. The mountain cradling the city I had seen many times when visiting El Paso with my wife Lynn, the city at its feet. *Lynnie, you should see this!* I thought. *Heck, we could have flown to El Paso ourselves!* I laughed out loud. We had come to her old hometown many times to visit her Mom and Dad.

Lynn, my former wife, was a kind, sweet, cute and personable sexy girl whom I met when she worked for me. Her Dad was base commander of Fort Bliss in El Paso. We were instantly attracted to one another when we met but hid our burgeoning relationship from others in the office. Eventually we made it known and lived together and then married. We had our ups and downs but kept at it, enjoying ourselves. We moved to Mar Vista and rented a house to start our family. But after trying to get pregnant with no success, Lynn had enough of the inconsistencies. We were growing apart. I was crushed but I knew she was right. We later became close friends and she worked for me again, putting up with me in a far different way than a wife does with her husband.

As I turned north and began to leave El Paso, off to my right and behind me, I was thinking of Lynn and the last time she flew with me. She was game and bold at the outset when I got my license. I rented a Grumman Tiger for a couple of trips we went on together in California, one on a movie scouting trip to Paso Robles. The movie was *Nitro*, starring Christopher George, of *Rat Patrol* fame, which would be made by his friend and my client at the time, Preston Pierce.

The last trip Lynn and I took together was when we were coming back from Las Vegas to Palm Desert. We had left Bermuda Dunes Airport (UDD) the day before, early in the morning at sunrise. The air over the desert was smooth as glass. It was a routine flight.

But coming back, we didn't get our butts going until after noon. Too much of a good time in Las Vegas. The desert heat was rising and the thermals bounced us around pretty good. "I'm going to die!" she screamed, as one elevator ride after another of the thermal effect was getting to her.

I had to grab her by the back of her shirt and sternly address her. She was sitting next to me in the co-pilot's seat: "We are not going to die! It's just the thermals. Try to ride with it! Okay?"

She meekly nodded back at me but the look on her face was one of terror. She was about to cry. I squeezed her arm affectionately and got back to the task at hand. Flying the airplane.

When we landed back at Bermuda Dunes, and I shut the engine shut off, it was eerily quiet in the cabin. Lynn looked over to me. Calmly she said, "That is the last time I am ever going flying with you."

Remembering the moment, I smiled. Lynn never did fly with me again. I was heartbroken that my wife would no longer share my passion but there was nothing more to be said about it. The look on her face in that plane is still firmly implanted with me. No way was she going to brave it out again. For no one. Not sharing my flying was another reason the marriage wasn't going to work even if I kept flying without her, taking care of myself and pursuing my passion.

I looked to my left. In the distance a humongous cumulus cloud was rising from the desert floor. A big thunderstorm was forming. I was glad I was ahead of it, with less than an hour more now to Roswell.

The controller's inquiry was still lingering. I needed to take action on this concern: "El Paso, Grumman Two Niner Lima, request eleven thousand five hundred feet."

Despite checking the charts again to verify my flight planning was correct, I decided to trust my gut, whatever the doubt might be. Another few thousand feet could not hurt and besides, smoother air would be more than likely.

I watched the thunderstorm grow slowly, building, hoping I was far enough away, which seemed about thirty to forty miles at nine o'clock.

I planned my descent. Pattern altitude was four thousand, six hundred seventy-one feet, and I was up at eleven thousand five hundred, a difference of almost seven thousand feet. I was flying over two miles a minute, so at a descent rate of five hundred feet per minute, a nice, leisurely descent, I would start down at about fifteen miles out.

Roswell was beginning to feel the effects from the growing thunderstorm. Scattered clouds were everywhere, tops at five thousand feet. I picked my way down through them and was cleared to land, a right traffic pattern for Runway 17. It was bumpy, the wind was howling, but straight down the runway, as I settled Two Niner Lima down, the wheels kissing the ground. I was grinning from ear to ear. First new place. Flight well done.

Time to find some aliens.

CHAPTER IX

————————————————————————————✈

LEG THREE
ROSWELL, NEW MEXICO

Ever since I was a toddler, flying saucers, space adventures, and the possibility of the existence of extraterrestrials and contact with them had fascinated me. I just had to go to Roswell. Flying to my next stop, Dallas from Phoenix, all in one day would have been in excess of at least seven hours, so I decided to make Roswell a fuel stop and check out this small town of legendary stories.

In 1947, the local newspaper released the news that a flying saucer crashed just outside this New Mexico city. Witnesses saw aliens alive, others dead, at the crash site. The government announced they had recovered a flying disc but then (I guess thinking about it a bit more) changed its story a few days later, claiming it was a weather balloon that broke up over a field outside of Roswell.

The legend was born, and the story continues, even to this day. I was determined to spend some time here to see for myself.

I arrived in Roswell around one p.m. local time and taxied Two Niner Lima onto a huge ramp in front of the AvFlight FBO. The tarmac was empty but for a small, idling Embraer Phenom 100 jet with Air Force markings. A young woman wearing a yellow vest ran out, and with her ground batons, waved me over to a parking place just past the Phenom 100. I trundled behind the Embraer and sharply turned to the right as she directed me to the tie-down space she commanded. Batons crossed, signaling me to stop, she had me park aside the Air Force jet.

As I always do, I quickly turned the ignition on and off, just in case, to make sure no electrical short was present in the ignition system, then pulled the mixture to idle, and the throttle to close. Two Niner Lima came to a quiet stop, the propeller, interestingly enough, stopping directly vertical, 12 o'clock to 6 o'clock. I chuckled, as that rarely happens. *Must be the aliens!*

The young lady, fighting the growing winds on the ramp, asked if I needed fuel. "Not yet," I told her. "I'll be staying for a few days, so I'll order later. But could I get some help carrying my luggage to the terminal?" We were far up on the tarmac and the AvFlight office was a good one hundred fifty yards away.

Before I completed my shut-down of cameras, headset, iPad and the rest, two young men arrived in a golf cart, and began tying down Two Niner Lima with some serious, double straps and fasteners. I unloaded my suitcase, small bags now filled with the iPad and iPhone, and backpack, and they put them all on the back of the cart.

"Do you want hangar space?" asked one of the young men. They both were in their twenties. Many a lineman like them work for an FBO to supplement their flying opportunities. I learned later neither were training to be pilots.

"No," I answered. "Do you think it is necessary?" I was thinking of the impending thunderstorm, the winds whipping over the wide-open tarmac, the sky growing darker.

"Your call. We always ask," came the reply.

I thanked them but declined. If it was to be that Two Niner Lima would be lifted away by the strength of the storm, well, so be it. Besides, I'd had her insured for all these years since her modification at a hull value of fifty thousand dollars, almost twice the value of the aircraft. I did that after I had modified the aircraft with Ken Blackman and upgraded my avionics to make sure if there was a claim, and the plane was a total loss, I could replace the entire plane including the avionics. The insurance companies who have insured Two Niner Lima all these years never questioned this hull value, probably figuring the risk *far di minimis* (in other words, not worth the effort) for this Grumman Yankee that I had souped up. I knew, however, if a claim were ever made, that's when the insurance company would begin its "What us, pay?" dance they are so good at.

The wind made attaching the canvas cover I carried a bit of a challenge but one of the boys helped me. I pulled the straps tight, as I knew there would be rain, and maybe even hail, with this coming storm. Then I patted Two Niner Lima on the nose for another flight well done, and hopped into the cart for the ride to the terminal.

When I checked in at the front desk the young lady behind the counter was, once again, as nice as could be. I didn't want Two Niner Lima refueled right then. Although some pilots do so at the time of arrival and tie-down, I never want the fuel to evaporate, as some of it would in the New Mexico desert heat.

"I'll call for refueling the day before my departure," I advised her. "And that'll be a question of what the weather's doing in Dallas."

All along my journey thus far, I have been watching the weather, its trends, and how it would be affecting those intended destinations, even days away. Texas was being besieged by a stationary high-pressure ridge and warm, moist air from Mexico was being pulled up and into that front, making a wet mess of all the state. I wasn't sure I would be able to get going after the few days I planned to be in Roswell.

It is exactly why I decided not to have any schedule. I didn't want to put pressure on myself to have to deal with any adverse weather just to get somewhere at a specific time. Better to just chill, see what the Universe is delivering by any such delay, and ride the wave to wherever it would take me.

I was still famished. "Do you have anything to eat?" I inquired after we finished checking Two Niner Lima in for her stay.

"Yes, around the corner. Help yourself."

Before I could leave the counter, a well-dressed young man came up to me. "Welcome to Roswell," he said. "My name is Mohammed. I am the manager here. Can I be of service?"

He was a handsome, well-fit man in his thirties, wearing a tie and jacket. He must have overheard the conversation, and he walked me around and over to the snacks. I asked if I could get a lift to the Days Inn, where I had made reservations for two nights. He smiled and told me he would be glad to take me. I took a bottle of water, along with an apple and orange, pretzels, and cookies, and told him I would just be a few minutes as I wanted to wash up and go to the bathroom.

Mohammed then drove me to the motel, pointing out the sites along the main drag, appropriately named Main Street. The main stretch of town was not too far from the airport and within a few minutes, he was pointing out the UFO Museum and the local shops, telling me not to miss the dining treats.

We talked a bit of politics, and his experience of moving to Roswell from Detroit, Michigan, where he ran the Av Flight facility, and then took a transfer to ROW to move up the company ladder. His story was telling. America at its best and worst.

"It has been an adjustment," he confessed, sharing that he was Muslim, and how in Detroit, it was no problem because there are many people of different colors and of different religions.

"I am an American," he told me. "I was born in Michigan. There was no problem where I grew up. Here? It is taking time."

I felt his obvious pain, to be sharing such sensitive thoughts right away. I wanted to offer him comfort and allay his isolation, sharing my discomfort experienced at times as a Jew, even though he was of Arabic descent.

"I understand what you mean, Mohammed," I said. "Being Jewish I have felt too many times the hostility of strangers. Because of my New York accent or whatever."

He nodded approvingly. I went on.

"I have travelled a lot around America, and I have a theory. See, you and I grew up amongst many different people. You in Detroit. Me in New York. No problem when we all mix together and deal with each other. But go to a place where everyone is white, and they have never met or dealt with different kinds, well, their walls go up. Their ignorance gets the better of them. The unknown drives their fears," I offered. "They just don't know any better. But I think in another few years, even that will change. That's what is going on now. Last hold of the old white folks!"

Trying to assuage any tension in the conversation, I gave a light laugh.

There was quiet for a moment. Then Mohammed nodded and said, "Well, all I ask is for people to sit down and listen, and hear me, and hear that I am just like them."

We bantered a bit more, moving to the banal in response to my inquiries about the city. I already felt the warmth, sensed good vibrations, and I had been here less than an hour when Mohammed pulled into the Days Inn parking lot, adjacent to the New Mexico Military Institute. We exchanged a warm good-bye and I thanked him profusely for his kindness, wishing him good luck and telling him I would see him before I left in a few days. I felt this professional and respectful young man's pain to belong and I made a mental note to send AvFlight my compliments on this fine manager at ROW.

The motel had my room ready before the three p.m. check-in time. Exhausted from the early morning departure and no sleep, I couldn't wait to get into the room and unpack. My knee was killing me and walking was putting me in extreme pain. The torn meniscus had been acting up since before my departure on this journey but now it was much worse. Rest and total chill for the rest of the day was in order. I hardly moved off the bed and got a good night's sleep.

My stay at the motel included the free breakfast so after some coffee in the room, checking e-mails and Facebook and reading the L.A. Times online, down I went. My knee felt somewhat better, the pain dramatically less than yesterday's unexpected flare-up. Explaining my dilemma, I had texted Ronnie, my friend in Dallas with whom I would be staying after Roswell, to ask if she had a good orthopedist to recommend. Thank God she knew someone and texted back she was on it. I needed another shot of cortisone to keep me going and I was kicking myself for not seeing my orthopedist before I left, despite thinking about it and going to every other doctor who was treating me. Bozo I can be at times. My fond nickname for Captain Bob when he strays.

Breakfast was surprisingly good. An omelet, some raisin bread toast, juice and another few cups of coffee got my motor running. I was excited to get down to the UFO Museum and see for myself if the story about the Roswell crash was all true. The chatter of foreign visitors (I made out German and Spanish) made me realize there are many who come to explore the question and who may just not believe the party line.

In the 1950s, three years after the Roswell incident, Hollywood churned out many movies about flying saucers, aliens, and their visits and encounters with Planet Earth. I was growing up on Long Island and this little boy was hooked. Anything that flew, whether plane, rocket ship, or spaceship from another planet, fascinated me.

I could identify the planes overhead on their way to Idyllwild Airport (now John F. Kennedy Airport), a mere ten or so miles give or take from my family home.

"Eastern!" I would call out. "National... American ... TWA!"

Seems Rockville Centre was on the approach into the airport. In those days, I was a proud junior cadet of the *Rocky Jones, Space Cadet* TV show. *Flash Gordon* stirred my imagination. The robot *Tobar the Great* frightened me.

I showered and put on my Incrediwear knee brace, then walked down the hill on Main Street, to the museum. It was a beautiful, sunny day. The wind behind the thunderstorm was pushing the warm desert air, clearing the sky, making the azure blue noticeably rich in the morning light. I was smiling and happy and just tickled walking down Main Street in Roswell, New Mexico, my own SETI. It made me think of *Contact*, my favorite movie. You know—that's the one where Jodie Foster does, indeed, find and meet them.

All the Main Street lamp posts had an alien silhouette painted on them. Every store took advantage of the town's rendezvous with the ETs. McDonald's was a huge spherical shape, as if a flying saucer had plopped down, right where it sat. Its neon sign proudly proclaimed, "World's Famous UFO McDonald's." Statues of aliens stood before many stores. It was amusing, not too insipid, just about right, promoting its unusual encounter with the right cachet of aliens sprinkled about. Just a small town taking advantage of its history.

Roswell has over one hundred thousand tourists per year and holds an annual UFO Fest every Fourth of July. I couldn't stop snapping pictures on my phone—every building with an alien reposing in front, even advertisements on posters. All had the kitsch alien theme.

But Roswell isn't only about aliens. It is the fifth largest city in New Mexico and a center for farming and dairy cattle. It served as the site of the first rocket tests by Robert Goddard and even has a minor league baseball team, rightly named the Roswell Invaders. I was impressed to learn of its many famous residents: John Denver, renown rock and country singer, Sam Donaldson, TV news impresario, Robert Goddard, rocket pioneer, and Nancy Lopez, famous golfer, among others. I spent some time at the statue honoring the city founders and reading about the history there at the town square. A Confederate soldier, Captain Joseph Calloway Le, made his way west following settlers from Missouri who had founded the town. He became the king pin behind its growth in the late Nineteenth Century.

I finally made it down to the museum. It was about a fifteen-minute walk from the Days Inn. My knee was killing me still and I was walking gingerly, with a slight limp, hoping Ronnie could arrange an orthopedist for me when I got to Dallas.

The museum is in an old, abandoned movie theatre. I signed the Guest Book and began my tour. Reading the story told by affidavits adorning the walls was mind-boggling. Key witnesses. Truth and lies. This lawyer felt it an open and shut case. Too much circumstantial evidence to doubt it. In fact, the affidavits sworn to by witnesses right before their deaths, convinced me even more. The government, with threats to their livelihoods and businesses, had ordered all of them to keep their accounts secret. Where there's smoke, there's fire, as they say. Of course, that might be my cynicism, learned so disturbingly and sadly from the *Pentagon Papers*, but to me, the evidence, some even direct percipient observation and tactile experiential recollections, had me certain the crash occurred and our government was covering it up.

I spent a few hours reading every post on the walls, looking at every picture, every re-creation, exploring the entire arena of extraterrestrials, all laid out in this museum. From the *Roswell Incident* to *Contact of the First Kind, Second Kind, and Third Kind*, the museum did a credible job presenting the facts and observations, asking the questions, presenting both sides of the query, honestly and directly.

The museum had many posters of movies I had seen, not only about the Roswell Incident but many of alien encounters. All of them I watched over and over on TV as a kid. They jumped out at me, stirring my memory of black and white images, watching with my little sister, hiding under the blanket, afraid of what would be coming next in *War of the Worlds*, *The Day the Earth Stood Still*, and *Forbidden Planet*.

I reveled in it all. The museum even had an extensive library where many, I was told, including those scholars from the University of New Mexico, do research on the subject. It blew me away to see all the books and shelves of documents and other items locked in glass file cabinets, and huge rooms filled with research and content. The Roswell crash was not a joke to this museum and library.

Right on! I thought, as I believed it to be true. And seeing for myself the overwhelming evidence, well—someday, my friends, someday we are all going to be in for one helluva surprise.

Roswell was everything I'd hoped and more. Even a possibility for future residence for me. I love New Mexico, the people, and its Native American history and culture. This city radiated contentment and had a tranquility about it that appealed to me. I vowed to come back someday, to spend more time in the area, and in town. It was that much fun and hit me in a very positive way.

It was past four p.m. when I got back to the room. My thoughts turned to flying and my next leg to Dallas. Texas was awash in convective activity, the weather emanating from the Gulf of New Mexico. A slow-moving low front was drifting eastward, spinning counterclockwise (as low pressure disturbances do) and right in front of my flight eastward.

Flight Service advised that I should be able to get into Dallas before the worst of it got there. I changed my route a bit to avoid some heavy rains forecast for Midland and Odessa, heading instead further south to Abilene for my fuel stop. I ordered some Buffalo Wings and a salad for dinner and went to bed before nine. I requested a five a.m. wake-up call. I had already asked the front desk to order me a taxi for six a.m.

Texas was before me. Halfway across the country. My first encounter with a new kind of weather with which I had never dealt, planned for or flown in. I was nervous and hoped I could sleep.

It was going to be a long day.

CHAPTER X

———————————————————————————→

LEG FOUR

June 5, 2019

ROW - ADS with fuel stop at ABI

Roswell, New Mexico, to Addison Airport, Dallas, Texas, with fuel stop at Abilene, Texas. Distance: 288 nm ROW-ABI.   170 nm ABI-ADS. Total: 458 nm.

Route: DMN - ABI Direct.

ABI –ADS Direct. Radar vectors through Dallas Class B airspace to ADS.

Start time (ROW): 7:06 a.m. (Mountain Time) Wheels up: 7:29 a.m.

Wheels down: 10:20 a.m. (Central time) Shut-Down time (ABI): 10:26 a.m.

Start time (ABI): 11:08 a.m. Wheels up: 11:29 a.m.

Wheels down: 12:54 p.m.

Shut down time (ADS): 1:02 p.m.

Log Entry: ROW – ABI: 2.4 hrs. Flight time: 1: 51.
Left early. Nice flight @ 7,500'. Few clouds into ABI. Excellent
landing. Beautiful airport. Pilot Cole helped w/DFW transition.
ABI – ADS: 2.3 hrs. Flight time: 1:25.
Wonderful flight. Beat wx into DFW. Convective activity build-
up. On top.   Sct. @ 7,500' – 9,000'. Class B clearance then had to
accept IFR clearance, rv (radar vectors) ADS.

I woke up—wide-awake—around two-thirty a.m., and after going to the bathroom, was hoping I could fall right back to sleep until my four forty-five alarm sounded. The cab would arrive soon enough. I needed to get some caffeine into me, even if my only choice was the weak motel make-your-own with pre-measured coffee in the little filter that slides into the one-cup coffee machine. I was restless and no sleeping position I tried worked, for the longest time. I did have some REM sleep but was still up around four-twenty a.m. I decided it was time to get going.

On my Journey, this trip would be my first foray into new weather. I was apprehensive. I was so used to flying in the southwest. The benign weather always present in California and east through Arizona was usually timid due to high pressure sitting off the California coast. New Mexico was more of the same, despite the rising terrain. But, now, going eastward into Texas and the southeast, I was facing unstable air and increased convective activity due to all the moist warm air coming out of Baja, California, and the Gulf of Mexico. In late spring and summer, it was a lot worse.

I was nonetheless prepared and diligent in my preparation for the upcoming encounters. I could see the clouds, so I could fly around them, under them, or on top of them, to some extent, as far up as Two Niner Lima's service ceiling limitation of thirteen thousand feet. My fear, however, was in the sudden precipitation and surprise of an imbedded thunderstorm. Or, the darkening sky and I am somewhere I should not be. This concern was why, despite holding an instrument rating, I did not want to fly under IFR (instrument flight rules).

I was committed only to fly VFR, or by visual flight rules. I didn't want to give myself the opportunity to press against weather with which I was unfamiliar and in which I had not regularly flown. Besides, a small plane is no test for inclement weather unless equipped and capable to handle it. There are, indeed, some single-engine, piston airplanes today, like the Cirrus GT, Mooney Acclaim, or Cessna TTX, that are more than capable of flying in such weather. They have enough power to top the clouds with anti-icing equipment and a service ceiling up to twenty-five thousand feet. But Two Niner Lima was a far cry from these modern, sophisticated singles, which were equipped with the same avionics found in jetliners. I was in no rush, nor would I dare test Two Niner Lima in bad weather.

I had installed the Stratus 3, a portable ADS-B in device, which captured and transmitted current weather to my iPad. It was working as advertised, showing me my exact location as I traversed over the aviation sectional map. It also showed any precipitation near my route. I was ready and prepared. Despite the apprehension, these added tools gave me some confidence to now confront my unknown.

I made a cup of coffee and sipped on the heated dark water, a far cry from my morning Peet's Major Dickason Dark Roast that I was so used to drinking over the years. But despite its weakness, even motel-room coffee was a comforting ritual to begin the day. I

called Flight Service to see how the weather was doing. My briefing the night before left me somewhat confident that high pressure
was building in Oklahoma, and I should be able to get into Dallas.
Maybe.

When the flight briefer said, "Good morning, Robert Young," I
just about dropped my coffee cup.

"How did you know it's me?" I asked incredulously.

"Well, you're in our computer. Two Niner Lima lists you as the
pilot. How can I help you?" replied the briefer.

Uncle Sam used to run flight service stations but over the last
five years or so, they have got out of the business of providing
weather services for pilots. Privatization they called it when they
put out the service for bid, and it became Lockheed-Martin Flight
Service. It was now run by another company. The briefers were
still the same and, notwithstanding this change, as professional
and capable as always.

That familiar exchange had me feeling optimistic. The briefing
was the same as the evening before. I had changed my route southward due to thunderstorms in north Texas and encroaching down
to Midland-Odessa, near Haskell Municipal Airport in Haskell,
Texas, which was to be my fuel stop. I would now stop for fuel
further south in Abilene and then see how the weather was doing
in Dallas.

I showered and, at five-fifty p.m as I was packing up my belongings and finishing getting dressed, the cab driver knocked on
the door. He was early and as anxious to get his day going as I was
to be moving on.

"Sure. Give me a few more minutes," I told him. "I'll be right
out."

After securing my belongings and doing a walk-around to
make sure I wasn't leaving anything behind, I left the Days Inn. It

was another flying routine I had incorporated into my daily life.

Inside the Chrysler van taxi was another gentleman. He was catching an early commercial flight on American Airlines out of ROW and the cab driver advised me he would be dropping him off first. I exchanged morning pleasantries and off we trundled back down Main Street, now on a direct shot back to the airport and Av Flight.

When I had called Av Flight the afternoon before to put in a fuel order to "top off all four tanks," I'd asked if Mohammed or someone else, as promised, would pick me up in the morning. They were unable to do so because early morning arrivals left no staff available for pick up. I just reckoned it was because I was a little guy with Two Niner Lima and not the big corporate jet pilot ordering hundreds of gallons of fuel. Nevertheless, I was doing what I needed to do for an early morning launch. Time was my enemy now. I didn't want to leave late and face too much convective build-up down the road in Texas.

Av Flight did, of course, continue to extend their professional courtesy to me by driving me from check-in out to Two Niner Lima, parked far away on the huge tarmac. Wendy, one of the staff members, and I got into a rather old gasoline golf cart. I was surprised

"It's not electric," I remarked as we loaded my bags into the back. "It's a real classic."

"I know, right?" She smiled. "Never a hitch with this baby. I love it!"

Little things, I guess she was saying, but I took it to mean she could rely on it time and time again. Sometimes the old reliable is just as good as a new arrival. Hey, if it ain't broke, don't fix it. Kind of why I kept my BMW 530i for twenty-two years.

I loaded up Two Niner Lima, still careful to keep most of the weight behind me and closer to the center of gravity, rather than further back in the cargo hold. There is one strap to tie down the small suitcase filled with my clothes, and then next to it, on both sides, I crammed in my small duffel bags. My heavy backpack I laid across the suitcase, and my suit bag, which I'd left on the plane, I placed on top as before.

This is an important pre-flight item necessary to check when flying. A plane "out of cg", or outside its center of gravity envelope, can be dangerous and the pilot can easily lose control. A classic example of this was the recent crash of a Boeing 747 climbing out of an airbase in Afghanistan. Cargo broke loose and slid back into the rear of the cavernous cargo area, forcing the nose upward and the plane out of control. The pilots had no chance to correct it. The plane pancaked into the ground.

Two Niner Lima started right up. I asked the Roswell ground controller for Flight Following direct to Abilene. He came right back to me:

"Two Niner Lima, are you GPS equipped for direct to Abilene?"

"Affirmative" I replied proudly. "Direct to Abilene on a heading of 095."

I was smiling because not only did I have my Garmin 530 in the panel to verify that, but my iPad and Foreflight had the flight all planned out. I was beginning to feel comfortable not only flying with it and watching my progress, but also with flight planning. Over lunch in Phoenix, Captain Jordan had taught me some tricks and I was getting the hang of digital flight planning. This modern stuff sure beat taking out my ruler and pencil and drawing my flight's route on the paper sectional map, measuring each leg, and guesstimating my time enroute.

He accepted my request. "Grumman 29 Lima, squawk 1623, departure 119.6."

We taxied out to Runway 17. Along the way, I passed all the American Airlines 737- MAXs being stored there in the desert air. It was stunning to see them all. Engines wrapped and sealed, all of them sitting sadly. Boeing had clearly been caught by its own arrogance and resulting malfeasance of its manufacture of this new airplane. Coupled with the deteriorating, diminishing (and supposedly overseeing) government agency, the FAA was a shell of its capable and competent self. Its funding was continually cut, making it difficult to supervise its own engineers and inspectors and insist that everything necessary be done in the certification process. It can only mean trouble when a private enterprise is its own inspector of what it's manufacturing for public use.

Passing by these new but tainted aircraft, I wasn't sure if they would ever fly again. I saw so many others, now relics, being cut up and discarded, littered about ROW, which had a factory here for that purpose. Just before the cab driver dropped me off, we passed by a fuselage in a huge bin, and I recognized the blues of Eastern Airlines. Its hockey-puck design, tilted and reposing in an awkward position, was not a part of the flying machine it once was. It was now literally trash in the heap.

So unfair, I thought. To this pilot, that was the cruelest fate a magnificent flying machine could suffer, and after EAL pilots had relied on them on countless journeys.

I had to adjust for density altitude again in the increasing heat of the morning. Two Niner Lima's takeoff roll slowly gathered speed and I rotated at seventy knots, slowly climbing in the desert air. I turned to a heading of 095 degrees after reaching a thousand feet above the ground. Departure control quickly had me up to seven thousand, five hundred feet.

New Mexico was, as advertised, plateaus and mesas. A vast land mass, green from all the rain, I peered down and could see the distinct plateaus. I was only three thousand, five hundred feet AGL (above ground level) at that point. I could see the distinct steps up and down of the mesas, just like I remembered learning about when I was a boy studying geography. Texas gave way to green, rich, fertile soil. It was huge. So much grass. Of course, good for all the cattle and growing whatever.

Abiline was reporting marginal VFR but that ATIS report was almost an hour old. As Forth Worth Center handed me off to Approach, it was now VFR, with scattered clouds. Down we went, for a right base onto Runway 17 Left. I advised the controller that I would have to stop my descent at forty-five hundred feet to stay clear of clouds. She would bring me closer and when the clouds dissipated, with ABI in the clear, I landed Two Niner Lima right on the money at this beautiful airport.

I was struck by the setting. As I had turned right from base to final, in the distance was a lake and some mountains. Maybe not mountains, but small hills. It appeared to a be a place to go and enjoy the water, to get away and find some cool relief from the Texas heat. I taxied in and the lineman guided me next in the line of a few King Airs and other aircraft. He signaled me to stop and shut down.

Famished by then, I decided to sit and eat something before I got going again, after I checked with Flight Service and re-fueled. As I was walking toward the FBO terminal, a fellow pilot was walking toward me to his airplane. It was parked next to mine.

"May I please ask you something, sir?" I inquired.

"Sure. What's up?"

He was a middle-aged man, about fifty, handsome in a rugged sort of Texas cowboy way, attired in shirt and jeans. His name was Cole and he had just flown in from Midland to do some flying with his son, who was based here in Abilene. Two Piper Saratogas, six-seater, 350 h.p. single- engine machines, sat side by side. I figured one was his, the other his son, but he was nowhere to be seen.

"Could you tell me the best way to get up to Dallas and transit the Class Bravo to Addison? I'm not from here and it's my first time. And with this weather—well, I am not so sure about it."

"Where you from?" he asked.

"Santa Monica. I just retired. Flying cross country, seeing friends."

"That's pretty neat. Well, don't you worry. All you have to do is fly up at seventy-five hundred feet. That will put you above most of the weather. Then, when you get to Dallas Approach, ask for clearance through Class B direct Addison. They're pretty friendly. They'll take you right across into Addison."

I thanked him and went inside. That was encouraging.

The FBO was quite the place, modern yet comfortable with big leather chairs and couches set about—the décor reeked of all things Texas. There was a stairway leading up to a second-floor lounge and flight planning room. I grabbed an apple and bottle of water and walked upstairs.

When I called Flight Service, the briefer confirmed everything was holding for now. They did not expect the weather and forming thunderstorms to do anything until early evening. I felt upbeat—I just might make it. Cole's advice and comforting words gave me some relief from my worry about the weather and my first time flying into Dallas.

I looked out from the lounge out at the tarmac. Two Niner Lima was last in the row of jets, King Airs and the two Saratogas. The smallest of the lot, but this pilot and his bird were equal to all the drivers of those bigger and faster planes. And, as Cole so kindly and graciously mentored this Texas rookie, we are all equals in this amazing fraternity of aviation and its crew.

Outside looked idyllic. Off to my left was the Abilene commercial terminal, this FBO set off to the right with its own runway as well. Green as far as the eye could see, the hills in the distance. It felt so comfortable here. Mary, just like Cole, was at the counter, gracious and making sure I had enough bottles of water. I paid her for the re-fuel and another apple and walked out to Two Niner Lima, with a bit of hop in my step.

The trip into Dallas was one of the most exciting and fun plane excursions I have experienced. Maybe it was because it was Dallas, Texas, and I was now half-way across the country on my journey. Maybe it was because of how it all turned out, but I was smiling the whole way through.

Despite having to keep climbing, all the way up to nine thousand feet to avoid the building clouds, I was tracking true on course. I was handed off to Dallas approach and made my request, as Cole had instructed.

"Roger, Grumman 29 Lima, cleared through Class Bravo. Maintain seventy-five hundred feet and fly heading of three hundred thirty."

I began my turn. Right in front of me, in the distance, the clouds were building and closing across my route. I advised the Controller I wouldn't be able to maintain VFR flight. "Unable, as it doesn't look like I will avoid the clouds."

"Are you IFR capable?" he asked.

"Affirmative, but I prefer not to as a bit rusty, and I don't have the charts."

"Fly and maintain current heading."

I had avoided one problem, but now the wall of clouds was

closing in on me. Even in this direction, I knew I couldn't maintain VFR. I quickly weighed my options. I had no choice. I would have to accept the offer of an IFR clearance. Quickly, I thought it through.

Recently, a few months before, I had flown an approach into Santa Monica when it went IFR. In that particular situation, the weather was no longer allowing visual flight rules flying (VFR), as the ceiling was less than 1000 feet and visiblity less than the required three miles. On my return from Camarillo that day, the marine layer made a faster afternoon appearance than I had anticipated. I had left Santa Monica to Tucson by going up through a diminishing marine layer, IFR to VFR on top. I knew this airplane and was not scared by the choice. I could do this. I had no other way out.

"Dallas, Grumman 29 Lima will accept IFR clearance, radar vectors to Addison."

"Roger, Grumman 29 Lima, cleared to Addison, radar vectors, turn right heading of two hundred fifty and descend and maintain five thousand feet."

I got onto the gauges. All I saw now is "Mother" —the attitude indicator, along with the directional gyro below it. I glanced up and saw, as I descended, that I would pass right between those two clouds, at the bottom of the one on the right as I approached them, and would only be in the soup for a few seconds. A few bumps as I passed through had me then break right out in between the layers of clouds.

I was on a heading crossing over DFW Airport, and the controller guided me onto downwind for ADS, and through a rain shower for about thirty seconds as I descended. I was beaming as the light rain pitter-pattered against the windshield and fuselage. Dallas was so green, and lakes were everywhere. The view, as John Glenn exclaimed, was "tremendous". I was cleared to intercept the final approach course and turned to land on Runway 35.

When Two Niner Lima touched down, I was ecstatic. ADS was a single runway, and I taxied off and asked Ground Control for "progressives to transient parking."

"No transient parking. Either Atlantic Aviation or Millionaire, sir."

I chose Atlantic since they were at Santa Monica and Millionaire, despite having been to a few over the years, just sounded expensive.

"Right turn and first left, Two Niner Lima."

Jets filled the ramp. Linemen were scurrying about one of the planes, with its engines running. One lineman, with his batons, was standing in front. Another lineman, also with batons, was further down on the ramp, motioning to me to taxi to him. I slowly passed the waiting jet, went up to the lineman and turned Two Niner Lima around by its brake differential to face my lineman and shut down.

Dallas, Texas. Yabba dabba doo!

I was half-way across the USA in Two Niner Lima, simply amazed we were here. And damn proud of myself as a pilot for handling the approach, descent, and landing so well.

I was smiling. For certain, it was a big Texas smile.

CHAPTER XI

————————————————————————————→

LEG FOUR

FRIENDS

Dallas had always held some interest for me since that dark day back in November 1963, when President Kennedy was gunned down. It was the end of innocence for many, me included, as we sat glued to our television sets. The haunting images in black and white were the perfect setting for the macabre events that changed all our lives. To this day, I can still hear the muffled sound of the slow, steady beat of those drums in the cold November air, the riderless horse, the casket of our slain leader lying on the same caisson that took Abraham Lincoln to his grave.

One never forgets. Nor forgives.

The City of Ill Repute became its label. I grew up quickly after that day, my adolescent eyes looking differently and questioning everything—from what my parents had taught me to the world interrupted. College was a few more years away, and there my sense of the world, and what is and what I believed *should* be, would be overwhelmed. I imagine many, as I do, wonder about that day. If only things had been different. If only the darkness of man and his evil could ever be turned to good. The Baby Boomers get a bad rap. We demanded our government deal straight with us and, incredulously, they still don't. The fight continues on, even to this day.

I had visited Dallas many years ago when I had a case there and associate counsel with whom I had to visit. I also wanted to visit Ronnie, who was my girlfriend in junior high school. Ronnie had moved there when she was a youngster and, when she got into high school, had fallen in love with a senior. She married her Charlie when he returned from Vietnam, and moved to Texas when he accepted a job offer there.

We'd always kept in touch and I had visited Dallas a few times, once to offer her support after her second divorce. We took her children out to a Renaissance Faire. On another visit, I cried my eyes out when visiting the Book Depository Museum. Walter Cronkite's voice was playing over the speakers in a recreation of where Lee Harvey Oswald was perched, looking out that sixth floor window. Again, muffled drumbeats haunted me.

No, it just couldn't be so.

There I was, a forty-five-year-old man with tears streaming down his face, the cruel despair from years before reawakened

In junior high, Ronnie was a cute, petite brunette, with a personality and smile that melted us boys. I was lucky enough to get her to wear my i.d. bracelet to show we were going steady. Ah, how simple things were then. It was sweet times back then—times of innocence, of new exploration of the opposite sex, of relationships, even those of naiveté and blossoming desires.

When you're a kid, you have no responsibilities but to please your parents. You don't yet understand about money or how the world works, so you go to school, get good grades (or else), and even score some goals and sink some baskets to make your parents proud. Or, in my case, to earn some stripes and be loved. Even with such demands, it's far from the madness of being an adult and earning a living. In spite of all the responsibilities heaped upon us children, my mom and dad would always remark, "Life only gets harder."

Like so many things, it took me years to finally grasp what the heck they were yakking about. Time and perspective shaped by our life experiences becomes our teacher. And so we yearn for our innocence. Or any chance to revisit it.

I remember the good times of being Ronnie's beau and our make-out sessions down in her basement. Finished basements were all the rage back east in those days, with parents building out space for their kids to protect their plastic-covered living rooms from what kids do—make a mess. Ronnie's basement was also furnished with twin beds—but there was always another friend on the other one.

The highlight was when her mom, Tilly, started down the steps yelling, "What's going on down there?"

Quickly, buttons were buttoned and zippers were zipped. Oh no—don't get the wrong idea. We barely got to second base in those days.

"Nothing, Mom!" Ronnie shouted, giving us a few seconds of cover. "Just watching TV."

My best friend Louis, entwined with Judy, literally bailed out, not waiting to see if Tilly would actually dare come all the way down those steps. He opened the basement window, pulled himself up and out, and jumped on his waiting bicycle. Judy, of course, never forgave his sudden departure.

In my younger days I was into brunettes. Years later I learned a valuable lesson of discovery and self-awareness through a self-improvement training course I took after my divorce from Lynn. It was called Life Spring and it taught me that liking and being fixed on only one thing (like brunettes) was rigid and locked me into a place where I was missing so much else. Like blondes and red-heads.

Simple, sure, but even that was a breakthrough from my in-grained behavior. Everything we want is outside our comfort zone, that secure little box where we reside, where we stay, keeping fear and the unknown away in order to be safe.

Safe.

That discovery unlocked so much for me. This Journey is a testament.

Ronnie and I had our fights, like boys and girls do, I guess, but we both fondly remember the time she'd had enough of my teasing. We sat right next to each other in the lunchroom, the girls at one table, the boys at another. Well, little Bobby Young went one step too far. She calmly, and with a look that said, "I'll get you good," took an ice cream bar and smeared it down my face. Even I laughed hysterically. Sharing the story with her in later years always made us howl.

All of us kids used to take the bus down to the beach. You could go anywhere in those days for twenty-five cents. Rockville Centre, on the south shore of Long Island, outside New York City where I grew up, was a few towns north of the beach. A gaggle of kids would all hop on the bus and go to Long Beach for some sun and swimming. Judy and Ellie and Ronnie. Louis. Frank. So many others. There I got to see a girl in a bikini the first time. I was thirteen, and Ronnie's burgeoning sexuality was impressive. My first glimpse of her naked breast, when she leaned over, was seared into my memory.

Ronnie and I didn't last very long, but it was not the heartbreaker others would be and we became fast friends. Special, sweet moments bound us together. Now, for a lifetime.

So, whenever I did get to Dallas, I always tried to see her. She had another marriage after the mirage of her first love vanished. That, too, ended in painful disappointment for her, after two kids. A husband who gambled and shot pool for a living became too much. She would later lose her son to a drug overdose, and then almost lose her daughter, who had brain cancer but won her battle.

Ronnie always had a smile, always called me on my birthday and stayed in touch, as did I with her. She was one of those friends who was always there for you, always with a smile and positive support. You have to think about those who remain, those who go, those who stay, in your life. Ronnie and I go way back, so of course I would see her on this journey.

Atlantic Aviation's terminal was a modern, glass building. Like Abilene, jets were abundant and despite the high rollers on the ramp, I wasn't surprised by the professional attitudes and welcome. A staff member took my bags in from Two Niner Lima while I went to the men's room to relieve my full bladder and wash my hands and face. It had been hot in the plane, so I took a paper towel, soaked it in cold water, and wiped of the sweat from my face. Then another one, with more cold water, I put it on my back of my neck and top of my head to cool me off a bit.

I am always amazed by that factoid: all the heat escapes from the top of your head. Must be something to do with the chakra there, or so they say. And why, when I am getting out of the shower—unless, of course, it's just too cold out—I go from hot to cool, not all the way to cold, dousing that seventh chakra. I read a long time ago that to keep balance and nourish this one, known as the

Crown Chakra, it is central to maintain strong feelings with the Universe and develop a deeper connection to it. You can bet that on this Journey, having surrendered to the Universe and beholden to where it might take me, I have been religious in addressing that ritual every morning when I shower.

I checked in with the receptionist to register Two Niner Lima. The pretty young lady was a brunette, and her name tag identified her as Ibesta. I was guessing she was of Arab descent and when I addressed her as it was spelled, she corrected me, explaining the "b" is pronounced as "v." So it was Ivesta. Now, I wasn't so sure—maybe Spanish instead of Arabian. I stopped myself labeling her like that, as her smile was as warm as her rectifying words. I didn't like that my mind was wondering about her race when she was so warm with a stranger.

Ibesta then asked me if I wanted Two Niner Lima to be hangared to which I, again, politely declined. When she told me the overnight fee was twenty dollars per night, I was a bit dismayed.

"I thought if you purchased fuel here it's waived. I will be doing so before departure."

"No, sir. Not here."

I was getting worried about money now. I had just made a big payment on my last credit card account, so I had some leeway, but twenty bucks a night, plus the fuel, had me anxious.

My choice of this FBO would cost me almost three hundred dollars, and I was running out of money. Fuel here was expensive, almost six dollars a gallon. Not like the four eighty-two in Abilene.

"Do you think it possible I could get a break on the overnight fee?" I queried. "I chose Atlantic over Millionaire—your competitor—because we have one in Santa Monica, and I would appreciate it if it could be reduced."

Most airports don't charge any fee if you buy fuel, or, at the worst, only charge five to seven dollars per night.

"Sure," she responded. "I'll ask my manager and let you know. Do you need a lift somewhere? We can take you in our courtesy van."

"Oh, that would be great! Give me a few minutes to get my bearings and I'll be ready. Thanks."

I went to sit down, sip on some water, and reflect.

The lobby was full. A bunch of men looking ready to go on a business trip on a waiting jet outside were on a sofa and some chairs toward the rear of the lobby. The FBO had a high ceiling, with a stairway to a second-floor lounge and more bathrooms. The wall facing the tarmac was all glass. I sat down and peered out, sipping on the complimentary bottle of water Ibesta had provided me.

I looked across the tarmac. Dallas, Texas. Addison Airport. The tower was right across from me. Here I was, halfway across America and going to see one of my dearest friends and her husband, Larry. I was looking forward to spending some quality time with them both. Ronnie and I had been in constant text communication since I left Phoenix, especially when my knee acted up and I needed her help to find an orthopedist. I had met Larry a few times. A very kind soul, extremely talented and capable, a restauranteur, wine connoisseur, and he loved his Ronnie. They were happy and content, or so I understood from Judy, Ronnie's longest b.f.f. (best friend forever) with whom I was also still very close.

Observing relationships has always been fascinating to me, watching and listening to see what might really be going on. Hell, in all my relationships, and all my searching over the years, each one was different. Each had its own nuances, but the dynamics were all similar. My love and how I held my partner were always something to be measured. It seemed I needed to be concerned, in some sense, of my personal growth and commitment to growing that love and nourishing it, even through many relationships, seeking and finding something of which I have not been so sure. I wondered now after all this time, after marriages and relationships and seeking something so esoteric and intangible as love—if this "love" thing, was real, or if something else binds us to another. One other. I am not sure it is even explainable, even knowing, as God knows, so many have tried over thousands of years.

Perhaps, it has always been in the doing, in experiencing that love. Or, perhaps it's circumstance, and who it is with whom you get to experience this connection. If it is in that common denominator in each of us, operating on the same frequency, a similar energy, the same wavelength, that we find a particular other, and are bound in some inextricable way, be it friend or lover.

Love, whatever that is or may be. For each of us, it has to be different. After all, it is my experiences, my eyes that see, my heart that feels. Not yours. You have your own. Hollywood has its take. I don't know—so I question—what love really is. Sure, it is closeness, and attraction, and even heat. Companionship and friendship. But, as I came to understand myself better, and women more, I realized there was much more to it. That emotional intimacy has become so important to me—the sharing, the understanding and being with another, friend or lover. Now on this journey, I am feeling so much of whatever it is from my friends and giving back all mine. Whether in relationship or not, it is what I wanted to see more of, and have more. This human interaction that binds us to each other.

Crazy as it sounds, before I left on this journey I couldn't stand people, and I was enjoying my solitude. The years of litigation had fried me and I was deplete of any care or concern about others' problems. I felt so stupid and ashamed of myself for having to file bankruptcy after going through so much money my father and mother had left me. I'd spent it on my baseball dreams, believing I could build a league and grow teams in Hawaii, always thinking I could and would succeed.

The athlete in me knew no limitations and had taught me that with hard work and effort I would always score that goal and get that win, no matter the odds. Beaten, depressed and in despair, I felt foolish and embarrassed by my blind commitment to that cause. Losing my home after the final nail from my brother's malfeasance was the last blow to my fragile ego. I just wanted to be left alone, to reflect, to gather my wits and strength, and continue. Bruce and Dolly's home, far away from the city, was my refuge.

Now, this trip is telling me otherwise and pulling me to others. I am eager to share our love and friendship from the life experiences we had, the unexplained connection of traveling together, our souls intertwined in some fashion. I felt like I was digging deeper, and my conversations and inquiries were deeper, more honest, more authentic than ever. I was enjoying people. I was trying to understand this magic of connection that has lasted all these years. My friends. I don't want to stop.

I felt so blessed and happy sitting there reflecting on my friends and my arrival into Dallas. Besides, I was so damn pleased with myself as the Pilot in Command of Two Niner Lima, accepting that IFR clearance even though rusty as heck, being here, half-way across the USA in my own plane. It was almost surreal, and I had to slow myself down a bit, take in this moment, and keep it all on an even keel.

I took out my phone and texted Ronnie I had arrived and was

on my way to her home. They had left a key for me under the mat. I would see them later in the afternoon when they both arrived home from work.

I slipped on my backpack and gathered my bags. Ibesta asked Doug, the boy standing next to the reception desk, to take me to where I needed to go. I gave him the address, he punched it into Waze, and remarked, "Very good. Only three point six miles away. Let's go!"

Doug was young, about twenty-five I would guess, working at Atlantic but not training to be a pilot. He was thinking about starting but was getting married soon and had the wedding to pay for and get past that before he knew what he would do. I encouraged him to consider it, like I had done with Jordan.

Like so many others, he was genuinely stupefied when I told him I was from Santa Monica and traveling across country on this Journey. That anyone would travel around the USA in Two Niner Lima seemed incredible to him. I think he was a bit jealous of, but encouraging, nonetheless.

We drove through Addison, a suburb within immediacy to the city. The green I had seen from above was as prominent throughout the streets. It was a clean city, not too much traffic at all. We were gabbing away as Doug pulled up to Ronnie and Larry's townhome. I thanked him, gave him a few dollars, then lugged my bags up the walk.

I managed to figure out the lock and key and went inside. Their home was stunning, as if right out of *Architectural Digest*. It was like I always felt when I returned home to Dewey after a few weeks away and entered my former beautiful home.

"Wow! This is a nice home!" I would say, even if it was my own and done by my own handiwork. My reaction opening the door as I stepped into Ronnie and Larry's home was exactly the same. "Nice home, indeed!"

There, in front of me, was a note, "Welcome to Dallas." Another note gave me instructions as to which room I would be staying in, and inviting me to help myself to some cheese, nuts and wine in the living room, and advising me they would see me after five.

I would soon learn that my friend loved to leave notes for me, as well as her husband. She ran a tight ship and kept her beautiful home in tip-top shape. Larry was truly her partner in this endeavor.

My stay of almost a full week was delightful. The warmth and concern from them was more than I could have expected. Ronnie and Larry took such good care of me. They fed me, wouldn't let me spend a dime at all, and just loved and nourished me. They went to work every day, and I had their magnificent home all to myself. I tried to contribute by making sure dishes were washed and laundry was folded—whatever I could do to chip in so my hosts would not feel like I was an interloper in their home.

Curiously, Larry would not accept my offer of help in the kitchen or in the house always insisting to do whatever it was by himself. He was inflicted with MS, his leg a bit bent and he walked with a cane. But that didn't slow him down nor did he ever let anyone feel pity for him. I think maybe that was why he refused my help, but I didn't push it.

I walked about the neighborhood to a Starbucks around the corner, enjoying that respite a few days, sipping on an iced coffee, observing the people. It was the same as everywhere. People on their computers tapping away. Some outside on their cell phones. I overheard a real estate agent, a young man, pushing and prodding his listener about the property he had for him.

Larry, Ronnie and I talked endlessly about politics, watching our evening's fill of CNN and MSNBC. I learned about Texas life and politics, how the state was changing dramatically over the years (leaning more left every year). What Dallas living was like. People, even in Texas, seemed the same as everywhere I had been.

Ronnie made sure to have lots of social activities for us, from taking me out to dinner, to going out with her many friends for dinner, as well as having a dinner party at her home. My friend was selling me on her Dallas, and I was nibbling at the bait. I was so surprised at how cheap housing was, gas was not an arm and a leg, and there was no state income tax.

Her many friends also made me consider living there. Observing their interaction at every dinner, I saw how close they all were. Everyone loved Ronnie and Larry, and the genuine concern everyone seemed to have for one another was noticeable. Maybe it was because I'm older now, and I appreciate those connections and sentiments, but I had felt the good vibes ever since Two Niner Lima broke through those clouds.

The last Saturday night I was there, when we were sitting around the dinner table at the party Ronnie hosted, I felt as if I was in an episode of *Seinfeld*. All of them kibitzed so well with each other, their timing of tease and love down to perfection. I became especially enamored with their friends Marc and his wife Paula. I had met them before, when Ronnie took me to a party at their magnificent home, another one right out of a magazine, but huge. A mansion. Marc had not worked pretty much ever, as his family made a fortune in meat packing in Fort Worth. He dabbled in the law. Paula was a stunning woman of seventy, with eyes of green and a big smile. She and Ronnie were raising their kids together, before Marc, when both were hit by divorces and life's hard knocks. Like all of us, they persisted, re-married, and were all still best of friends for so many years. Their affinity was obvious.

Marc was a funny, dry man. He was short like me, slight of build, but it was his demeanor and delivery that captured me. No pretense. Quiet. Unassuming. But with a wit so quick, delivered in a dry, and quiet slight Texas drawl, he held the floor. I really liked him.

Ronnie had ordered in Chinese food and Marc's fortune cookie said he had a secret admirer. When we said our goodbyes, I confessed to him it was me and told him I hoped we would keep in touch. He felt the same, so I made a new friend. I thought, *Well, hey, maybe Dallas is a possibility*.

I also spent an afternoon with Sean and Bobby, two college friends from Brown. Sean and I played soccer together there and what I remember about him was that he had this long stride and could run like the wind. We knew each other as teammates but I hadn't spent much time with him until, an accomplished journalist, he was in Los Angeles writing for the *LA Times*. I had seen Bobby a few years back at a Brown mini-reunion Sean had put together, and to which he invited me, so it was good to see their mugs again and feel the love.

We'd all been jocks at Brown and enjoyed reminiscing about the glory days at our university alma mater, and how amazed we were at the University it has become. We remembered friends we all still knew and had in common, some gone now, others battling their own stuff. Bobby had some serious back issues. He was an amazing All-State Texas football player, although he was really too small for football. He was about my height—and he was fast. Sean regaled me with some of his legendary exploits on the local football field at St. Mark's, a private school in Dallas they had both attended. I remember Bobby at Brown, as the star freshman and big contributor on the varsity, despite his size.

We wolfed down delicious hamburgers at Chip's, a Dallas favorite. On the way back to Bobby's home, we drove by the site of the Robert E. Lee statue, which had been removed a few weeks before. Both shared with me the strong influence the Confederacy still had in Dallas, their concern about racial issues, and what progress they have witnessed over their lives in their hometown. It was a special afternoon. The connection we shared, the bond, this inexplicable love of other souls with whom I have shared the journey, whom I have touched (and been touched by) had me so happy. Sean dropped me off at my hotel late in the afternoon.

Dallas had an air museum at Love Field to which, the day before my departure, I was eager to go. But at Sunday brunch the day before I would go, a hellacious thunderstorm interrupted our get together. Larry and Ronnie had invited their kids and spouses to join us, and we were all enjoying hearing about the progress the kids had made in their own lives.

Taking stock of the darkening skies, I decided to check this upcoming storm on the MyRadar app. It had started to rain and the red eye of the storm, confirmed the severe weather.

"This is going to be bad," I said. "It's heading straight for us!"

Sure enough, all hell broke loose. Thunder and lightning, rain going sideways and coming down so hard you could hardly see outside. The atrium in the middle of the house backed up.

"It's clogged!" Larry said, jumping into the two inches of water, still in his shoes. The rising water was seeping into the house. He quickly pulled the drain up and the water receded while the storm continued to pound away. Later, we learned a crane had tumbled and crashed into an apartment building nearby, killing a young woman. The scattered remnants of many trees littered across Addison were evident the next morning when Larry drove me to the airport for my morning flight to Houston.

The weather was my concern and, with this storm, I was learning more about how fast it can come at you from the nearby Gulf of Mexico. I was using MyRadar and repeatedly checking Foreflight for the weather forecast for Houston and New Orleans, where I'd be heading next. Flight Service had advised that a high-pressure ridge was building over Oklahoma, keeping most of the storms a hundred miles or so off the coast. It would last four to five days, so I had my opening to go to Houston and then over to New Orleans. I would leave on the first day it was holding and not push my luck.

I got to the Frontiers of Flight early, taking an Uber over. But, because of the storm, the electricity was off in this area. the hand-written note pasted onto the front door informed me:

MUSEUM CLOSED. NO POWER.

I walked around and was able to see pretty much all of it inside through the windows. There was a bountiful static display outside the building. The sight of a Southwest Airlines Boeing 737-200 and some military aircraft had me enjoying being there despite the closure.

Walking behind the building, I peered out at Love Field. I looked hard, remembering . . . images of the blood-stained car and widow, Mrs. Jacqueline Kennedy, standing aside as officials loaded her husband's casket onto Air Force One. I looked out to see if I could remember the building where she'd stood. But my view that day, with Southwest airliners landing in front of me, in color, the sun shining brightly, didn't correlate to those faded black and white TV images and the horror from so long ago.

Feeling nourished, complete, and loved after my time with good friends, I was ready to move on. I packed and checked in with Flight Service, confirming their weather prognosis. In Dallas, I saw a place to which to possibly move. I had met wonderful new friends and, reveling in our connections, I relished the old.

I could have stayed for another few months, but it was time to continue the Journey.

CHAPTER XI

---✈

LEG FIVE

June 11, 2019
ADS - SGR
Addison Airport, Dallas, Texas, to Sugar Land Regional Airport, Houston, Texas Distance: 242 nm
Route: ADS – Direct SGR
Start Time: 10:18 a.m.
Wheels up: 10:29 a.m.
Wheels down: 12:03 p.m. (Central time)
Shut-Down Time: 12:03 p.m.

Log Entry: ADS - SGR: 2.1 hrs. Flight time: 1:34
Good flite. Lights, Camera, Action! Forgot to turn on all on TO. Step climbs to smooth air @5,500' + 10 kts tailwind. Houston approach down to 2,000' bumpy. Bad ldg but saved it after bounce.

My window would be holding for four to five days, so I wasn't in a rush to beat the weather. I would have enough time to spend in Houston and then get to New Orleans without too much hassle. Larry offered to take me back to Addison Airport, which happened to be around the corner from his office. With warm feelings for Ronnie's beau, I gave him a hearty hug and kiss on the cheek when I departed. He'd never hesitated to make me feel welcome. Their generosity, love and support had me soaring to the next stop.

When I said my goodbyes that morning and walked into Atlantic Aviation, it was almost nine-thirty. It was a beautiful day for flying, not a cloud in the sky. Passengers and crew filled the lobby, and the tarmac was active with jets lined up, waiting to be on their way.

Again, Ibesta was behind the counter, where I needed to check out and pay for my fuel. She had left a message for me on Thursday afternoon, but I had missed her when I called back Saturday. I was hoping to catch a break on the overnight fee. Lucky me— she advised they would cut it down to fifteen dollars per night. Well, money is money and I was running low, so any savings was a blessing.

I found a baggage cart, like those a bell boy in a hotel might use, loaded my bags onto it and rolled it out the back door Ibesta had pointed out.

After that hellacious storm, I was concerned about Two Niner Lima. But there she stood, off to the side of the terminal, no hail or wind damage discernible. She seemed poised and eager to go as I unsnapped the canvas cover and laid my bags on the wing walk. I took the wheel chocks out from under the front and main wheels as I walked around the plane to undo the snaps. Then I unlocked the canopy and slid it back full aft. After loading up the baggage compartment, putting my iPhone, Stratus 3, iPad, and keys on the glare shield, I took my fuel analyzer from the back storage compartment behind the pilot's seat and began my walk-around. This fuel analyzer is an eight-inch clear plastic tube with a thick plastic pin a few inches in length fastened to its top.

One of the first things a pilot learns in training to fly is doing the walk-around. It's part of our checklist—it's up to the pilot's discerning eye to make sure the plane is airworthy and ready to go. I have had Two Niner Lima for so long that I could do this in my sleep. Doing it in a meticulous, same direction flow every time, as is specified, makes for routine and habit. Just like looking over your instrument panel in a certain way, in a flow across the panel, as Captain Ron taught me. That's how I approach the walk-around, as I am sure all pilots do.

I can still recall Bill Beecher, my first instructor, walking along with me when I was just learning to fly in a Cessna 150. At each position to verify, we would stop, and he would explain what he was looking for and what we should see to approve and then move on. Every plane is the same, and when I see a First Officer doing the walk-around on an airliner, I always smile at the common task we all have, no matter what equipment we're flying.

First to be checked on Two Niner Lima are the fuel ports under the left wing, almost at the point where the wing joins the fuselage. There are two spring valves right next to each other, one for the main tank and the other for the auxiliary tank. I filled the fuel analyzer with a few inches of fuel and confirmed it was the correct fuel—100 octane low lead. Now the only aviation fuel in use, it should be a light blue in color. Light blue it was. Before they stopped making 80 octane low lead, the distinction in color was obvious, as 80 octane was pink.

I also look for any sediment or particles, checking to make sure there's no contamination in the fuel. Nor should there be any water, always an issue in wet climates, possibly because of fuel contamination in a storage tank. This had happened to my friend Alireza, who parks his plane next to mine at SMO, when he filled up his Grumman Tiger last spring. If water is present in the fuel, the pilot will see water as a distinct volume of liquid at the bottom of the analyzer, as water is heavier than gasoline. Water weighs eight pounds per gallon, while gasoline weighs six pounds per gallon. Alireza, as any pilot would, was draining his tanks when I last saw him, testing and retesting, again and again, to make sure the water was out of his bird's fuel tanks.

The walk-around continues outboard along the left wing. First I look at the flaps on the back of the wing to make sure there's no apparent damage on the left flap in its retracted position. I then move next outward to check the ailerons by moving them up and down, verifying that the yoke moves in the proper directions, and the ailerons are secure, not loose. I will check my flight controls as well, when I am seated, to again confirm they are operating properly. A loose aileron could result in some significant vibration and tear away from the aircraft, which would mean the pilot wouldn't be able to turn properly. Or, God forbid, bad vibrations would begin a structural flutter which, even in Two Niner Lima, could be catastrophic.

Ailerons were a creative new idea developed by an early aviator, Glenn Curtis who, in contrast with the Wright Brothers' original designs, created this easier way to turn the airplane in conjunction with rudder input. Reading about this innovation by Curtis, and about the Wright Brothers' original wing warping designs, particular Wilbur's intense patent fights against Curtis, shed background and detail of the early days when the science of flying took hold. (See *Birdmen: The Wright Brothers, Glenn Curtis, and the Battle* to Control the Skies by Lawrence Goldstone, and The Wright Brothers by David McCulloch.) It changed my perspective on walk-arounds of Two Niner Lima as a flying machine, with its particular performing parts. I had to be thorough, from the ailerons on the wing, to the curvature of the wing on top and the flat surface on its bottom that creates the magic of lift, and to the engine propeller, twisted in a certain way. I read anything I can find about aviation and these fascinating accounts in particular were adjuncts to my continued education as a pilot.

Now, at the end of the wing, I flex it slightly and check underneath, peering all the way down its flat under surface to verify no parts are hanging or amiss and the wing is clean. I also check that the left main tire is property inflated.

Each fuel tank cap is on top of the wing at its end so I then opened it to verify that the lineman had filled each tank to the top, to full, matching what I paid for and confirming that I had enough fuel to make this leg. I had checked its quantity before when I opened Two Niner Lima up, looking at the fuel gauges on each side of the front of the cockpit to verify by sight that the tanks were full. Checking the level in the tanks confirmed that observation.

The walk around continues as I check the leading edge of the left wing, making sure the front edge is clean, and there are no dents from rain or hail damage after being tied down at ADS. Hail was on the tail-end of the storm that blew through Addison a few days before, so I am puzzled but relieved when I find no damage. Looking at the side of the building, I had to think that maybe, in some way, the terminal had acted as a wind block for Two Niner Lima, and we lucked out.

Getting back to my task, I continued on to the fuselage, checking to make sure the static port, which is part of the gyro instruments vacuum lines, is free from any debris. I then confirm by a slight lifting motion that the engine compartment is, in fact, secured, which brings me facing Two Niner Lima and looking at her head-on.

At this juncture, I stick my hand into the open inlets of the cowling on each side of her propeller, making sure no bird's nest or other debris is present. I check the propeller blades, confirming no dents or nicks are present. A nick of some depth could cause the propeller to vibrate so badly it could tear away from the plane which, if found, is a matter of great concern. Over my years of flying, that has occurred twice, and each time, my mechanic filed down the slight nick and indent and I had no issues. Every year, along with the aircraft, the tensile strength, along with the entire propeller, also undergoes its annual inspection.

While inspecting the propeller, I opened the access panel to the engine compartment on top of the cowling and unscrewed the dip stick to verify that Two Niner Lima has a minimum of six quarts of oil of its eight-quart maximum. On my pre-journey inspection, Bill's Air, my mechanics at SMO, had added new oil. When I started, it was full but now it was just above six quarts. I could replenish the oil in New Orleans. I put the dipstick back and turned it once and a half, not too tight, as the heat and pressure when flying would make it tighter anyway.

Peering around in the engine compartment, I made sure there were no loose wires and everything seemed to be attached, then I closed the compartment. Now at the right static port, I completed my walk around on the right wing, doing everything I'd done on the left side of the aircraft, but in reverse. Only when I came to the tail, the horizontal stabilizer and the rudder, did my inspection look for more than the obvious defects. There, affixed to the stabilizer, is a cotter pin, which is essential to confirm it is securely in place, controlling the trim wheel used to "trim" out the control forces and make it easier to handle and fly the machine. Without that cotter pin in and secured, I would be out of luck. Wrestling the aircraft in the sky would not be a pretty picture.

I have done as many walk-arounds as flights in Two Niner Lima and other aircraft I flew, from the Cessna 150 in which I soloed, to the Grumman Tigers and Cheetahs I flew when earning my private pilot certificate, to the Piper Archers and Dakotas I rented after Grumman ceased doing business when Gulfstream decided it could make more money selling its business jets than bothering with small planes. Something I always think about grabbed me from the very beginning and made me a fatalist. As diligent as I was, I could not peer into the engine compartment and see a piston ready to break, or a wire ready to melt and cause a fire, or some other hazard just waiting to happen. As a result, and because I kept coming back without any calamity or malfunction occurring, I began to believe it was all a matter of fate (if and when the day ever comes).

It did on July 4, 2016, when my throttle jammed and I had to make an emergency engine-out landing at Van Nuys. Working my way through the problem—thinking, assessing, and breathing through my fear and anxiety—I was able to take it to a happy ending. But when trouble-shooting post-flight after landing, I discovered that a broken butterfly valve attached to the throttle cable had lodged in the carburetor. It was a reminder—not even the preflight and walk around can always assure a risk-free flight.

But, other than this incident, I am always aware of the inherent risk pilots engage in every time I take to the air.

"Never rush the walk-around," my instructor Bill Beecher always commanded. "It spells death so use your checklist and take your time."

His admonition, chastising me one day when all I wanted was to get going again on another lesson, had me pause. Bill was a mild-mannered older gentleman who never raised his voice, but that warning, and his serious tone stayed with me. Every checklist and the methodical and orderly walk-around were needed to give me some assurance the aircraft was good to go.

Two Niner Lima fired up again after only a few turns of the prop. After obtaining ATIS, I checked in with Clearance Delivery and requested Class Bravo Clearance up to five thousand, five hundred feet, direct to Sugar Land Regional Airport in Houston. "Upon request. Contact ground."

I switched over to Ground control, advised that I had the weather information, and started down Taxiway B (Bravo) to Runway 15. Sometimes, as I taxi, I do housekeeping chores, putting in certain frequencies and getting the Garmin 530 ready with its destination and the format laid out the way I like. I was putting in a few frequencies to save myself the chore at the run-up when my head set crackled:

"Grumman Two Niner Lima, Ground, we have your clearance. Ready to copy?"

"Grumman Two Niner Lima. Roger. Ready to copy."

"Grumman Two Niner Lima is cleared through the Class Bravo airspace. Fly runway heading. Climb and maintain two thousand feet. Contact departure on 124.3 Squawk 1623."

I wrote this down on my note pad, in short-hand I was taught when I obtained my IFR and Commercial ratings. Then I read back the clearance to the controller.

"RH. ↑ Two thousand. 124. 3. 1623."

"Read back correct. Contact tower after run-up."

I pulled into the run-up area. It was a beautiful morning. The sky was all blue above me, not a cloud in sight. I completed my run up and then contacted Tower as instructed, holding short of Runway 15, awaiting my release as a few planes arrived, one right after the other, at ADS. Looking to my right down the final approach path, I didn't see any more aircraft on final approach. I was next.

Then, so out of place it startled me, my iPhone rang. It was Larry. I was curious but my mind was elsewhere, my thoughts on my imminent departure. I couldn't pick up, as the phone was set to be my video recorder, lodged in its position in the cradle on the glare shield.

Besides, I was concentrating now about the take-off—but I was concerned. Why was he calling now?

"Grumman Two Niner Lima, cleared for take-off. Runway 15. Winds Calm. Fly runway heading."

"Grumman Two Niner Lima, Cleared for take-off, Runway 15. Runway heading."

I pushed in the throttle and rolled out, checked my directional gyro to line up the runway heading on it, and quickly accelerated, pulling back ever so slowly. After Two Niner Lima reached seventy knots, off we went. Up and straight out to two thousand feet, where I trimmed her out, awaiting the next step climb to five thousand, five hundred feet.

When the controller noticed I had no transponder code and asked if I was squawking 1623, I realized I was thrown a-kilter. In my training I learned a pneumonic trick to remind me to turn on all my lights, then the transponder, and then to advance the throttle by saying, "Lights, Camera, Action!" when I was about to take the active runway for departure. The controller's inquiry pointed out that I had not performed this habitual task, failing to turn on the transponder to activate my assigned squawk code. I had also failed to turn on my lights. Larry's call had interrupted me at a crucial and solemn time right before take-off.

I quickly turned on the transponder.

"Grumman Two Niner Lima squawking 1623." I sure as heck didn't want to admit I was a Bozo and not a professional discharging my basic pilot duty.

"Roger, Grumman Two Niner Lima. Radar Contact. Two thousand feet. Climb and maintain three thousand, five hundred feet."

Up we went and as we did, the air became smoother, climbing up and over the distinct haze line about three thousand feet. I saw all of southern Texas laid out before me. Mainly farmland. I wondered about each farm, all the families below, living in this state, being a Texan, and the identity associated with that bravura (or so this New Yorker thought). What must it be like, living this rural life, farms so spread out amongst the green fields and grasses? In the distance, I saw a smokestack, maybe of a utility plant servicing the area. Another few tall buildings rose in the distance. I thought it must be a hotel or casino, looking strangely out of place amidst the flat farmland.

The controller then brought us up to five thousand, five hundred feet, and I was still heading south. We were showing one hundred forty-three to one hundred forty-six knots on the Garmin 530 and, verified by Foreflight on the iPad, we had a ten-plus knots tailwind. Ah, a tailwind and clear skies. A pilot's dream. It would be a short flight

When I approached the Houston Class B airspace, the descent down to two thousand feet had Two Niner Lima rocking a bit, from the building convective activity near the Gulf. ATIS reported the winds at three hundred thirty, right for the tailwind I had, and Runway 33 in use.

The controller handed me off to the tower and cleared me for landing on Runway 33, left traffic. I reported on down-wind, kept a bit of extra speed on final, floated a bit, bounced, added a juice of power to break the bounce descent, then smoothly touched down.

The airport was set within a beautiful, green wooded area. I taxied to the transient parking off to the left of the main terminal, the lineman, as always, guiding me with his batons. When I shut down a fuel truck pulled up. I refused fuel then, preferring to wait until the night before departure to re-fuel so the gasoline wouldn't have an opportunity to evaporate in the heat. Now, I was getting the hang of shutting down. Another lineman pulled up in a golf cart and helped me unload my bags.

Lastly, I took a picture of Two Niner Lima before he drove me to the terminal. Focusing my iPhone, I framed Two Niner Lima against the tower and the modern terminal, confirming another successful step in our journey. Houston, Texas. The sign on the front doors greeted me with "Welcome to Sugar Land." There was even a Starbucks inside the plush lobby.

I went through my routine—checking in, washing up, buying a cup of coffee and taking a little time to ponder and reflect. I was pleased. Another step along the way successfully navigated. I texted my friend, Corey, younger brother of my high school pal Michael, to let him know I was down and would Uber to him in half an hour or so, at a lunch meeting he was attending.

I was eager to see NASA, the purpose of my stop, and admire the greatest endeavors this country had ever accomplished.

CHAPTER XII

———————————————————————————————✈

LEG FIVE

FRIENDS

The half hour drifted by as I observed the folks coming and going in and out of the plush terminal of the Sugar Land Regional Airport. It was relaxing for me not to keep moving, to pick up and go and rush on to the next place. I was dilly-dallying here just because I could, and how rare is that for any of us harried souls to simply sit and be still with our thoughts, to watch and listen. I wanted to catch my breath before engaging with Houston, my next adventure.

A fortyish blonde woman, nattily over-dressed, Gucci bag dangling, with a teenager in tow, sat down next to me, and I started a conversation with them. Mother and daughter, I gathered from the looks of them. I wondered what they did and how they did it, to be in a place like this. It was like they were diving into a movie screen and becoming actors in this play of mine. Me? Well, I'm a private pilot flying across the country in my small two-seater, making a dream come true.

"Yes, I came all the way from Santa Monica," I responded in

answer to the mother's query. "After I see NASA and Houston for a few days, next stop is New Orleans. And where are you heading?"

"We're taking our daughter Betsy out to Abilene to see the family," she replied. I imagined a huge ranch or compound, old Southern Texas money, oil money, and going to see the grandparents who provided all this for her. I didn't want to ask. Imagination is the best way to travel in this movie.

"What's it like living in L.A.?" Betsy jumped in. "Seems so glamorous."

She was probably seventeen or so, blonde hair tied in a ponytail, wearing flats, jeans, and a madras shirt, sleeves rolled up. She seemed to be one of those pert, wholesome kids whose inquisitiveness and wonder are written all over her face, clearly her mother's daughter—not yet on her own and not having shed the imprint.

"Oh, not so," I told her as I took another swig of water, washing down the last of my coffee and feeding my still parched thirst.

"I mean, I was an entertainment lawyer for a long time, and after a while you get used to the celebrities. Not like you run into them every day. But glamourous—not really. We're just like everyone else, work hard, do what everyone does, I guess. But I get to live in a pretty neat place that has the best weather. And no humidity!"

"I hope I'll get there one day!" mused Betsy, and I saw that glazed look into what she hoped was her future. I envied her youth and how she had the whole world in front of her. My sobering thought was, *Oh, dear Betsy—life is harder than you can ever imagine, and that dreamy look? Well, life can get pretty rocky and smite you good, girl.*

But, I said, "It's a pretty cool place, so make sure you do!"

The seed was planted, and for sure, Betsy would be there one day, like thousands of others who come, dreaming their dreams. I was no different. Ever since Willie and the Giants left New York, California was some far away, magical land, where the sun shone endlessly, the girls were prettier than you could imagine, and your dreams could come true. It casts its spell and never lets go.

Now, seeing that starry look of innocence, it jarred me—starkly and contrary to my thoughts and the reality of sitting there so far away from home. I was still searching. My dreams never did come true. Or, maybe they did, and I'd done exactly what I was supposed to do. I shuddered a bit as the Eagles song, *Wasted Time*, popped into my mind. No, the Universe provides, and every step is part of the journey to get you to here, to today, at Sugar Land Regional.

Go West, young man. Go West. Horace Greely and Manifest Destiny spoke to me then, as the pull to explore what is out there, whatever it is, and whatever it was that keeps us looking, still pulls at me now. Maybe everything is the way it's supposed to be. But we think there is more and keep searching. Are others so fulfilled they need not? Or dare not?

Just then, Betsy's Dad (I gathered) came over from the reception desk and advised his girls it was time to go. I nodded and we exchanged best wishes, and they left. Two young pilots accompanied them to an aircraft waiting outside. For sure, a jet.

This was a recently built airport, I had read before my arrival, and the new terminal reeked in elite status, clearly not one for the masses. Private FBOs like this reflect its clientele, as did Atlantic Aviation at Addison Airport in Dallas, the Signature at John Wayne Airport in Orange County, California. It is a different way to fly, to traverse the country by private plane, whether by jet, turbo prop, or piston, big or small, even down to the size of Two Niner Lima. It was first cabin, and even if I only flew a two-seater, I didn't feel like an interloper. After all, we pilots are the exception and command equal status, right? Or so I wanted to believe.

Of course, the rich don't think like that, with their noses too far up in the air to notice anyone or anything outside their privileged world. You get used to privilege, I guess, and it must be hard to give it up or dare risk its taint and jeopardize the gilded life. How did the song go? Oh, yes, Don Henley crooned: *It all can change in a New York minute.* Frank even said it better: *Riding high in April, shot down in May.*

Those tunes rang true for me now.

Here, at the Sugar Land airport, there is no TSA. There are no lines, no crowds. No airline agent checked me in or searched my bags or put them on a conveyor belt for screening. No, I just walked out carrying my bags. Sometimes, when I think about that—well, how much crime and contraband really does move this way—by private aviation at places like this? Everything is so wide open. Maybe it was because of the unwritten code amongst pilots and elite travelers not to mess up this pretty darn good thing we have going.

It is a long way down. Trust me on that.

My brief time of reflection over for the moment, I punched up Uber and ran to the bathroom before they came. Once over fifty, a lesson I learned and practiced diligently was never pass up a bathroom before moving on. To my chagrin, the App advised me that my driver would arrive in three minutes, so I did my business quickly and got my bags out to the curb just as Nary pulled up in his Nissan.

I'd taken a few Ubers in Dallas and now, here I was in Houston, with Nary. I learned he was a logistic engineer from Nigeria who specialized in pipelines for natural gas. Business was not so good and he'd been recently laid off, so he was earning extra money driving for Uber. He liked America but now without work, it was a bit more difficult for him and his family. He didn't want to go back to Africa even though his parents and siblings were still there. The incongruity of it all intrigued me. A foreigner, black, an engineer in the oil business, unable to find work in the oil capital of Texas, smack dab in the deep south. Something didn't fit.

We were heading clear to the other side of the sprawling metropolis. I had thought Corey's home was near the airport but it was not. The plan was for me to meet him at the Capitol Grille, and then he would drive me to his home.

My first glance of Houston from the elevated freeway disappointed me. So flat, hazy, and hot. We were on Interstate 10, heading east. Traffic was a bear as rush hour was building. The city appeared to be so spread out and sprawling, lacking the closeness and green intimacy I experienced in Dallas. Downtown loomed out of the haze. A metropolis.

That changed when Corey and I were headed to his home in the Heights area, near the old but now gentrified part of the city. From what I could see, downtown looked like any downtown, with its tall, glass office buildings jutting upward alongside the freeway. As did so much else. We passed by shopping centers with the familiar names. Target. Walmart. CVS. AMC. No matter where we go in America, everything looks the same. There's comfort in that, but so far in Houston I wasn't finding that same vibe I'd experienced in Dallas or Roswell or Tucson. It seemed a bit more like Phoenix, but Phoenix, lying in the Valley of the Sun surrounded by those incredible mountains, beneath a sky that stretches on forever, had it beat. I was unimpressed.

The Heights was an older neighborhood with lots of trees, more compact and dotted with many Victorian homes. It had a bit warmer feeling to it. Corey was educating me about the city, and the area in which he lived. Taking it all in, I asked questions, wanting to know more. Each new place was an opportunity for me to learn as much about it, for future home considerations.

Corey had gone through his own hell in the past fifteen years. He had made a fortune in Galveston but the SEC got a bug up its butt and came after him. After years of litigation, he lost everything. Then his wife became ill and had a liver transplant, after which she died when she could not stay off the wagon. His now girlfriend, Karen, was a sweet, sexy, warm soul from California. A doctor, she had relocated to Texas for work and met Corey online. They seemed smitten with each other and in sync.

After Corey showed me to my room, with the admonition to keep my door closed to keep the cats out, we went to a Houston favorite for a hamburger. I added Hop Daddy Burger Bar in Houston to my list of favorite burger joints (finding the best ones is another quest I've been on for years). Lots of them now, always trying to make the best, unique burger, but give it to me rare, please. Grill the onions, add lettuce, tomato and ketchup, and let the quality meat speak for itself. Cassell's in L.A. has been leading my list, which includes In N' Out, Hamburger Hamlet, The Counter, and even my local haunt at SMO, The Spitfire Grill, right up there in the City of Angels.

We went back to Corey's home, sat down and began to talk. He poured us both a glass of wine and we chilled with some of his medicinal marijuana. Life had rocked him and now he was working hard again, using his Texas contacts to create and develop real estate deals. He was on the precipice of putting together a syndication and taking two marijuana businesses into a Canadian company to take them public. I marveled at his energy. He was two years younger than me but at sixty-nine, his energy and ambition far exceeded my past two years of seeming resignation and defeat. I didn't want to risk anything or make the effort anymore. He did. It got me thinking.

In response to my comment about how similar our paths were and how inspiring it was to see his positive energy (something I had lost), he said, "I liked being rich. I don't like being poor. Simple. I am not going to be, so I am busting my ass now."

What it got me thinking about was my decision to go on this journey, to no longer have a desire to "play the game" after so much pain and defeat. I had lost my confidence. I wasn't sure of myself anymore. When you think you can score at will, or always succeed no matter the obstacles-well, nothing can stop you. But after losing my family money, getting sick, thinking I was about to die, not having the success I'd envisioned and seeing the arc of my career and business ventures perhaps ending—truthfully, I'd been resigned. There wasn't much—besides Two Niner Lima—that had any appeal.

Now, hearing my friend speak, watching his animated confidence, I felt something stirring within. It reminded me of what my dad always told me:

"Don't ever quit. Keep fighting. Just keep getting to tomorrow. The judge could die."

"Whatever do you mean by that, Dad?" I remember asking him, many years ago, years removed from our separation when I'd gone out west instead of to Court Street and his firm. My question came at a time much later when we got closer and eventually became friends.

"When I was a young lawyer, I had a case in front of an old

judge who was just killing me," he explained. "I thought it was a decent case but every time I went before him, I could tell he had it in for me. I kept stalling, trying everything I could think of, taking more of his wrath for my delays. And then one morning I got a call from the court. The Judge had died and the case was reassigned to a new judge, who was a friend of mine. And wouldn't you know it? After that, I won every motion, even won the case! So, my son, don't quit. Just keep getting to tomorrow. The judge could die!"

Dad was laughing, telling me that story. Oh, you know fathers, they have lots of stories. Many are not real, but they provide lessons for the child. And my father had many stories. Sidney Young was one tough guy. He had signed a contract with the New York Giants right out of Brooklyn College, but when the "Home Run King" slipped on some ice and broke his elbow, his dreams of a professional baseball career were over. Instead of going to spring training, he put himself through law school, attending classes at night.

"Baseball players are bums," my Grandma Pauline told him. "Stop wasting your time with baseball."

So instead, he became one of the leading real estate lawyers in New York, representing some pretty big names, from Fred Trump to his son, Donald, to Harry Lefrak and the building of Lefrak City, Leona Helmsley, just name them. Lindenbaum & Young was central to their success. Abe Lindenbaum, my dad's partner, was City Planning Commissioner under three mayors for over twenty years.

"If you wanted to build something in New York, you dealt with Lindenbaum & Young," my father once told me. "We'd send builders and real estate moguls downtown first, to see Bunny," he added, referring to his partner by his nickname. "And we'd tell them to take care of Bunny." He rubbed his thumb and forefinger together.

"Then come back to me to take care of all the zoning and paper-work."

I got it. Money takes care of everything.

Dawn couldn't come soon enough. My excitement grew as I drank some coffee and had a few bites of toast. I was eager to get to the Johnson Space Center and see NASA. A boyhood dream was about to come true.

In every space launch I had watched religiously since a young boy, control was handed over to Cap Com and Flight Control in Houston as soon as it cleared the launch tower at Cape Canaveral. When the sign came into view, and the Redstone rocket stood tall on display (along with a full-scale replica of the Space Shuttle sitting atop the Boeing 747 shuttle aircraft carrier), looming in front of me, I was in awe. I could hardly wait for the Uber driver to stop the car and let me out.

While in Dallas, I had purchased my ticket online and now here I was, entering the Space Center Houston Museum. I presented my ticket, entered the lobby, and came to a full stop so I could take it all in. Wow! I felt like a little kid, going into the candy store. With so many goodies before me, where to go first to sample these delights? The simplest way, I decided, was left to right.

I spent hours exploring the history of NASA and manned space flight exploration, from yesterday to today to tomorrow, onward to the Moon again and soon off to Mars. I saw up close the history I had witnessed: the Mercury 9 Space Capsule, *Faith 7*, which L. Gordon Cooper flew, the last of the Mercury astronauts to go into space in 1963, circling the globe for twenty-two orbits, spending over thirty-four hours in space. I was fifteen when I gulped down every bit of news on the only three available TV channels, and in print in *Newsday*.

And there it was, scorched, the name faded and blistered from re-entry.

Years later, Tom Wolfe's *The Right Stuff*, both the book and movie, honored the seven men who began our reach for the stars. Actors, including Ed Harris, Dennis Quaid and Sam Shephard beautifully portrayed the first group of space explorers, who knew they were the first and led the mission with teamwork and dedication, brave souls who made a contribution.

From Mercury to Gemini to Apollo, all the space programs, capsules, and even the moon rocks, had me enthralled. Every exhibit, portraying our progress exploring space (what I had lived vicariously before) was now right before me, and I was living it again. Standing in awe, I saw and read about all we had gone through and what this country had accomplished within eight years, heeding the clarion of a young President who, determined to put a man on the moon and return him safely, had laid down the gauntlet. And even if President Kennedy knew it was essential to our Cold War with the Soviet Union, it was still amazing to see it all under one roof. Making it even more special was that it was on the Fiftieth Anniversary of that incredible accomplishment—achieving President Kennedy's challenge.

Having followed my namesake, astronaut John Young, on his many missions, from Gemini to Apollo and the moon, and then the first to ride the space shuttle, I made sure to take pictures of his mission patch. Besides Young's name, along with the others, the patch has a design of the mission woven into it, with the names encircling the glorious representation of what they did. Smiling, I saw me, Captain Bob Young, as an astronaut on Apollo 10, on my way to the stars. I imagined myself with Eugene Stafford and Gene Cernan going around the moon, doing one final test, then landing on the lunar surface. Then, in my fantasy, I was on Apollo 16 with Charles Duke and Ken Mattingly, among the first to ride the fiery launch of space shuttle Columbia. If only.

A boy can dream, can't he?

Moving on through the exhibits, I read and studied what NASA was planning for the exploration of Mars. I hope I'm still alive for that. I always remember what Grandpa Benjamin told me in 1969, after we landed on the moon — a remarkable achievement.

"I never *ever* believed this possible, and I can't believe it happened in my lifetime!" he told me — not surprising since he was a boy raised in the Bronx in the late Nineteenth Century. It had taken him and his father (my namesake) who had emigrated from Odessa in 1881, a whole day to go to Jamaica by horse and buggy.

Who would have ever thunk it? Mars? Actually, many would not but I always thought it possible. Just a matter of time.

After many hours inside, I went outside and walked down the Astronaut Access Arm to the Space Shuttle, wondering what it must have been like, making those last steps before going into space, wondering if they would return. If you saw the Challenger explosion, or the Columbia disintegration, or heard the news flash when the tragic flash electrical fire killed the crew of Apollo One, you could understand what it must have been like for those brave souls.

Every pilot is aware of the inherent risk of flying. Climbing into a space capsule, the top rung of our ladder, couldn't have been any different from every time I climb up and into Two Niner Lima. Maybe worse, but only because of the odds. After all, these pilots were at the mercy of explosives, along for the ride until they could be pilots in space. Gus Grissom, one of the original Mercury 7 astronauts, was set to be the first man on the moon but a frayed wire on Apollo One sparked, causing a cabin fire during a launch rehearsal, killing him, Roger Chaffee and Ed White, the first man to walk in space.

Every pilot, I suspect, shares this apprehension, as I do. How could we not be aware of the inherent risk, relying on a machine and our skills and experience to get us through? But while we all feel it, it quickly disappears when I slip into the left seat. Doing my checklist and other preflight chores keeps my mind on the task.

In his classic examination of the beginnings of the space age, Tom Wolfe describes the lack of many bail outs from doomed test planes in the early days of jet travel. Test pilots risked their lives exploring new machines that were built to go faster and faster, beyond the sound barrier. When something went awry, as it often did, bailing out was the last thing on their minds.

No, at Edwards Air Force Base, high up in the California desert north of Los Angeles, these test pilots would keep trying to troubleshoot their ailing aircraft to right their stricken ship and keep it flying—all the way down until it crashed into the desert below.

"Fly the airplane!" Bill Beecher had said, and I knew exactly what he was talking about.

I finished my exploration of the Space Shuttle Carrier, reading all the details of the strengthened Boeing 747. She and her replica shuttle stood over eight stories high in Independence Plaza. She was huge. Relishing all the stories portrayed on her decks, I thought back to the day she was carrying the Endeavour space shuttle over Los Angeles, right over my home. She flew at fifteen hundred feet that day above Dewey, for her last fly-by enroute into LAX to be set up for exhibit in the California Science Museum at the University of Southern California. No airliner ever came that close, as they were restricted on the same downwind leg into LAX at six thousand to seven thousand feet. But not this honored guest.

I hopped on a tram and saw the remainder of the Johnson Space Center Campus. The docent took the microphone and told us of the history as we rambled on. Built on what was supposed to be an extension of the Rice University campus, many were squat 3-story buildings, classroom buildings converted, numbered, and referred to by that moniker instead of for what each did. Building 2. B2. Not the Teague Auditorium it was. Building 11. B11. Not the Cafeteria. Building 10. B10. Not Engineering Fabrication. All served some functions for NASA in this business of space exploration.

The tram took us to the Space Vehicle Mockup Facility where NASA had duplicates of everything it had put into space. Amazingly, right there in front of me was the Apollo capsule and LEM (Lunar Excursion Module) where the astronauts on the ground worked feverishly to find a way to create oxygen out of junk to keep Jim Lovell and his Apollo 13 crew alive. We saw the new Orion capsule and parts of the International Space Station and each module that had been added to it. The building was over a couple of football fields long and displayed row upon row of our history and ongoing exploration of space.

The last stop of the tour was Rocket Park, where stood the Redstone Rocket that had launched Alan Shepard into space in 1961. Americans were thrilled when we put our first man up there, even it was a fifteen-minute suborbital ride. I remember it well, listening on my transistor radio, a seventh grader hearing the beginning of man's reach for the stars.

Adjacent was a long, low building that housed the Saturn V, the biggest rocket ever created. When it came to life, our guide explained, people standing on the shore of the Banana River three miles away could feel the ground shake. The marvelous sound rumbled across the divide where thousands gathered to watch this behemoth, carrying man's hopes and dreams, travel up and away. Amazingly, the sound came after the rocket lifted, but came it did. The rocket (three hundred sixty-three feet tall, bigger than the Statue of Liberty) rose ever so slowly, its five F-1 engines building up its speed to escape gravity, six and a half million pounds of roaring fury inching skyward with three astronauts on board, counting on this machine to do its job perfectly. Praying, maybe.

I was overwhelmed. The amazing events and people who made such history, and who are striving for more, was all there. But all I could feel at the end of the day, as I sat in the cafeteria, was sadness. Whatever happened to the country I love—the country that did all these incredible things, mastered new technology, and explored the new frontier? I was saddened and still fear I'm bearing witness to the end of the America as I knew her over my lifetime. The fall of an empire.

I was always a firm believer and supporter of NASA, the agency that has brought us all such pride, along with countless innovations. What is going on that we forget our call for greatness?

Have we lost our will, our drive, our common commitment to each other? No, sadly I concluded that all we seem to think about is money and amassing personal wealth, the greed from corporations and lobbyists doing their bidding, the banks grinding us all, seeping into us, sapping our sense of purpose. Where was our commitment to do what must be done for the betterment of all?

"Of the People, By the People, For the People" seems to have been lost, with a party now consumed by its need for power, even to the extent its members will disavow their oaths to the Constitution. Can't they see we are all in this together?

Make America Great Again, my ass. I don't even recognize the place anymore.

It is unsettling that we seem to have chosen our demise, and that selfishness and greed prevails over all else, getting the better of us. That wasn't the American way I knew and in which I grew up. We're forgetting what made us great—and I had just spent hours bathing in it. I was so unsettled when I went back to Corey's for dinner.

I didn't have any answers. I don't know what will be, but I knew when we were better. And when we were one.

I hoped I would live long enough to see this aberration stopped and the downward spiral reversed.

And to see man step on Mars.

CHAPTER XIII

LEG SIX

June 13, 2019 SGR - NEW
Sugar Land Regional Airport,
Houston, Texas to Lakefront Airport, New Orleans, Louisiana
Distance: 295 nm
Route: SGR – Direct NEW
Start time: 10:26 a.m.
Wheels up: 10:43 a.m.
Wheels down: 12:55 p.m. Shut-Down time: 1:00 p.m.

Logbook Entry: SGR-NEW. 2.8 hrs. Flying time: 2:12 hrs. Nice flight @7,500′ Dir NEW. Above cloud tops. Bases @ 4,500′. New Orleans Approach cleared into Class B Dir NEW. Descended to 4,500′ then 2,500′. Excllnt ldg.

The excitement of NASA coupled with the disconnect I had experienced with all the conflict in our country had us engaged in political discourse my last evening in Houston. MSNBC was background noise on the tv, satisfying our daily fix in a world gone mad. Karen was making us a potluck leftover dinner of chicken and rice. Corey and I were scheming, trying to see how our recent forays into the exploding cannabis business might be a fit. We ended it all early and I got a decent sleep. Houston was well worth the stop. NASA was a boy's dream come true despite the reality check afterwards, and the neighborhood was worth consideration as a future domicile for me, although the vibe did not seem as embracing to me as it had been in Dallas.

Trying to put a finger on the contrast in experiences I had, I tossed a bit before finally falling asleep. NASA had been so invigorating, uplifting me and (what it always did for all of us) lifting my spirit, along with each spacecraft or Space Shuttle sent soaring.

Now what I keep hearing is the noise, the racket, the constant conflict. If only we could just change channels. *Pfft!* No more insanity. Ah, yes . . . some soothing classical musical to calm our jangled nerves and find some refuge, please. If only.

The left seat in Two Niner Lima was my escape.

On his way to a meeting, Corey took me over to SGR and dropped me off around ten a.m. I was excited to be passing the half-way mark across America and to be on my way to seeing my dearest friends, Paul and Martha. Wanting to chill and relax with them in New Orleans, I planned to stay there for a while. Zeke, as Paul had been known for years, had long ago, when financial disaster struck, graciously offered me his third-floor bedroom for as long as I needed it, if things got rough. I wanted to see if New Orleans (NOLA) was another possibility of refuge if needed to regain my bearings. NOLA is always fun, anyway. I had no doubt it would be nourishing for my soul because of my friends, and the amazing cuisine for which the city is known would further nourish my tummy.

It was a beautiful day and the weather was cooperating. I paid for my fuel and a nice young man named Doug helped me load my bags onto the golf cart before driving me to Two Niner Lima, which I'd parked a good walk from the terminal. We got to talking and he presented me with his business card after I told him that I was from Los Angeles and was an entertainment attorney. He was in the film business he said and would see me out there soon. Another dreamer—but I wished him well.

Who am I to judge when I have pursued my dream—this adventure? I told him I had a client with whom I could put him in touch, who might be helpful. He thanked me, gave me a quick hug, and I settled down to the task at hand. Sometimes love and connection happens when you least expect it.

I quickly went through the preflight routine, got the iPhone into its cradle, the iPad set up on the yoke. My walk-around was perfunctory. No rushing now. I had plenty of time to get to New Orleans. The weather was good and I hadn't gotten up so early to beat it, as I'd had to do a few legs before. I even managed a decent night's sleep. My spirits were soaring.

I requested flight following services all the way to New Orleans with ground control, selecting five thousand, five hundred feet altitude all the way there. My clearance came as I was taxiing. When I was preparing for my commercial license, which allows a pilot to fly for hire, not like a private pilot who cannot be paid but can get his expenses shared, I learned to write down clearances. There's a small pad affixed to my metal lap board on which I write the instructions I receive from a controller, while flying or taxiing. In the past, I would just repeat them, but this way, I could always refer back, if need be. And, as I did as a law student and a lawyer taking copious notes, I developed my own shorthand. Arrows pointing up and down for *climb or descend*. Hz for *haze*. New math signs, greater than or less than, for *at or below* or *above but not below*. My own madness, I guess, but I much prefer to think it as efficient as the right stuff.

Two Niner Lima seemed to have some extra pep that day. I finished my run-up and   taxied to Runway 17.

"Good morning, Sugar Land Tower. Grumman Two Niner Lima, ready to go, Runway 17, straight-out departure."

"Roger, Grumman Two Niner Lima, hold short for landing traffic."

I looked to my right to see a big Gulfstream business jet swooping down like a Klingon Bird of Prey. Wary of possible wake turbulence, I made a mental note to watch its touch-down point. Something Two Niner Lima could not overcome if caught in it when we lifted off.

I learned this early lesson in my flight training about how deadly it could be when Vanna White lost her fiancé because of it, at Van Nuys Airport. He was landing on Runway 16L, seconds after a California National Guard C-130 had touched down on the adjacent runway, 16R. The hurricane-like wing-tip vortices blowing over to the shorter general aviation runway were too much for the small aircraft he was flying, and he crashed.

Pilots are always learning from such accidents. "There but for the grace of God . . ."

"Grumman Two Niner Lima, cleared for takeoff. Wind calm. Fly heading 110. Maintain 2,000.

Wind calm made me sure I could hold my rotation past the touchdown point of the Gulfstream, even if a minute or so had gone by. We gathered up speed and instead of my usual pull-back ever so slowly on the yoke at sixty-five knots, I held a bit more forward pressure until seventy-five knots. Then I released it, and even before I could slowly pull back, Two Niner Lima leaped off the runway. I put in more downward nose trim, making sure we had no problems with the weight in the baggage compartment, and off we climbed.

Sugar Land Tower handed me off to Houston Departure Control as I passed through twelve hundred feet and Houston continued my heading direction. They had me climb up to three thousand feet, stopping me at my cruise altitude there because I was still in the Terminal Control Area just below its ceiling for that section of the TCA. We were heading south, almost over Galveston already.

The Gulf of Mexico was coming closer. I had been waiting for Houston Departure to clear me up to fifty-five hundred feet and on course, a left turn along the coast to New Orleans. I waited for the instruction.

I waited some more.

Now, it seemed I needed to say something. The Gulf of Mexico was getting closer and it appeared I was outside the TCA.

"Houston Departure, Grumman Two Niner Lima, request five thousand, five hundred feet and resume own navigation."

"Roger, Two Niner Lima. Didn't forget about you. Up to five thousand, five hundred feet and resume own navigation."

After so many years of flying, I have learned (as I have in life) that if you don't ask, you don't get. Of course, pilots want to obey the rules and do as they are told, but if there's ever an emergency (or doubt, as in this case) nobody will be upset with your asking or doing. Pilot in Command is the ultimate authority for a safe flight and that authority is defined in the Federal Aviation Regulations (FARs).

It's a lesson learned many years ago from the tragic crash of an Avianca Boeing 707 running out of fuel when approaching JFK, and if it was because they were a foreign crew, or if there was a misunderstanding in the cockpit, or the failure of the pilot and co-pilot to declare an emergency when the aircraft is sucking fumes—part of every pilot's training. Open your mouth. ATC (Aircraft Traffic Control) would much prefer a pilot make a request to dealing with death and carnage.

At five thousand, five hundred feet, the air was smooth, as it always is above the haze layer. The convective activity would begin further down the road into Louisiana, which looked very wet, lush and green. Water was everywhere interspersed with marshland breaking it up.

The Bayou.

Clouds were building as we climbed, going up to seven thousand, five hundred feet to get above them and maintain a smooth flight. We were clicking along at one hundred forty-five to one hundred fifty knots, with a nice tail wind of ten knots plus. The closer I got to New Orleans, the more the clouds built up. Soon, New Orleans Approach had me descend to four thousand, five hundred feet, just below the base of the clouds, and it got a bit bumpier. By the end of the day, with all the moisture from the gulf coming over the hot land, cumulus clouds were building, giving me a firsthand look at how a thunderstorm grows. Sooner or later, as a mature thunderstorm, they would disgorge their moisture.

Before I made contact with approach, I picked up the ATIS (Automatic Terminal Information System), which broadcast the current weather at Lakefront—a little trick I picked up in pilot training.

We broke out below the clouds, and I was taken aback by the view. There before me was the mighty Mississippi River, brown, of course! The Big Muddy, winding and twisting its way to the City of New Orleans, faintly visible in the distance. Wow!

I had seen so many pictures of this river over the years, but this view from my perch in the left seat of Ten Niner Lima thrilled me when I saw it winding and meandering onward to New Orleans in the distance, so brown that the moniker clicked. Big Muddy, indeed!

I was following along on Foreflight on my iPad, my little plane inching forward along the magenta course line, direct to Lakefront Airport. It isn't so easy to pick out an airport when you're descending, especially into a new environment to which you have never flown, at the same time you're trying to pick it out amongst the buildings in the city.

I decided to ask for help. Why not? Being a stranger in a strange land has its benefits. "Approach, Grumman Two Niner Lima unfamiliar. First time here. Request vectors."

I knew Lakefront was landing Runway 36 and I was planning a left-base entry but just couldn't pick it out. The ride was getting even bumpier, a grudging acknowledgement to the rapidly heating and rising air over this Gulf city.

"Grumman Two Niner Lima, fly direct Louis Armstrong Airport, then fly runway heading of 110 until you have airport in sight. Contact Lakefront Tower at 119.9 Welcome to New Orleans."

I was just coming up to the City's main airport and as I passed over it, flying over its Runway 11, I could finally see Lakefront Airport. I changed frequencies.

"Lakefront Tower, Grumman Two Niner Lima, 2,500' just passing Louis Armstrong, inbound for landing, with Mike. Request Left base entry."

"Roger, Grumman Two Niner Lima. Left base approved. Cleared to land, Runway 36."

"Grumman Two Niner Lima, Cleared to land, Runway 36."

If it sounds redundant, it is deliberately so, to repeat and read back clearances and directions the controller issues so as to avoid any misunderstandings. There is no room for error in a discipline that is unforgiving. One mistake could mean life or death. You can't pull over to the side of the road and figure it out.

Landing takes extreme focus. I have my own routine: stretch myself a bit in Two Niner Lima. My height is five feet, seven and a half inches, and Two Niner Lima, even for a smaller man like me, is not the most comfortable place to hang out. Three hours of sitting is about as long as I want to make it. Besides, I only have three and a half hours of fuel, and need that half hour, or five gallons remaining, for the required reserve under Visual Flight Rules (VFR).

So, I stretched myself out, leaned back and forth and took a few breaths. On other approaches and landings, if time allows, or the bladder isn't bursting, I'll take a swig of some water.

Now, it was time to slow the airplane down.

Learning to fly by instruments is all about using power settings to get the airplane to perform in a certain way, depending on your pitch and attitude. I developed my own for Two Niner Lima. Twenty-five hundred rpm to descend at five hundred feet per minute. Slow down to pattern altitude and proceed in the pattern at twenty-one hundred rpm. Once established at that power setting, I trim out the aircraft for my downwind leg speed of one hundred five knots. More trim to ninety-five knots on base, descending now at sixteen hundred to seventeen hundred rpm. A bit more trim to get my final approach speed to ninety knots, eighty-five knots over the fence. Here, since I was entering the pattern on a left-base entry, I was slowing down to 105 knots, where I dropped out the first increment of flaps, using more flaps to adjust my height on the approach.

I turned final and it was another *wow!* moment. Right there in front of me, stretched out, as if into Lake Ponchartrain, was Runway 36. I was right on the money, ninety knots on final. The wheels kissed the ground and I made one of my better landings, remembering (as I do most of the time when beginning my flare) to look down to the end of the runway.

Welcome to NOLA. I was jazzed!

CHAPTER XIV

————————————————————————————✈

LEG SIX

FRIENDS

My right knee was throbbing intensely, so I was eager to get out of Two Niner Lima. The cortisone shot in Dallas didn't seem to take and, during the flight, I was flexing my right knee repeatedly, trying to ease the constant, pulsating pain. I cursed my bad luck. With the two shots I'd had before, the torn meniscus pain subsided and I felt like new. I had hoped this one would take somewhat. Or at least, my fading olfactory and taste senses would be rejuvenated—by the magic medical potion, especially now to relish even more NOLA's exquisite cuisine.

Enough moaning, I thought. Grin and bear it. It hurt, but it was tolerable.

Slowly, I brought Two Niner Lima to a stop, following the red plastic baton instructions from the lineman parking me right in front of the only fixed base operator here at Lakefront, Flightline First. A three-story building, it was an old square, WWII-like beige concrete structure. The tarmac in front was empty—only Two Niner Lima parked there now, off to one side. I smiled. I had followed the same signals every lineman uses at every airport, as comforting as the controllers' familiar jargon which had guided me thus far.

I had always wanted to do that—signal directions to guide those big airliners in. When I was in college, I had applied at T.F. Green Airport in Providence but they rejected me because I wasn't union. It remained a dream unfulfilled.

Sliding the canopy back, I responded to the lineman's inquiry, declining any re-fueling as I hoped to be in New Orleans, for about two weeks, chilling and enjoying my friends. After shutting Two Niner Lima down I finished my post-flight chores, unplugging the iPhone and undoing the iPad from its cradle, and placing them on top of my bag of ice and snacks.

There is a certain way to exit a Grumman. First, stand up. Then kick the seat back with your inside heel, stand on the spar (which also is the main fuel tank running horizontally and raised above the floor under the raised seatback), and step out with your outside leg onto the wing on the wing walk. That is the rough surface painted black abutting the fuselage and running from the front of the wing back to the trailing edge upon which one walks, thus its name.

It was good to get up and stretch my aching knee. The pain was not so bad now, big baby that I was. My ensuing self-diagnosis concluded the cramped quarters from the repeated recent flights was exacerbating the torn meniscus.

The lineman was a lanky young boy, in his early twenties who greeted me with, "This a Grumman,?"

"Why, yes, David. Why do you ask?" I replied, seeing his nametag. It was a habit I developed over the years, perhaps taught by someone. Or maybe I picked it up from some spiritual or self-improvement course. I've taken a few in my life, seeking answers and enlightenment. Using someone's name when you meet them personalizes the conversation and humanizes the interaction. It surprises most.

"Well, I took some lessons in a Tiger once. Which one is this?"

"Oh, this is a modified Yankee," I told him. "One hundred sixty horsepower. When I ran out the original one hundred eight horsepower engine, I put in the bigger engine, a dorsal fin, and a new panel. My rocket ship!"

I was beaming.

"I just retired and flew her all the way from Santa Monica."

"Wow! Really? Sweet. That's amazing." He seemed stunned that this old guy showed up in a two-seater from so far away. "How long will you be here?"

"Not sure. Probably ten days. Maybe a couple of weeks."

"Okay. Make sure you leave the brake off. You want it hangered?"

"No, that won't be necessary. Can you help me in with my bags?"

"Sure. Let me grab a cart. I'll be right back."

I inserted the gust lock into the hole in the yoke. It really isn't your typical lock, but rather a metal pin which fits in holes in the rod attached to the yoke, with a metal jutting flag attached noting: "REMOVE BEFORE FLIGHT."

Incredibly, yes—some pilots have tragically taken off with the gust lock still in position. Another key reason to follow the checklist and not rush around an airplane. The gust lock prevents the ailerons from moving and checking it was my last chore, along with making sure the ignition and master switch were off. I have been remiss at times, and once when I was a student, I left the master on, which drained the battery. The flight school was not pleased.

Stretching back into the baggage compartment I pulled out my bags. By the time I'd clambered down, David had returned with a hotel baggage cart. We walked into the FBO where I checked in, then went down to the men's room to freshen up. Martha had just texted me that she was five minutes away. David left the cart with my bags by the front door and I slumped into the nearest chair, staring out the front window awaiting Martha's arrival. I was going to enjoy chilling out for a good chunk of time. I was beat.

Martha drove up and I went out to greet her. A blonde, fair-skinned, beautiful woman, she is one of the nicest peoples I have ever met, as is her husband, and it was great to see my old friend. Zeke got it perfect with this kind Southern lady. We loaded up her Lexus and drove back to their home, through the streets of New Orleans.

It is an old city, with the usual glass buildings, high rises down-town, and stores jutting out in the oddest buildings. There's no visible uniformity, like in Los Angeles and its strip malls convert-ed from gas stations. No, here was St. Charles. Carollton. The old trolley line running down the middle—overall, an elegant, stately place filled with older homes, tree-lined streets, and wide boule-vards.

There was a quaintness amidst the antiquity. I looked for any damage that remained after the terrible flooding from Hurricane Katrina and the breach of the levee. Unlike the last time I'd visit-ed, five months after that horror, I saw no waterlines. Our drive evoked fond memories of my previous visits. NOLA has its own personality and I was eager to explore it and see if living here could be a possibility.

Zeke had bought his Georgian style home years ago in 1987. It was near Audubon Park, on Henry Clay Street, amongst other streets honoring like Confederate statesmen, confirming that I was, indeed, in the deep South. Standing three stories, with a beautiful pool in its backyard, it was the perfect spot for a needed respite with friends. Martha showed me upstairs to my room and left me to unpack. I took out my chargers and plugs, found the outlets, and started recharging all my flying equipment as well as my iPhone and iPad.

With the aviation gadgets I'd added to Two Niner Lima, I had done well in being prepared. I also supplemented them with a Flight Gear Battery Pack, a great backup for the iPhone and iPad I was using in flight. The Stratus 3, coupled with ForeFlight by a Bluetooth connection, was also a bonanza for me. Instead of taking out my ruler and drawing out my route with a pencil, as I had done for years, and writing down all the way points and stops with the correct frequencies I would make, now I was using Foreflight solely for my flight planning and following along on the Nav Log it automatically prepared for each flight. This new technology was surely the way to go. New surpassing the old. Thank you, Captain Jordan.

I was eager for Zeke to come home from work. I wanted to see how my friend was doing. A few years ago he encountered some health issues, and like me with a stent-repaired heart, was dealing with the everyday concerns of mortality aa a more prominent portion of one's reality staring at us. I didn't dwell on it much anymore, as I had when I first received those three stents. You just know time is so precious, more so when a diagnosed frailty is your companion every day. Now I wanted to know how my friend was faring.

I had joked with friends before departure that many of the people I hoped to see I might never see again. Whether it would be my demise or theirs, I had first earmarked this trip as a Farewell Tour. Now, don't get me wrong—I don't think I'm going to die tomorrow. When I was younger, even at sixty (but long before the impact of heart disease hit me), I was going to live forever. Hell, I thought for some years I was another Dorian Grey. I mean, my name is Young!

God laughed for sure, and my comeuppance has me pushing and laughing right along, knowing the exit off the stage, left or right, is nearer than ever before.

Martha briefly shared with me Zeke's present state after I asked how all this was going for her. She smiled.

"I just worry about Zeke and do my best to keep it all going."

Nothing more needed to be said. We all just had to keep it going.

Paul came home and we greeted each other as we always do. Hug and kiss on the lips. Many say that's strange for men, or at least heterosexual men, but I feel open and loving and hey, maybe a bit of my gay side comes out when I express myself to my male friends like that. I got that from his father, Hank, maybe the nicest guy I have ever known. He always had a sweet, kind word for every one of his son's friends. Hank, and his beloved wife, Flo, were like surrogate parents where the boys from Brown would find unconditional love and support. It was our escape, a place where we were made to feel special, away from the abuse many of us suffered and endured as children. Hank would greet every one of us with a hug and a kiss, calling us Honey and Sweetheart. Not a gay bone in his body, of course, just the epitome of love and affection for his son's friends.

They lived a modest life, in an apartment in Flatbush, and raised a son and daughter.

Sadly, Paul's sister, Elise, was in a car accident shortly after getting married, and then in a coma for years, for which Zeke took on the financial responsibility because he'd done quite well as a partner in a New Orleans law firm. Not only because he could, but because he was the kind of guy who just did, without asking. He had so much love in him, like his dad, and there wasn't anything he wouldn't do for his family, never mind his friends. Out of the blue, and over the years, a framed picture, or book, or some notion reflecting my love of the Lakers or Dodgers or flying, would arrive from Z.

Just because. He was that kind of guy.

I had first met him when we were both eighteen and freshmen together at college. He lived down the hall from me in a dormitory which housed all the freshmen. He was Paul then, later to be Zeke. Our college pals nicknamed me Fox after I started scoring a lot of goals for our undefeated freshman soccer team, like my older brother had. He had preceded me there, and the soccer coach had bestowed the same moniker on him. Paul had met Billy, with whom I played soccer and became another close friend and fraternity brother, rooming together as sophomores. We all hit it off, although I couldn't drink a lick—not like they all could.

At first, I was jealous of Paul, whom everyone seemed to revere. Until we got close, and I knew him more, I felt humbled by his easy way with people. In some odd way I felt incomplete, not as well-liked and received, and that I was competing with him. I had always been like him, and yet when I got to Brown, amidst so many capable, talented, and intelligent people, I felt insecure, was less outgoing, and a bit unsure of Me, preferring my refuge on the soccer field where I made a name for myself right away.

College is the place to enable an adolescent to transition into adulthood and find his or her way. I was no different. I grew up those four years, understanding that there were always so many talented and better people, athletes, scholars, or what have you, out in the world. Learning to find myself and navigate through life was the challenge I had to face.

College should be available for everyone. Not just for the learning and academics, but to give everyone the blessing and opportunity to grow, find themselves, and be ready for the world as better and more capable citizens. Simple.

Paul became Zeke and we traveled our four years in Providence together, remaining friends over our individual journeys, seeing each other often at college reunions and other festivities in which he made sure to include me, from his fabulous rockin' wedding to Martha in the early 1990s, or celebrating his parents' fiftieth anniversary. Zeke brought us all together because, well, he was Zeke.

It was good to see him. He looked dapper in his suit, coming home from the office. It was wonderful to feel his positive energy, with no apparent signs of illness.

We shared our common fears of ageing, our mortality, and our aroused awareness of our frailty, now both with maladies. Zeke, being the man he is, expressed his concern about Martha should something happen to him and his reality similar to mine.

"I know exactly what you mean. A day doesn't go by with stents in me that I don't think I'm dying tomorrow."

I was desperately trying to comfort my friend. We both looked at each other silently. No more words were needed but I wanted more. I wanted to shake that fear and drive looming death away from my friend and me, at least twenty or thirty years away. We had shared so much and I didn't want it to end.

Of course, I know it is inevitable and it is coming. But deep down, I am waging my own fight, doing something and every-thing at full tilt, every day, avoiding the thoughts, not wanting to see it coming.

Just then Martha walked into the kitchen where we were sit-ting around the island on our stools. Her cheerful smile and jabber about all the plans she'd made for me the few weeks I would be in their home and beloved city interrupted our awkward silence.

My time in NOLA was one for a decent rest and respite. All the excitement of the trip, along with new flying challenges in new environments had me exhausted. I was determined to lollygag and do nothing, an art that I have become quite good at perfect-ing. Oh, sure, I've worked hard and partied even harder, but doing nothing—now that takes planning. And it takes planning to treat your Self to the solitude of being with yourself and tuning in to the world about you, without distracting yourself with chores, to just *being*. It was a bit Zen but something that I felt nourished me, even if to others it seemed lazy.

Like my dear Dad, who would see my little sister and me on the family room couch, engrossed in *The Three Stooges* on TV and say, "Get off the couch and do something!" Looking back years later, I remembered that my parents never stood still. They were always doing something, and God forbid their children would not achieve or be productive. It was an energy I did not want anymore. I was turning inward, exploring, and doing nothing was my way to find some inner peace. After forty-five years of being a lawyer and han-dling other people's problems, I needed a break. Solitude afforded me that. As did the left seat of Two Niner Lima.

So, now in NOLA, I wanted to take a pause, continue my writ-ing, and rest and rejuvenate with my dear friends. I was not disappointed. Daily walks through Audubon Park got me back into some semblance of shape, my blood moving, with a good sweat worked up in the high humidity of the Gulf city. I broke out my stretch bands and brought some tone back to my arms and shoulders. I wrote. I swam.

Zeke continued to work hard and we never did pick up our conversation again. He has been a senior partner in a law firm for years, and had become an expert counselor in his field of government energy and regulation. Martha is a capable and loving host, and they both spared no expense in their generosity and kindness, sharing their New Orleans with me and opening their lovely home for my refuge. Whether it was taking me to a book signing of Ron Swoboda's new book about the 1969 Mets, or dinner at Galatoire's amidst the nouveau and established at New Orleans' finest restaurant, with fish so fresh they must have been caught moments before. Their generosity to their old friend knew no bounds.

We had lunch at the Napoleon Café, a scrumptious salad of NOLA delights. We walked the sights around Jackson Square, and up to the levees, seeing how precarious the city sat, adjacent to the Big Muddy. I reveled in its history, examining the remnants of first the French, then the Spanish, and then Thomas Jefferson making one of the best deals ever with the Louisiana Purchase. I didn't much care for Bourbon Street. Too much debauchery to suit my taste. Too noisy, too crowded with drunks and revelers, reminding me of a same but different Venice Beach crowd.

Nonetheless, my days in NOLA were filled and busy. I felt loved and nourished.

The highlight was when Enid came down from New York to visit. My sweet love, my high school classmate whom I finally found after years of wondering where she was. I would ask my

friends over, I swear, the last ten or so years, "Do you know whatever happened to Enid?" No one had heard from her.

Then, one day, lo and behold (as she tells the story), I was looking for her on Facebook, and there she was. She had decided to add
her maiden name to her profile, and we made an instant connection. It soon became obvious something was brewing between us.
She had been married for forever and was still searching, pained
by her choices but resigned to stay in an unfulfilling marriage, until her best friend suddenly died from deep vein thrombosis. Alive
and healthy one second, dead the next. Enid knew it was her time,
before it was too late—and suddenly Bobby Young, her crush from
eighth grade, is back in her life. We have been enjoying ourselves
immensely, comfortable with our own Selves, and each other, and
clearly in lust and love. Yes, even older folks can still burn the mid-
night oil!

Enid, as she always does, made fast friends with Martha and
Zeke, and it was a joy to see. I was tickled for Enid and their raves
after she left made me beam. We saw *Toy Story 4*, ate brunch at the
Camillia Grill, and saw Ellis Marsalis. Watching this maestro perform at an intimate dinner club from front row seats, and seeing
the new World War II Museum and all its aircraft exhibits, topped
off an amazing two weeks.

The South seemed pleasant enough—just don't talk politics.
Zeke and Martha shared with me stories of their friends and as-
sociates, living in the South, many of whom were Trumpsters and
Republicans. Paul, after all, was a Brooklyn boy. You can't get more
Yankee than that.

But this was the deep South where the Confederacy still beats
strong within the hearts of many. My hosts told me the removal of
Robert E. Lee's statue had provoked great anger. The empty pedes-

tal, standing almost thirty feet high, still remains but seems naked without the general. I couldn't understand why they didn't take down the pedestal as well. It was the same in Dallas. No, I thought, when the Confederacy lost the Civil War, they said the hell with Reconstruction and erected statues of all their leaders even though history showed they were traitors to the Union. To those continuing the hatred and bigotry they were heroes, but even more important than the tribute was letting people of color know who was still in charge.

The remaining pedestal said the same to me. A little bit left to remind everyone in this southern city.

To remind all of us.

People were polite enough, and you didn't talk about it, but there was a reason why Louisiana remained firmly in the red state column. And, that was, as Zeke explained, even if New Orleans was predominantly Democratic, still the deep South. The African-American population was thinned out by Hurricane Katrina and the horrors suffered in the Ninth Ward. Many whose homes had been swept away when flood waters rose to over nine feet never returned.

But, as Zeke explained when we were down in Jackson Square, near the natural levee and where the first settlers set up shop, that natural rise of the land had spared that part of the city. But, not where the engineers thought they could keep the water out with their man-made levees. Another lack of hubris. Like the Titanic. The Challenger disaster.

Man can be too arrogant for his own good.

It was a fine line, after all, staying for more than a few days. We all know fish stinks after three days, and that seems to be the line not to cross as a guest. Every stop I made I was ever so conscious of that admonition and careful not to do anything too stupid to wear out my welcome. Here, I was even more sensitive to my friends, as they had welcomed me for the two weeks I'd planned. I made sure to pitch in, washing dishes, buying this or that, doing whatever was needed to help Martha with her countless tasks running the household and taking care of her beloved husband.

Martha, Zeke, and I enjoyed our last evening together before my departure. Wine and a Martha cooked dinner with my dear friends. I wanted to make sure to tell Paul how much he meant to me. And, honestly, I wasn't sure when I would see him and Martha again. With him dealing with his health issues, and me not a hundred percent, that was in question.

"Thank you, guys, for being so wonderful and so hospitable these past few weeks. You both mean so much to me and this was just what the Doctor ordered. And, I love you, man. You have been always such an inspiration for me and such a good friend. Thank you."

I hugged him. He seemed puzzled, looking at me quizzically, as if to say, "Yeah, but so what?" But he didn't say anything. Maybe he understood that I was telling him how I felt just in case. I didn't linger but politely excused myself, as it was time to pack and go to bed.

As the two weeks came to an end, I was rested and ready to travel on. The weather was cooperating. I cancelled my plans to visit Florida when my good buddy Michael begged off because of issues with his son. I couldn't reach Captain Ron to make it to Orlando to see him, Nel-Ann, and dear Claudia. My friends on the east coast of Florida were waiting for me, but with money becoming an issue, I decided to head north to Wilmington to see Andre, meet his beloved Joanne, and find out if North Carolina could be a possible residence.

I had played high school soccer with Andre, and was somewhat of a mentor to him then, a senior taking the sophomore under his wing, as Roger L. and my dear cousin Roger G. had done with me. Andre blossomed into a super star in high school and college but then the Viet Nam war interrupted his life. I wanted to hear more about this sensitive soul I had become close to through the magic of Facebook and try to learn about this boy who had befriended a teammate way back when.

On Foreflight I was planning the flight up to North Carolina. Up to Albany, Georgia and then on to Myrtle Beach, South Carolina, before a few more minutes to Wilmington. It would be a long day, over seven hours of flying, with two fuel stops. Flight Service gave me the all-clear report. Martha was going to get up early and take me over to Lakefront bright and early. I wanted to be airborne first thing as I was getting a handle on flying in the south and southeast.

Best do so before the convective activity brings those afternoon thunderstorms.

My excitement was growing.

I would see the Atlantic Ocean the next day, if all went well.

Damn, I thought. I am almost there.

Across America.

CHAPTER XV

———————————————————————————→

LEG SEVEN

June 27, 2019

NEW-ILM with fuel stops at ABY and MYR

Lakefront Airport, New Orleans, LA, to Southeast Regional Airport, Albany, GA to Myrtle Beach International Airport, Myrtle Beach, SC, to Wilmington International Airport, Wilmington, NC

Distance: 314 nm NEW-ABY. 296 nm ABY-MYR. 62 nm MYR-ILM

Total: 672 nm.

Route: NEW-ABY Direct. ABY-MYR Direct. MYR-ILM Direct.

Start time (NEW): 7:28 a.m. (CentralTime) Wheels up: 7:46 a.m.

Wheels down: 10:13 a.m. (Eastern time)

Shut-Down time (ABY): 10:17 a.m.

Start time (ABY): 12:13 p.m.

Wheels up: 12:29 p.m.

Wheels down: 3:30 p.m.

Shut down time (MYR): 3:41 p.m.

Start time (MYR): 4:05 p.m. Wheels up: 4:14 p.m.

Wheels down: 4:50 p.m.

Shut down time (ILM): 4:53 p.m.

Log Entry: NEW-ABY: 3.1 hrs. Flight time: 2:27.
Good flite @ 5,500'/very hazy/smooth/ cleared up fur-
ther east near ABY /clouds build up near ABY
ABY – MYR: 3.2 hrs. Flight time: 3:01.
Wow! East coast! Clouds build up- 5,500'-7,500'-9,000'-11,500'.
Descent from over 40 mi out/ Diverted by ATC to check on pos-
sible crash of C-130/Charleston thunderstorm /Tried to take pic
on final- Idiot!

MYR-ILM: 0.8 hrs. Flight time 0:36.
Sweet flite. Replenished myself @ MYR. Up coast / 3,500' – smooth
over ocean. Straight-in apprch R-6. Off-set approach per ATC to
follow TBM / excllnt ldg

Martha, bless her soul, was up as early as I. Once again, I didn't do too much sleeping before a big day of flying. I got out of bed and went downstairs around five a.m., where I had a cup of cold brew coffee to get things moving. First time ever that I had this cold brew. It's a concentrate into which you pour boiling water and voila! Really good coffee. Not like my favorite Major Dickason's, but it still got the body moving.

Martha had packed up some snacks. I went upstairs to shower, get dressed, and pack last-minute items into my suitcase, backpack and small duffel bag. When I went down at six-thirty ready to go, Zeke was waiting for me in the kitchen. I thanked him again, held him tight, and Martha and I were off to Lakefront Airport. The city was starting its hustle and bustle but there was very little traffic at this hour of the morning.

Martha dropped me off with a big goodbye hug and I went into Flight Line to square things away. I took a bit of a hit. Overnight parking was ten bucks a night, not as pricy as Addison (where I'd managed to finagle down from twenty dollars to fifteen) but it, plus the fuel, cost me three hundred for the two-week visit. But it was worth it. I felt so good having been with my dear friends, and anyway, my Social Security check had just posted so I had enough to make it up to Wilmington and keep on going all the way to my final destination.

Grabbing a baggage cart I quickly loaded on my stuff. Two Niner Lima was all alone on the tarmac. I placed the bags on the wing walk, took off her cover, and verified that she had, in fact, been refueled. Besides ascertaining the fuel gauges showed full, I also opened up each tank and checked them visually.

As I was doing so, I noticed Two Niner Lima had little green dots all over the white portions of the top of the fuselage, and all on her nose. One of the linemen came over to see if I was okay and to retrieve the baggage cart. While he was removing the chocks, I asked what happened, pointing to the bright green dots all over my girl.

"You must have hit a swarm of mosquitos."

"Green mosquitos?" I asked incredulously.

"Oh, yes. Real big ones. Seems they just get attracted to the planes, and then die there. Happens to everyone."

I was flabbergasted. Poor Two Niner Lima. I put the bags into the baggage compartment, did my preflight cockpit chores and, as I did my walk-around, I told her we would get her washed soon enough, once up north. She fired up right away.

The weather was being extra kind to us this morning. There were high cirrus clouds at twenty-five thousand feet, cooling the air more than on most NOLA days. With the sun behind the clouds, it would be far cooler flying than on a usual hot, sunny day—a relief, even with the sunshade I'd installed before departure from SMO. Having the shade, instead of the previous debilitating fishbowl all glass canopy environment, had been a life saver this entire trip.

On my taxi instructions I erred and had to do a 180-degree turn to get on the correct runway as per ground control instructions, down Taxiway Bravo to Kilo for an intersection departure on Runway 18 Right. I wasn't concerned about giving up a few feet of concrete and didn't insist on a full runway departure. I had over five thousand feet left, ample room, and the air was not so hot as to make the density altitude a problem for Two Niner Lima.

But now I was having difficulty loading my destination of KABY (Albany, Georgia) into the Garmin 530.

This all-in-one navigation and radio device gave Two Niner Lima a suffix of Gulf, or G, so our type aircraft for Air Traffic Control (ATC) tracking purposes was an AA-1A/G. Each aircraft model is important to the controller looking at the radar screen. He or she has to spatially fit each aircraft into the flow in order to guide the traffic, whether it's a little Beenchcraft Baron twin engine or a big Boeing 737.

In common parlance, Two Niner Lima is an American Aviation aircraft, her original manufacturer, which was based in Cleveland back in 1971. Our model was a 1A, the first change in the original two-seat model they built, and we were Gulf, meaning we had GPS capabilities on board. That would be important for certain instructions and/or approaches Two Niner Lima could take from the controller and fly. While presenting the same information, my iPad, with its Stratus 3 connection, was portable. In the eyes of the FAA, it's only temporary and can only be used to supplement my GPS, not as a primary source of navigation. When the Garmin 530 was designated, its installation certified as part of the aircraft. Thus, the moniker.

On powering up, when I started to load in the destination for the first leg so I could track it onboard the 530 and my iPad, a message flashed:

"All data installed has been lost."

I didn't understand it until I tried repeatedly to set my destination as Southeast Regional Airport, or KABY. The 530 did not recognize it as a "valid identifier." *Well*, I figured, *at least I have my iPad, with the Stratus feeding it, and the same information, so I'll be okay.* But it wasn't working. After trying to enter KABY a few times (with no luck), I got so frustrated I gave up. The 530 would still provide me with our airspeed and a moving map of sorts, and although not exact, it was not a no-go item. I thought Two Niner Lima must have been hit by lightning. There was enough going on during the two weeks she sat outside but I wasn't sure. I decided not to dwell on it. Time to get going.

With my flight instruments and radio frequencies all set up, run-up was complete. The tower cleared us for takeoff, and we were on our way. Two Niner Lima climbed quickly, seeming a bit friskier in the cooler morning air. We headed out over Lake Pontchartrain on a right downwind departure and on to a heading of 075 degrees, direct Albany, Georgia.

We climbed up to five thousand, five hundred feet and hugged the coast, angling northeast. Mobile, Alabama, soon passed by off my left wing and I couldn't help thinking about its history. As a young boy, growing up in the northeast, I knew my community was not immune to racism and bigotry. Mobile, as planted in my nine-year old consciousness, was a place where the civil rights movement gained serious traction. Being Jewish was not easy in those days but it was nowhere near what a person of color had to go through. As I grew up, I also knew the times they were a changin' and doing so right there in Mobile and the rest of the South.

The fiction of an America void of this disease irked me so when I began to mull it from my vantage point. It is hard to fathom that such hatred and beliefs still persist. That this is, sadly, who we really are. It remains such an anathema to me, as that was not what we were supposed to be about, and what I now realize, naively believed, what I was taught.

Mobile, Alabama, from five thousand, five hundred feet, its downtown sticking up and out in the haze, seemed peaceful. I couldn't see hate and discrimination and bigotry from Two Niner Lima. Racism wasn't obvious, not a landmark I could point out and say, "Ah-ha, there it is." No, it was invisible, silent, like it really is—insidious, sucking out the good in all of us, rotten to the core.

I remembered what the Apollo 8 astronauts reminded us of, here on the good Planet Earth, with their historic mission. There were no boundaries of nations on this beautiful ball of blue they saw from space. We were all one. No countries, no borders, just one blue ball sitting out in the dark void of space where we were all living together in this universe.

I felt the same as I looked down at Mobile. From Two Niner Lima, I couldn't see the differences. There were no demarcations of black or white. Just another peaceful city passing serenely by. If only that was the reality.

The haze lightened and the familiar sight of farmland and towns, dotted about the landscape below, began anew. America had this homogenous look, and I was feeling so much love for this land. We are so all the same.

After Mobile Approach handed me off to JAX Center, I showed I was a newbie when I advised upon reporting in, "Jacksonville Center, Grumman Two Niner Lima, five thousand, five hundred feet (instead of "JAX" Center). Subsequently, listening to transmissions of other pilots, I gathered that's how it should have been. As they took me into Albany, I felt convective activity building up below me. The clouds dotting the sky, now more plentiful, were like little cotton puffs spilled out of their box. A straight in approach to Runway 4 set me up for the good landing I made. I taxied in to the only FBO on the field, Eagles of America Albany.

It was a cozy airport, with the FBO reflecting warmth and Southern charm. Ms. Tammy greeted me, I arranged for fuel, and then sat down in the comfortable leather chair in the small and cozy lounge to nosh on Martha's snacks of fruit. Feeding my chocolate fix, I also wolfed down a Snickers bar I had stashed on board.

At four dollars and forty cents a gallon, fuel prices here were the cheapest thus far on the entire trip, almost a dollar less than most other FBOs. I reckoned it was because of the proximity to the refineries in the Gulf states versus locations further away. But who really knows, these days, how these bandits set their prices? Nothing makes much sense anymore. You pay the Man and what say do we really have?

Sure, I can check the prices at any airport as I go, but this is where I needed to stop enroute to North Carolina, dictated by the fuel limitations of Two Niner Lima. I had met my three-hour fuel limit, so I had to stop or otherwise cut into my reserves. ABY turned out to be a welcome surprise, not only because of its fuel prices but because of the kind and solicitous Ms. Tammy, who, like others, couldn't believe I had flown all this way from California.

After we exchanged pleasantries and I had my snacks, I reflected on the last forty-five minutes coming into ABY, considering the convective build-up. I'd planned to fly at fifty-five hundred feet and now was thinking we would have to be higher. I would make that decision when I got airborne. After one more trip to the bathroom, I bid Ms. Tammy adieu and headed out to a refueled Two Niner Lima. I got a kick when I saw a small red carpet laid out at the foot of the wing walk. "First Cabin!" it screamed. Oh, yes, for sure! I chuckled and felt like a big-shot for a moment, finishing my cursory walk-around.

We taxied out. Ground control came back and gave me my clearance direct to Myrtle Beach, along with my squawk code and departure frequency for JAX Center. During my respite with Ms. Tammy, I checked the weather on my phone, and had to improvise and change my next destination. A thunderstorm over Charleston, South Carolina, had negated that first choice for my next fuel stop. Having heard so much about that charming city, I wanted to stop for a late lunch. It would leave me plenty of daylight to make it up to Wilmington before dinner.

I did a complete run-up even though it was the second flight of the day. I was in no hurry and always felt it was best be sure, so why not take the extra few minutes, power the engine up to 1,800 rpm and check things out.

It was that mind set I had always followed (well, okay, most of the time) throughout my almost forty years of flying. Best be sure, rather than be cursing yourself on the way down in an emergency you might have prevented if you had only performed that check list.

Albany Tower cleared us right away for a straight-out departure on Runway 4. I saw soon enough that my chosen altitude of fifty-five hundred feet wasn't going to be enough to get above the building clouds. Just as I was contemplating if I should climb up to seventy-five hundred feet, the JAX Center controller broke into my thoughts.

"Grumman Two Niner Lima, JAX Center. Do you see smoke at your one o'clock position, about fifteen miles?"

I looked through the hazy sky below the clouds in that direction and saw nothing. "Negative, JAX. No smoke. Grumman Two Niner Lima."

"Grumman Two Niner Lima, we have a report that a C-130 crashed at Moultrie Airport.

Would you mind going down and taking a look?"

"No problem. Grumman Two Niner Lima leaving fifty-five hundred feet. Give me heading and distance to the airport."

Peering out toward the one o'clock position, I reduced power down to twenty-five hundred rpm and began to descend.

"Roger, Grumman Two Niner Lima. Fly heading of one hundred fifteen degrees. Cleared down to twenty-five hundred feet."

"Let me know."

I still saw nothing. I was now down to twenty-five hundred feet, coming straight up to and over an airport, but I wasn't sure if it was Moultrie or not. It didn't seem like it was, but my inexperience with Foreflight had me hesitate to confirm my exact location over which airport when I looked down to check it on my iPad.

"JAX Center, Grumman Two Niner Lima still sees no smoke. Negative on smoke. I am just over an airport and don't see anything."

"Roger, Grumman Two Niner Lima. Thanks for your help. Resume own navigation.

Altitude at your discretion."

With that invitation I decided to climb up and over the clouds.

"Roger, Grumman Two Niner Lima. Climbing. Up to seventy-five hundred feet. Resuming own navigation."

I quickly turned back on course and began my climb, now avoiding too many clouds.

Finally on top of them, I could see so many churning and building. The afternoon heat was doing its magic, cloud-building miracles. Far off to my right, I saw a huge thunderstorm. The anvil from its top, so big and foreboding, indicating a mature thunderstorm, stretched for miles. I guesstimated we were a good twenty miles or so away from it. In my path, directly in front of me, I saw building clouds, which forced me to weave my way between them—first up to ninety-five hundred feet, then up to eleven thousand, five hundred. But the air was smooth, despite the ten-knot headwind which had us crawling on top and in between the clouds.

It was a good thing I didn't dare try Charleston. Over the frequency, still with JAX Center as I angled up to South Carolina, the controller was reporting heavy rain, lightning, and microbursts—all sorts of havoc affecting the approaches into Charleston. He was saying that many of the incoming pilots were declaring missed approaches, and some were choosing to go to their alternate airports. *Say intentions* seemed to be the operative buzz words.

One look out my right wing told me why. This anvil-topped thunderstorm stretched a good fifty-plus miles long. I wanted to give it an even wider berth but clouds on my left were building higher than my altitude, and I had only a narrow pathway forward through two building cumulus clouds ahead of me. I was flying through this building line of storms, running north-south direct to and ending in Charleston with this Mother of all thunderstorms.

I sneaked through that last corridor and was past the line of building clouds. The thunderstorm, still off to my right over Charleston, was receding. And then I saw it—the Atlantic Ocean, about fifty miles ahead. The sky was clear. No more clouds. I broke out into a big grin.

"Damn! Oh, my God. I did it. Flew across the country!"

I was quite pleased with myself, for sure, but I brought myself back to the task at hand. JAX handed me off to Myrtle Beach Approach. I had already tuned into the MYR ATIS and advised I had the information.

"Roger, Grumman Two Niner Lima. Begin descent down to twenty-five hundred feet. Maintain VFR."

I was forty miles out. I had already calculated that from eleven thousand five hundred feet a leisurely descent rate of five hundred feet wouldn't hurt my ears with a too-rapid descent. To avoid being affected by the change in altitude pressure, I had to start my descent at around eighteen minutes out, or thirty-six miles. Good enough, it was time.

Throttling down to twenty-five hundred rpm, I achieved my five hundred feet per minute rate. The air was smooth. Tower cleared me for a right base entry to Runway 18. As I turned final, there lay the Atlantic Ocean in front of me.

Wow!

The wheels kissed the ground. We rolled out and I slowly taxied in to the plush, modern glass terminal of Myrtle Beach Aviation.

Both Two Niner Lima and I were smiling like smug, proverbial Cheshire cats. Seeing the Atlantic Ocean on final had me stoked and I was reveling in the joy of crossing America. I exited the B(ravo) taxiway onto the main terminal parking area. Rows of planes, mostly jets and single-engine turboprops, as well as many twins and a bunch of Cirrus aircraft, were parked one after another—a sure sign that the rich did, indeed, cavort and play at this resort town.

As I exited off the taxiway, pausing to figure out where to park, a golf cart with flashing lights and a rearward facing "Follow Me" sign on its roof moved toward me, coming out of the second row of planes parked on the tarmac. The driver wanted me to follow him, and that I did, as he brought me to the far end and the last row, midway up. There waiting was a lineman, his red batons held high, signaling me to have Two Niner Lima come face him. Then, bringing his batons to an X in front of him, he signaled me to stop. I braked and began my shut down procedure. Mixture out, throttle full off, ignition quickly off then back on to make sure there was no electrical short. Confirming electricity would indeed stop. Ignition now off, I put the keys on the glare shield, slid the canopy open, greeted the lineman sauntering over, and requested fuel.

The general aviation terminal building here at Myrtle Beach was impressive. Glass walls two stories high wrapped around the three sides facing out eastward to the Atlantic. Sunlight streamed into a huge seating area filled with plush, leather couches and chairs. Each seating area was designated by its grouping on its own woven rug. Of all the FBOs I had visited on my journey, this was *numero uno*, the cream of the crop, hands down. Just like what I observed about the planes parked on the tarmac, the building, and its beautifully decorated interior that seemed right out of *Architectural Digest*, stated clearly who their customers were. I had heard much about Myrtle Beach and the playground it was, and this front line was a clear indication where the privileged few headed and played. I laughed to myself. Once again, Two Niner Lima and I just moseyed on in, like every pilot and his plane, no matter who he was or what he was flying. We were just as entitled and privileged as those disembarking from the biggest and fanciest Gulfstream jet on the tarmac, with every pilot treated as equal.

In no rush, I decided to relax for a bit. After refreshing myself in the men's room, I sat down, ate some more chocolate and the last of Martha's snacks. I texted Andre that I had just landed telling him I was going to check the weather and would advise him of my approximate ETA and where to meet me. After looking up the weather on my Foreflight App I texted back and advised him I would see him at Air Wilmington around four thirty to four forty-five.

To my surprise, Andre texted me right back:

"I'm already at the terminal where you fly in and park. Been here for about 1.5 hours." A happy face emoji accompanied his text.

"Okay. Great!" I responded. "Getting ready to pay for fuel and walk out to plane. See you soon!"

I relaxed a few more minutes. It would be a short hop up to Wilmington but so far it had been a very, *very* long day. I had been up for over twelve hours since the early morning, flown across five states and over six hundred miles, so I wanted to make sure to catch my breath and be ready for the half-hour trip coming up.

After a few more minutes, eyes closed, relaxing and expressing my gratitude for the day's journey almost done, I got up, paid for the fuel and got a ride out to Two Niner Lima. A brief walk around, verifying again the fuel was at the tops of the tanks matching the fuel sight for each tank inside the cockpit, and confirming the rest of Two Niner Lima was good to go, I hopped in and fired her up.

We took off again on Runway 18, out over the Atlantic, and turned left, hugging the coast for a bit. As we climbed out and over the ocean up to thirty-five hundred feet, the air was smooth. It usually is over cooler water instead of a heated land mass, much like when Two Niner Lima and I traversed the Southern California coast. But this time, going north, the land was on my left. I compared the views—the mountainous terrain out west and the Pacific coast to the flat territory of South Carolina receding behind me. As we cut over the land on our direct course, things got more interesting, with the heated afternoon air rising from the earth and giving us repeated bumps along the way. I was, of course, below the haze layer boundary, above me at about five thousand feet, but I decided to ride it out.

As I neared Wilmington, I got the ATIS, confirming Runway 6 was in use, and thus, I requested a straight-in approach. Approach control agreed, vectored me slightly to the west to get behind a Dahler TBM, a single-engine turboprop I dreamed would someday, maybe, be mine. I confirmed my visual contact with this traffic and then contacted the tower.

Coming up to Wilmington I was on a long final approach, enough time to grab my phone and take some pictures. I was nestled alongside the Cape May River, which poured out into the Atlantic. A jostle of turbulence had me drop the phone and bark at the pilot:

"Idiot! Fly the airplane!"

And, needing no further reminder, that I did. I lined Two Niner Lima up again, facing the Atlantic Ocean. The view of the city and the Ocean filled me with joy and accomplishment. I was even more exhilarated when, with a perfect landing, the wheels kissed the ground.

It was an excellent but very long day. It got even better as I rolled to a stop and my dear, old friend Andre approached Two Niner Lima with a big smile. I shut down, hopped out, and embraced him.

Time to find out about North Carolina and my former teammate.

CHAPTER XVI

LEG EIGHT

FRIENDS

I was curious, to say the least, about my Facebook friend and old teammate. He had been so warm and friendly since we reconnected via Facebook, not only inviting me to his home on my journey, but sharing with me, and others, his life. I was eager to see the young boy I knew, now a grown man, who many years ago I had mentored. I was more curious to know what he remembered about our relationship, me, and who I was—all in search of me, now, here, today.

He strolled out onto the tarmac as I unloaded Two Niner Lima and finished my post-flight duties. We hugged like old friends. Never mind that I'd hardly known Andre except as a young burgeoning star player, as I was. We played together at South Side High School on Long Island over fifty years ago, when he was a sophomore and I was a senior. He was then but fifteen, skinny, fast as the wind—and boy, could he play soccer.

Now, here was a grown man. I looked into his face, and saw

that boy, but barely. I would soon learn of the man he had become and how life and the circumstances of his birth and color of his skin impacted him and shaped him.

But our joy to see each other was indisputable. To me the question seemed to be why as we were, really, two strangers, other than sharing our present day lives on Facebook. It would be a fascinating three days with him and his wife Joanne.

We walked into Wilmington Air and I checked in with the young lady behind the counter. It seems as if most every FBO has the pretty, young face behind the counter. Who could not help being smitten upon her welcome? And distracted. Although I understood the sales concept behind it all, I did recognize and catch my typical male reaction. Sometimes, confronted with a face of an angel in front of me, this boy can find himself thinking elsewhere. So, I turned up the volume on my personal control system, focused and concentrated on the facts, the costs, and when I would need to check in and request fuel.

Not like so many years ago when a darling Canon saleswoman would come to my law office and I would be a smitten puppy dog. She sold me a lot of equipment my office never needed. Time has me a bit more tempered and grounded, the puppy now an old dog who knows all too well the effect those tricks will have on me. So, Captain Bob was concentrating now, closing down his flight into Wilmington and securing Two Niner Lima — not allowing himself to be lured by her smiles and his own illusory thoughts of conquest and young flesh. I guess there must be some evolution after all. I chuckled to myself.

I went to the men's room to wash the day's grime and heat off me and relieve my bladder, then Andre and I were off to his home in Wilmington. On the way, he shared with me some of himself, how he was when we last saw each other, and how the Viet Nam War had shaped his life.

It was a pleasant trip through Wilmington. Situated near the mouth of the Cape May River, which empties into the Atlantic Ocean, it was another town to consider for future residential possibilities. More northern than southern, Wilmington is not at all like New Orleans with her stately homes. It has the more modern look of Houston and Dallas. But I liked the vibe. Andre's home is situated outside the city proper, which sits naturally alongside the river and expands outward. Like my now former house on Dewey Street, his was nestled in a cul de sac at the end of the street where tall maple trees surrounded it.

Andre suggested we stop and grab a beer before going home. We pulled into a shopping center, parked and went into the bar where, he told me, he often goes to hang out with other Vietnam vets. In this, his own personal *Cheers*, the barkeeps greeted him by name and he introduced me proudly as his old friend who just flew his plane across the country.

Now, everyone seems to react the same. "Whoa!"

"Really? You did what?"

Further explanation from Andre brought a few more admirable looks, especially when he showed a picture of us standing in front of Two Niner Lima and Wilmington Air. More than likely the small size of the plane, or so I thought, was making people react with surprise, thinking that I must be crazy to fly all the way in that thing. Andre posted our smiling faces on Facebook and so many who knew us both reacted with love to see old friends and teammates together again.

It pained me to learn of Andre's journey. I remembered the skinny, polite young boy I had befriended and guided a long time ago when I was an elder leader of a team. That was what I did.

Made everyone feel a part of it. Didn't matter who he was or what he did. Whether the manager or a scrub, everyone was a part of the team. I have that gift of compassion and empathy. I can sense and feel people, or "read" them, as I am told. And, as a law student and lawyer, I've learned to use it by simple observation.

I realized my gift when I had to learn more about me, as I'd not been the mega-superstar athlete like my brother. I had to find my way. Find *me*. And the one thing I recognized I had, and excelled in, was my heart and ability to be with people in a positive way. I wish I had done more self-exploration a long time ago. I know now it would have led me into coaching and teaching which, from my experience as an adult coaching kids' soccer, had brought me the greatest joy. Other than flying, of course. But looking back (and with no regrets) at the time I got out of law school and refused to go into the family law firm with all the inherent family issues, I just went out and got a job. So, the law called and that is what I did.

In high school soccer, I had played center forward while Andre played left inside. The effective formation, in those days, employed a 5-3-2. As I had been when a sophomore, he was a starter on a heavily laden senior team. But he excelled. I can still see him standing there next to me on a kick-off, his curly hair, dark complexion, and slight build, looking at me for leadership and direction. Eager and confident, he was way ahead of so many and, as I learned now, he would far exceed my exploits and become a super star in high school and college.

He didn't remember much about us. He did recall where we had both played on the front line, and he recalled Art Raynor, our coach, with whom he had become friends until Art's death a few years ago. Mr. Raynor, as we knew him then, was a darn good coach and mentor to adolescents. He understood the game and had a good rapport with his players.

My senior year in high school was his first year as Varsity Soccer Coach. He taught me how to kick after our night opener against Oceanside, another high school located in a nearby town and a natural rival. I had a "gimme," as they say, when I broke open, one on one on the goalie at about ten yards out. I kicked it over the goal and made the game a lot closer than it needed to be.

I remembered that miss all too well. We played under the lights. It was the first game of our season every season, and fans were packing the stands. Even more uncanny, and for whatever reason, I remember those easy ones that I missed more than those goals I scored. Even from my college career, while I scored a bunch, it was the ones I missed that still haunt this ex-jock. Like the time against the University of Pennsylvania when I let a corner kick go right by me thinking it would go in. Just a simple nod of my noggin and it was a sure goal, but my reticence let it slide across the end line and not into the net. Or the penalty kick in my last home game against Columbia when, again, I tried to be cute. I placed the shot with the inside of my foot to the right side, not hard enough like I normally did with my instep—and the goalie got to it. Ouch! Again, my reticence had me not going full blast. The mind sure can play with you.

At our next practice after that Oceanside miss, Coach Raynor took me aside, saying he wanted to watch me kick. When he saw I was kicking with my toe and not my instep, he approached me. Still, to this day, I remember that conversation.

"Okay," he said. "I've been watching you kick for a while now. What were you thinking about when you missed that shot the other night?"

"I don't know. I just wanted to kick it as hard as I could toward one side, and I missed."

"You missed because you're kicking all wrong. You're kicking with your toe. You can't expect to have any control that way. Here, let me show you how."

Mr. Raynor then showed me how to kick with my instep. He motioned to the goalie to get ready. Then he turned to me and said, as he demonstrated:

"Get over the ball and your foot will follow through on the laces!"

"Or you can use the inside of your foot and try to place the ball—if you have the time."

"And always shoot down and low away."

Boom! Boom! Boom! One after the other.

I stood back and watched in awe, my seventeen-year-old mouth agape, as this then thirtyish year old placed the ball in the net. First, like a rocket, with the nets giving way as the ball hit the twine. Then, a few times over, with his instep; then with inside of his feet. Each move exemplified power—him getting over the ball, the ball taking flight like a rocket. With authority, as we players call it.

"Practice this against a wall," he told me. "With your speed, you should score a hundred goals this year!"

He smiled. I felt my coach care about me.

He was the first real coach I had in my athletic career. My brother, who was my coach my Freshman year in college, was another, but by then, coaches weren't teaching fundamentals. They were about strategy and fielding the best players. You didn't play at Brown University if you didn't have the skills by then. Having won the Ivy League title six years in a row, Brown was a collegiate powerhouse in those days. My senior year we lost for the first time in seven years.

But it was Art Raynor who made me a real soccer player, finally, with some understanding of the skills needed to be better. He taught us the strategy of attack, pulling our defense up and behind the offense. All as one unit, moving back and forth, in unison, attacking and defending. Everyone was involved in the offense and defense.

And did I ever practice. Kicking against the garage, I developed a powerful instep shot—dare I say, a cannon of a shot. I confirmed my progress by knocking out too many wooden panels in the garage door, until my father had enough and declared he was done repairing the garage door. He advised me, somewhat sternly, to go to the school yard and shoot against the brick wall.

I didn't score a hundred in my senior year, but enough to be Second Team All-Nassau County. Some of my best friends remain from that squad and memories of our glory days still warm this former jock. I like to play Bruce Springsteen's *Glory Days* now and then. It's a nice reminder of the athlete I was, all five feet, seven and a half inches of me. There's nothing like the thrill of victory—or the agony of defeat—with the sense of community a team has when pulling together, win or lose. Even with the body exhausted, the mind is satisfied by the effort rewarded. Win or lose, I understood what brought success, on and off the field. It was no accident.

I also understood you couldn't do it alone.

Athletics taught me that essential discipline. It exposed me to team play, and how everyone, no matter what his or her status, be it star or bench warmer, was a part of it. In whatever one would attempt, getting down to it, day in and day out, separates success from failure.

Preparation and hard work in practice paid off in games. Working with teammates in harmony was an underlying benefit. Being fit was essential to do the assigned task. Again and again, until the kick became second nature. Coach Raynor inspired these lessons and they carried over, into to the rest of my life.

Like they did in flying.

Maintaining one's status and proficiency is essential. Preparing for a flight. Calling weather service. Making sure Two Niner Lima was ready to go. I have spent hours of repetitive, hard work practicing landings and take-offs, slow flight, instrument approaches, and flying solely by instruments. Over and over. Two Niner Lima has become a part of me. All the hard work would pay off in a successful flight, as it has so far, with this journey across the USA. The air traffic controllers are my teammates, working in harmony with Two Niner Lima and me, as we cross the vast expanse.

I always was able to draw upon those lessons Coach Raynor laid out. Practice. Discipline. Understanding the task at hand. It always becomes obvious to me when, like the perfect landing, it only happens when you set up the final approach. When the sweet sound of the tires embracing the ground is the reward for a perfect landing.

Perhaps I have taken those lesson too far. Maybe they have even been too much. I was certain of my abilities to score goals on the soccer field, and I took that confidence into every endeavor. I always believed I could score and win. No matter what I was doing, I always felt I would succeed.

Lately, though, after all I had gone through, I hadn't been so sure—until this point in my journey. With every stop along the way, I felt a bit more restored, a bit more like that boy who could score every time he walked onto the field.

Andre had another somewhat painful story to share. His father was a lot like mine.

Demanding, narcissistic, but not just emotionally abusive. No, his dad was also physically abusive. I had no clue back then and it was a shock to hear it. His pain was still evident, but as he told me of the confrontations, his strength was even more apparent. He had used his anger and pain to move himself forward and become a success.

So, I realized as I quietly listened, he, too, was burdened by an older brother's path and the excessive demands of a difficult parent. He, likewise, had carried the emotional pain as best he could, wrapped in anger. His athleticism carried him and defined him. He, too, knew he would succeed.

But, alas, Andre had no choice but to battle one more unchangeable fact: the color of his skin.

Opening up, he shared with me how much anger he'd held inside back then. He claimed he had few friends, although I was suspect about that. He was way too personable. But I felt the pain and disappointment when he explained how intense his anger had been. He believed his "friends" were only nice to him because he scored goals. He had viewed everyone with deep suspicion. Worse, he explained, because as a person of color, he had experienced such deep prejudice and racial taunts all too frequently. When he'd stood and played next to me on the soccer pitch, I had taken him under my wing. I didn't see anyone or anything but a teammate in uniform wearing our same school colors. There was, and still remained, a certain affinity and comradery. I had no idea that we were so alike.

I, too, still carry that anger deep inside, wrestling with the pain.

I often wonder about why it is we feel such comfort and closeness with some, but with others, we feel wary and distant. Energy vibrations? Similar backgrounds? It never fails to surprise me as I listen to an individual, look into his or her eyes, watch how they respond, how they communicate, and measure my response. Older now, I am more likely to trust my intuition and go with my gut. When I was younger, and far less aware, I thought too much, always analyzing, thinking, wondering. I was like a young Woody Allen but not as facile at communicating. Nor did I know my own self as well as I think I do now, since I've started tuning into the energy and possibilities the Universe is presenting to me.

It was just easy with Andre. Then, as I recall, and now. But my heart ached more when he told me that despite being enrolled in college, he was drafted and after his physical, put on a bus and inducted immediately. I felt horrified—that this could have happened didn't seem legally possible.

But, then again, I am white. I realized when he looked at me with such sadness in his eyes that, of course, it happens every day to people of color. The random traffic stops for no reason, the questioning of what you might be doing in a white neighborhood.

I hate that this terrible disease, so insidious in our species, eats away at our country.

I asked both Andre and Joanne about their experiences of racism. Joanne is his high school sweetheart and wife of almost fifty years. Quiet and soft spoken, she told me how she went after an opposing high school coach who had openly displayed his racist attitude by imploring his players to get that "monkey." She confronted him right there on the field, and the ensuing melee became a story of legendary proportions in the annals of South Side Soccer history.

They had lived most of their mixed-race marriage in New York and Colorado before retiring to North Carolina, as Andre, an explosives expert trained by the Army, worked for the government after he found himself a bit lost as a young adult.

Sometimes, as Andre shared some stories, the obvious happened more often than not. Andre recalled numerous times police officers pulling him over, frequently in North Carolina, but he knew the law, had no fear, and would calmly explain to the officer why it was wrong to have pulled him over. Since there was no violation, it was clearly because of his race. His government employment and life experience gave him the strength to stand up for himself. And coupled with his experience as a munitions expert defusing bombs—well, hell, he had no fear, not even when a cop pulled him over.

I marveled at his strength, and his *cahones,* and wondered if I was anywhere that strong. Despite excellence in so many domains, be it on the soccer field, courtroom, or with people, I still had my doubts about me. I haven't been able to get a handle on that self-doubt. Perhaps it's from not feeling loved by my father, but I am still unable to shake the pain of inadequacy even now. I tend to mull it over too much, or dance with it too long.

My journey thus far had renewed me and brought me new confidence. As Andre talked, I was far less critical of me, seeing a universal, common pain a father can cause. But it really didn't matter. One way or the other, we all have our Viet Nam, and we each confront the devil with whom we must dance. Andre's came every time he had to defuse a bomb. The insanity of the war, ambushes, doing things he never dreamed he was capable of, was his. The insanity of war made him steel against any foe.

I understood. My dance was with that disconnect as to what others perceived from the outside looking in, wrestling with the lingering pain inflicted, questioning, wondering, doubting *me.* Dancing with that Beast. It was only in the left seat I did not. No one could touch me there. After all, it was just Two Niner Lima and me. No one to judge or criticize. No, I was capably handling a machine and flying it through the air, proficiently, expertly, as I am Captain Bob. All the way across America.

I spent a pleasant few days with Andre and Joanne. I liked Wilmington and enjoyed his friends and the city. We dined along the Cape May River, picnicked at an outdoor concert listening to a local band play good old rock n' roll, and drank lots of morning coffee on their porch. Joanne warmed to me and opened up about her life. I marveled at her composure and strength, never mind her obvious love and affection for Andre. My questions became more direct about their life together and the hurdles they'd had to get over, even if they had to take on the rotten disease eating away at all of us—the one which none of us should be burdened.

They were happy and content in Wilmington, and I was pleased I'd gotten to know this man I'd put my arm around so long ago.

My brother-in-law had called and asked me to surprise my baby sister early for her sixty-fifth birthday, so I cut my visit short and made plans to head up to Virginia Beach. I would be flying into Norfolk and the weather held promise for only a few more days. I told Jack to make sure she was at their home when I arrived.

But first I would stop at Kitty Hawk, in Kill Devils Hill, North Carolina, to pay homage to the Wright Brothers and where it all began. I had read the latest biographies about these famous first flyers and I couldn't miss stopping at their national monument on the way up the coast.

CHAPTER XVII

————————————————————————————————→✈

LEG NINE

June 29, 2019 ILM-FFA-ORF

Wilmington International Airport, Wilmington, NC, to First Flight America, Kill Devil Hills, NC, to Norfolk International Airport, Norfolk, VA

Distance: 152 nm ILM-FFA. 58 nm FFA-ORF. Total: 210 nm.

Route: ILM-FFA Direct.

FFA-ORF Direct.

Start time (ILM): 10:16 a.m. Wheels up: 10:31 a.m.

Wheels down: 11:20 a.m.

Shut-Down time (FFA): 11:41 a.m.

Start time (FFA): 2:21 p.m. Wheels up: 2:33 p.m.

Wheels down: 3:05 p.m.

Shut down time (ORF): 3:13 p.m.

Log Entry: ILM-FFA:1.5 hrs. Flight time: 1:10.

To FFA-Wright Bros. Monument. Btyfl little airport right next to Monument. Stunned when overflew and down inlet to ocean and

saw it. Wow! Good speed control/over trees.
FFA-ORF: .9 hrs. Flight time: 0:33.
First time at even + 500' – 4,500'. A bit bumpy. Used smarts to get
flight following when contacted King City Tower freq. Needed
vectors to airport. Nice view of harbor.

Again, I had a restless sleep, anticipating the next day. I awoke early to good weather. The night before I had checked with Flight Service, and all was looking good for my jaunt up to First Flight America Airport to visit the Wright Brother's monument, then up to Norfolk to surprise my sister in Virginia Beach.

Joanne insisted on breakfast and prepared some scrambled eggs and toast before she left for the beach with her friends. We had a warm goodbye hug and I promised I would be back soon.

Andre and I sat drinking coffee and chatting on their screened-in porch. I was enjoying Andre and his wife so much I really didn't want to go, but with the weather holding and my brother-in-law arranging the surprise for my sister, I didn't want to stay longer and be hemmed in if the weather started to change, as it was predicted.

I still don't trust weathermen a hundred percent, even though they're so much better now than when I was a kid in the Fifties. Before satellites and monitors, the science of meteorology was hit and miss. Not today. My briefing included checking in with Flight Service after I check the weather on Foreflight, look at various maps to verify the terminal forecasts, including cloud coverage, surface winds, and pressure changes, from which I could get a reasonable idea about weather conditions for my route. My Radar gave me a quick glance, as well, at actual convective activity and precipitation.

The morning, before the summer sun started heating up the day, was relatively cooler but I knew the heat would bring with it the all too familiar humidity. Living in California all these years has made me immune from that dampness and choking heat, so until this adventure I'd forgotten what it was like. But making my way across the south and now up the east coast, there was no way to avoid it. Just the way it is. Comes with the territory. I was enjoying the cool morning air with my friends, and Andre and I were glowing in our reacquaintance.

Breakfast filled me up and I excused myself to shower and pack. I was aiming for wheels up sometime between ten and eleven a.m., figuring about an hour and a half flying time to FFA. I would have a few hours to enjoy my stop at our flight mecca, then another half hour or so flying time to Norfolk. That would put me into ORF before any afternoon to early evening thunderstorm could build up.

I got myself together and Andre and I headed out to the airport. Instead of just dropping me off, he insisted on helping me with my pre-flight and then he hung with me a bit before my departure. We checked in at the reception counter, I paid the fuel tab and a few overnights parking stay, and we trundled out to Two Niner Lima on the standard hotel baggage cart loaded with mine.

I removed Two Niner Lima's canvas cover, a necessity to keep the heat and sun from baking the interior and exposing the radios and navigation equipment to excessive and damaging heat. Andre handed my bags up to me while I stood on the wing walk making sure to position them to keep the weight across that center of gravity right behind the seats.

Jumping down, I included my buddy in my pilot's tasks, explaining what I was doing, as he asked what I was doing and looking for. This man I would have in any trench beside me, to fight the good fight, or whatever the battle could be, solid as he was when I stood by him on the Hempstead Lake soccer field that South Side

High School called its home pitch. Even more so today, molded by his life's experiences, into the real mensch he was.

I got to the engine access department, which has a little door to peer in. There, I can check the oil dip stick and look to see if anything is amiss. I look for any oil leak, any loose wires, anything noticeable to indicate something was not right. After years of doing so, I have yet to see a problem in there. My check of the oil showed I was a quart low. The oil reservoir for the Lycoming 0-320 engine is eight quarts, but I usually never let it go too far below six quarts. The dip stick, like in an automobile, showed just over five. Taking no chances, I waved down a lineman and requested an additional quart of Shell 100, the aviation oil I've been using for years. This would delay my departure a bit, but with the weather clear and short flights ahead of me for the day, I was not concerned about the fifteen minutes or so departure would be pushed back.

We finished the walk around and gabbed a bit before the lineman came back with the quart of oil and a funnel. For whatever reason, company policy was that the pilot replenished the oil, not the lineman. So, I did. We handed him the empty quart container, and I turned to my friend, smiled, and thanked him for being there for me again.

Our hug said it all, a loving goodbye between two old friends and teammates.

I clambered aboard, fastened my seat belt, and activated the Bose Active Noise Reduction headset, slipping it on, the microphone jutting from the right ear cup on the right side of my face, as per my usual set up. As it was a short flight of about an hour and fifteen minutes and I wanted to just take pictures on the way, I chose not to place the iPhone in its holder coupled to the ATC communications.

Two Niner Lima fired right up and after getting the ATIS, I contacted ground, requesting flight following up to First Flight America Airport. We taxied out, got our clearance and squawk code on the way, and went through our run-up. All was good to go and as I taxied up to Runway 6, I requested a straight-out departure as my heading would be 055 degrees.

"Grumman Two Niner Lima, Winds calm, Runway 6, cleared for take-off."

"Roger, Grumman Two Niner Lima, Runway 6, cleared for take-off."

I could have sworn Two Niner Lima had some extra pep in her roll as she rapidly accelerated and off we climbed. The tower directed me to contact Wilmington Departure and I greeted them accordingly.

"Wilmington Departure, Good morning, Grumman Two Niner Lima, twelve hundred feet climbing to thirty-five hundred.

"Good morning, Grumman Two Niner Lima, Altimeter 29.96 feet."

I settled back now to enjoy the flight. I trimmed out Two Niner Lima at thirty-five hundred feet to take it all in. It was the first time in a while I was flying so much lower than I had previously.

Even if it was a bit hazy as we flew north over North Carolina, I was enjoying the scenery. A few miles west of me, the coast was visible through the haze. It reminded me of all of the country, all so green, fields and farms spotted throughout. Here, however, it was a bit different from the flatlands of the Midwest and the South. North Carolina was heavily forested with rivers flowing intermittently from west to east, out to the Atlantic. Houses and towns seemed to be cut out amongst the trees, the roads like arteries running from them, only to disappear amidst the green blanket.

How idyllic the towns and scenery I was passing slowly above seemed to be. New Bern. Jacksonville. Later I would learn that many of the towns I was spotting were some of the first settlements in the New World. That made sense to me as they were off the coast, up the river (which afforded protection) with a port at which to dock. They were a refuge away from the Atlantic Ocean which had no natural harbors on its coastline. Wilmington was the same, situated inland from the ocean.

First Flight America was in the Outer Banks, at Kill Devil Hills, North Carolina.

My route of flight was direct and. as I approached, I began my descent down to the pattern altitude of eight hundred twelve feet. Then I headed up an inlet toward the ocean to prepare for a left downwind approach. The Atlantic sparkled a rich, deep turquois color that had me admiring its distinct luminescence. The beach, crowded with summer tourists, became more visible as we got closer. When Two Niner Lima was down to pattern altitude, I set her downwind approach speed for one hundred five knots and put out a notch of flaps.

The airport runway was hidden behind some trees and when I was able to see more clearly, I started turning onto the down-wind approach leg over the bright ocean. I was looking west-ward when—there it was—the obelisk Monument representing the Wright Brothers achievement. It was a glistening, white spire standing on top of Devil's Hill. The sun was hitting it perfectly and it seemed to be lit up.

On seeing it, I was so stoked I said to myself, out loud:

"Okay! Wow! Just don't fuck up the landing!"

The pilot in me now recognized the precariousness of the im-pending landing and snapped me out of my giddiness.

I concentrated now on getting into the tiny strip—three thousand feet long and sixty feet wide—surrounded by tall pine trees. As I was planning my base turn at a forty-five-degree angle to my touch down point, I noticed a television tower which on final would interrupt my base turn. I decided to turn sooner than I wanted to avoid tangling with that steel Godzilla.

Seeing it, I got a bit nervous. I sat up straighter and slowed down to my final approach speed of ninety knots. I didn't want to carry too much speed and land long, as too much speed results in floating before touchdown to bleed off the excess airspeed—and then enough runway might become an issue.

I put out all my flaps as I made my base turn, trimmed for eighty-five knots, then quickly turned to the left onto final approach, came over the trees with room to spare and then down onto Runway 21.

Runway 21, just like at my home base, Santa Monica.

I smiled as we taxied to the transient tie-down spaces and I saw the Wright Brothers Monument atop the hill awaiting me.

This was not your typical airport. We taxied up to a wooden fence amidst other planes parked in front of a small building. No fancy, huge glass FBO as I had encountered elsewhere. No—FFA was, of course, a National Park, and the Park Service did a wonderful job putting in the landing strip for flyers like me to make the holy pilgrimage.

I shut down and secured Two Niner Lima. I pulled the cover over the seats and up to the glareshield to hide the iPad and Stratus which I placed on the floor in front of the co-pilot's seat, out of the sun and direct heat. Likewise, I took my headset off, and put it on the floor (making sure to shut it off to preserve its battery power). I took the small insulated bag Andre had given me, bigger than the one I had, into which he'd stocked me up with bottles of water and a few pieces of fruit. Locking Two Niner Lima, I turned around on the wing walk and took in the sacred view.

The fence stood in front of a small, wood siding house with a porch wrapped around two sides. Picnic tables surrounded it and I saw some families eating and enjoying themselves in the serene setting. It was a warm day, so the shade looked inviting. A sign on the fence read:

"Welcome to KFFA

Pilots register at Pilot's Facility

Aircraft parking limited to 24 hours

Night take-offs and landings prohibited."

I hopped down and opened the gate, walked through and went up onto the porch. There was a bronzed metal plaque on the building:

"Wright Brothers National Memorial Pilot Facility

A gift from the members of the

Aircraft Owners and Pilot Association

Ensuring Aviation's Future."

Well, I'll be darned! AOPA did something so nice! I wasn't happy with that organization these days, but this made me smile. I had been a member since I started flying back in 1979 so I was proud to have contributed to this monument. I had felt a kinship with AOPA for many years, mainly because John S. Yodice, the general counsel, who also wrote a monthly column in their *Pilot* magazine, had been a boss of mine. I had managed to land a clerkship with him back in 1972, when AOPA was headquartered in Bethesda, Maryland, a suburb outside D.C. where I attended law school. I would ride my motorcycle out to perform various legal tasks for him and AOPA. I recall many times answering the phone and speaking with member pilots. I had to learn fast where to get information and it sparked in me an idea to get a job with the government after graduation at the FAA or NTSB. Alas, I was unsuccessful and then a job offer in LA clinched my destiny. John Yodice was a good guy and I met and communicated with him a few times over the years before he recently retired.

I went to the bathroom at the back of the building then came out to drink some water and eat a few snacks before exploring the monument and the visitor's center and walking the hallowed grounds of the first flight.

Awestruck, I hiked up to the top of the hill and inspected the monument. When Orville and Wilbur mastered powered flight in the early 1900s, the hill was a massive sand dune. Today it's all covered with grass, planted in 1929 to stabilize the hill beneath the monument. Steps today make it easier to get to the top, leading up from a concrete path.

Climbing the hill was strenuous. With every step up the slope, soft deep sand caused me to slip part way back down. The Wright brothers also had to carry their heavy gliders up the hill for each flight. These tireless efforts paid as they mastered their flight controls.

I am enamored with the scientific approach and commitment these pioneers of aviation employed to this new science. In a wind tunnel they created back in Dayton they even worked out their principles and incorporated them into their ever-evolving designs. Their mastery of flying principles with their Wright Glider before attaching an engine to achieve man's first powered flight reflected their methodical and determined approach to this new realm.

I reached the top of the hill. There, the monument stood. On one side:

WILBUR WRIGHT

ORVILLE WRIGHT

In Commemoration of the Conquest of the Air.

GENIUS

Erected by the Congress of the United States

Begun 1928

Dedicated 1932

I circled around the monument. There lay the Atlantic Ocean, surrounding the island. Looking back now at what I had just seen on approach to FFA, I saw the markers for where those first flights started and ended. About thirty or so visitors were walking along the path toward the re-creation of the Wright's workshop, living quarters and the Visitor's Center.

Enjoying the view, I closed my eyes and tried to imagine being there with the brothers in the early Twentieth Century when Kitty Hawk and the Outer Banks were bleak and sparse and not so populated. I could almost feel the howling wind atop the hill, capturing the lift of the glider when they pushed off again and again as they mastered their new dominion.

I was conscious of the time as I wanted to land at Norfolk by three p.m. and Uber to my sister's house by four, all in order to surprise her. So I took a bunch of pictures, then walked down the hill and there I saw it. The launch rail was still in place—the rail upon which the first powered aircraft moved downward on a dolly, gathering enough speed to break the surly bonds of earth for the first time ever.

A painting in a glass plaque described it:

Getting off the Ground

After four years of scientific research and rigorous experimentation, and with their 1903 Flyer on the rail, the Wrights are set to fly. In unison, they each pulled down on a propeller. The engine roars to life and the propellers whip through the air; only a restraining wire keeps the Flyer in place. Orville climbs onto the machine and positions himself into the hip-cradle. He releases the restraining wire and the machine slowly moves forward. Wilbur runs alongside to steady the machine. After traveling 40 feet down the rail, the Flyer lifts into the air, ushering in the Age of Flight.

I looked down the rail, then closed my eyes, imagining that cold, windy December day. I opened my eyes and walked to the first marker, a white rock about three and a half feet tall, a couple of feet wide. There were three more in a row, separated by many feet in between.

END OF 1ˢᵀ FLIGHT

Time: 12 Seconds

Distance: 120 feet

December 17, 1903

Pilot: Orville

The next three markers indicated the next flights on that day. Wilbur bested his brother, reaching one hundred seventy-five feet. Orville topped him at two hundred feet. And then Wilbur smashed both their marks with a fourth and final first day flight of eight hundred fifty-two feet.

I was speechless. A jet roared overhead, a fighter jet of sorts, like an F-15 or F-35. It went by so low, fast and loud I couldn't tell. But as I stared at the rail where it all began I thought, *Oh, how wonderful to see that now*. It all started one hundred sixteen years ago, with eight hundred and fifty-two feet. And to think, in a few years man will set foot on Mars.

Amazing what we can do when we want to.

Hello, America.

I felt the same as I did when I walked through NASA and saw our accomplishments in the new frontier of space, thinking how painful it was to see man's greatness being destroyed by avarice and the lust for power. I felt an imbuing rise of self-confidence in the doing of it—crossing this huge continent in Two Niner Lima, reaching the Atlantic Ocean, my journey soon to be finished and mission accomplished.

America needs a new destination. Badly.

I hurried into the Visitor's Center and read more of the Wright Brother's history. There, it was all laid out, from their humble beginnings in a bicycle shop in Dayton, Ohio, to their crowning success at Kitty Hawk on December 17, 1903. I felt a special comradery with these pioneers. Oh, not like I was Magellan, finding the New World in Two Niner Lima, but almost. For me, it was a new world and new beginning. An adventure of a lifetime had been mine with this trip and here I was, at the beginning of it all. I was humbled and amazed how far aviation, and I, had come.

A replica of the Flyer was in a glass exhibit room. Staring out the windows, I could see in the distance the Monument to this incredible achievement. The picture I took said it all. Not too shabby, Orville and Wilbur. Talk about making a contribution! Wow!!

It was coming up to two p.m., so I started walking back to Two Niner Lima for the rendezvous with my sister. It would be a short flight from FFA to ORF, Norfolk International Airport—fifty-eight nautical miles, with flying time projected to be thirty-three minutes. After the long walk back to the Pilot's Facility I sat at a picnic bench and taped a live message to post on Facebook, sharing my euphoria on walking the hallowed grounds. I wouldn't post it until after I arrived at my sister's home, in case she was online. I didn't want to ruin the surprise.

It was time to go. A bit tired after the long trek from New Orleans, I hoped to spend a nice week with my sister and her husband. I wanted to regroup my Self before the last leg up to Danbury and the finish of this eastward march of my adventure. Thrilled by my pilgrimage to Kitty Hawk, I was pleased I had paid homage to the men who started it all.

I wasn't a bit tired as I walked back through the gate and onto the tarmac to Two Niner Lima. She was parked adjacent to the fence at the gate, and I was ready for the short flight ahead of me.

There was no ATIS (Automatic Terminal Information Service) but AWOS (Automatic Weather Observation Service) automatically took the same measurements for wind speed and direction, barometric pressure, and dew point and temperature readings. The big difference between an ATIS at an airport with a control tower versus an uncontrolled field was the voice announcing the hourly weather. Here, it was an automated machine, and spoke in that distant, robot mechanical voice. With a control tower, the controller will broadcast the ATIS for a particular hour and speak it in human speak. Better yet, with a live human, pilots also get information on the runway in use, and landing and taking off on which specified runway. With AWOS, like in any uncontrolled airport, you had to check the wind direction, then check the windsock to confirm it—not only the direction but also the speed (by seeing how extended it was)—then take off in the direction you wished.

Seeing the windsock blowing straight down Runway 21, I announced on the Unicom frequency my intention to depart on that runway. Just before I did, a Bonanza V-tail landed on it.

"First Flight Traffic, Grumman Two Niner Lima, back taxiing down Runway 21 for departure."

There was no taxiway, just the landing strip, Runway 21. I looked on the downwind, base, and final approach paths to see if any landing traffic was coming in. I heard nothing. I saw no other planes in the landing pattern so I started to taxi.

At the beginning of Runway 21, there was a slight turn around, which I followed onto and turned to do my engine run-up and check Two Niner Lima. She responded as she always had, all in the green and ready to go. I checked my iPad for the departure and destination frequencies and put Cherry Point Departure, Norfolk ATIS and Ground into COM 1   and COM 2. We were all set.

"First Flight Traffic, Grumman Two Niner Lima taking Runway 21 for departure. Straight-out."

Easing the throttle forward, I put Two Niner Lima into position. Although she had performed ably so far, the tall, towering pine trees (all thirty to forty feet high) at the end of the runway got the butterflies flapping. I didn't think it would be a problem but to make sure, I held Two Niner Lima with her brakes pressed firmly down, my feet arching on top of the rudder pedals. Pushing the throttle into full position, I watched the RPMs on the tachometer spin up.

I took my feet off the brakes, and we accelerated.

I wanted to be airborne by half the runway, just in case, so I had quickly gone over the emergency checklist to do what must be done if I hadn't reached seventy knots by the half-way point. Power to idle, brakes, rudder correction as necessary, stop.

Two Niner Lima must have sensed my preparation and, as she had done so many times before, she accelerated rapidly, rotating at seventy knots before the halfway point and clearing the trees easily.

I climbed through one thousand feet and banked left. It was the first time in the entire Journey that I would be flying at even plus five hundred feet, or on a heading between one hundred eighty and three hundred sixty degrees.

I announced my intentions as I departed the FFA airspace: "First Flight Traffic, Grumman Two Niner Lima off Runway 21, one thousand feet for forty-five hundred feet, turning left on to a heading of three hundred forty-one degrees. Good day!"

The air was a bit bumpy as we climbed but once over the haze layer, we smoothed out. My route of flight took me between the Outer Bank Islands, up and through a quiet, non-operational military operations area and then direct to Norfolk.

The sky was getting its afternoon dose of convective activity, with many clouds building up above me. I was at the base of them all and I breathed a sigh of relief that I wouldn't have to climb over or go through them, or deal with them at all on this short hop.

I couldn't raise Cherry Point Departure for flight following my take off, and not having those extra eyes guiding me had me a bit apprehensive. See and be seen is, of course, legal, but having a controller watching for conflicting traffic with radar (his extra set of eyes) makes you far more comfortable.

I wasn't sure who to contact then. Perhaps I was out of radio range. I was passing by King City Airport, and thought, of course, to contact them. They would know.

"King City Airport, Good afternoon, Grumman Two Niner Lima, at forty-five hundred feet, a few miles east of you. Requesting frequency for flight following this sector."

"Good afternoon, Grumman Two Niner Lima. King City Tower. Contact Norfolk Approach at one hundred twenty-five point two, this sector. Have a good flight."

"Roger, King City. Thanks for your help. Grumman Two Niner Lima. Good day."

I called Norfolk approach and was with them all the way remaining. I was heading straight towards the city, above a row of Navy ships docked on one of the port inlets. I couldn't be sure I was seeing the airport, although it appeared as a sliver off to my right side, growing larger.

Rather than stumble blindly, I asked for vectors. The controller steered me in that direction, deftly handing me off to Norfolk Tower.

"Norfolk Tower, Grumman Two Niner Lima, on the forty-five for Runway 23, with Mike."

"Roger, Grumman Two Niner Lima, cleared to land Runway 23. You are following a Delta Embraer on a short final."

"Roger, we have the Delta. Grumman Two Niner Lima, cleared to land, Runway 23."

It was a long taxi to the Signature FBO, all the way on the other side of the airport, opposite the passenger terminal. But the linemen had heard I was coming after I had inquired about transient parking. The red batons were moving, waving me in to park, and then a golf cart came scurrying up from the modern, beige brick and glass building.

Relieved and excited to get going, I shut down and went through the post-flight routine. When it was done, I grabbed my suitcase, backpack and small duffel bag. As the lineman loaded up the golf cart, I took a few pictures of Two Niner Lima and covered her up. Then off we went.

After a stop at the bathroom to wash the day's flying off, I went to reception where the woman behind the counter steered me to some water and fruit. Between bites of apple and sips of water, I punched up Uber. My ride would be there in less than five minutes.

The surprise was on!

Pre-Flight at Santa Monica Airport Before Departure

All washed and ready to go

Cockpit with newly purchased sunshade installed

Ready to begin pre-flight

Baggage compartment fully packed and loaded

Gia

29L parked at Deming with ICE hangars looming in the background

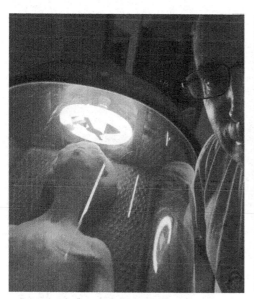

Examining the "remains" of alien found at the crash site

Relaxing with my new friend celebrating July 4th Independence Day

Street lamps adorned on Main Street with Alien motif

Dunkin' Donuts sign with flying saucer shaped McDonald's behind

Alien Salsa

Roswell's own baseball team - The Invaders

Dallas

At the end of the row parked for fuel at Abilene, TX

IFR into Dallas and Addison (ADS)

NASA

The missions flown by my namesake, astronaut John Young

The Space Shuttle Access Arm. Walking down the long corridor to lift-off

All our space hardware under one roof

Mercury capsule "Faith Seven", flown by Gordon Cooper

Redstone rocket with Mercury capsule affixed

Apollo 17 Command Module

New Orleans

Arrival into NOLA

Audubon Park

Up to North Carolina

Passing by Mobile, Alabama

Beautiful FBO at Myrtle Beach, South Carolina (MYR)

First Flight America

Two Niner Lima at First Flight America

Wright Brothers' Monument on top of Devil's Hill

Capt. Bob paying homage

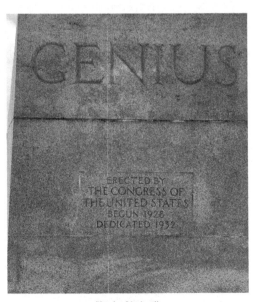

"Genius," indeed!

The Wright Brothers. On Hallowed Ground

These markers indicate the first four powered flights made by the Wright Brothers

The Wright Flyer looks back at Devil's Hill and the Monument to its accomplishment

Leg Nine. Part Two. CDW-DXR

Up to Danbury from Caldwell and passing by New York City in the haze

A happy Capt. Bob upon arrival @ DXR

Back to SoCal

Climbing into 29L

"Points of View"

Return. Leg Two. AGC-VLL

Lake Erie

29L tied down tight and safe, bracing for the storm

Return. Leg Four. Colorado

The Stanley Hotel, Estes Park, CO

The view from my bed. Drake, CO

Return. Leg Five. LVS- TCS

Approaching storm from Baja has 29L begin its climb up to 13,000'

Tied down at TCS

Return. Leg Six. TCS-GYR-SMO

Beautiful morning sunrise at TCS before departure.

Elephant Butte Lake

Salton Sea, Indio, CA

Approaching the threshold of Runway 21 at SMO, shortened by 1,500'

29L back home in tie-down space # 821 @ Proteus Air

A proud Capt. Bob acknowledging his able companion 29L on a journey well done

CHAPTER XVIII

---✈

LEG NINE

FRIENDS
MY SISTER

My little sister, my baby sister, my dear Wendy Florence Young, has always been my pal and biggest fan. I was the baby of the family for six years, the third of three children, when Wendy came along and took away my spoiled status. I never resented her arrival and, indeed, she was a special, wonderfully gifted child. Everyone cooed and ah'd and just adored the cutest little girl. Happy and loved, she was the apple of all our eyes.

Wendy grew up as the last of four children. My older brother and sister were not so close to us once they got into high school. My brother went off to college when I was twelve and Wendy was six. By then my older sister was a teenager, so it was Wendy and I who hung out together, and we developed a very special, close bond that has grown deeper over the years.

Now, she is my only family.

I was her protector then, and my dad's last edict to me in his final days was, "Take care of your sister," and so I did. I kept her out of lawsuits caused by our older brother. When the Trust made distributions, I ate the taxes on gains and generally shielded her as best I could. I never bothered her with the details nor shared with her the brunt of my brother's shenanigans.

When we were children, especially when I got older, I was often her babysitter. We watched all the kids TV shows, developing with each other our slapstick sense of humor and repartee. Laurel and Hardy, Abbot and Costello, and The Three Stooges regaled us. Sandy Becker, Officer Joe Bolton, and Soupy Sales kept us in stitches. Zachary's Monster Madness would scare the bejezus out of us.

I walked her to kindergarten and first grade, with my friends razzing us, throwing leaves on us, all in good cheer. We went ice skating at the local pond, big brother taking his little sister. We played basketball in our driveway court—hoops, as she called it. I was always Walt Frazier or Bill Bradley of my beloved Knicks, posting her down low, and otherwise doing what big brothers did: loving and playing with my little sister but making sure I had a playmate and defender who couldn't defend.

We did everything together.

I left for college when she was twelve and shortly after, my sister's life changed. Something happened in summer camp when she was thirteen, and she suddenly came home. Although she never talked about it my suspicion remains that she was molested by a camp counselor. Thereafter, for a good number of years, she fought anorexia, a terrible disease.

Anorexia Nervosa is an eating disorder in which people have an intense fear of gaining weight and become dangerously thin. It is more common in females and is potentially life-threatening. People with anorexia tend to be high achievers, performing well in school, sports, work and other activities. They tend to be perfectionists with obsessive, anxious, or depressive symptoms. It usually begins around the time of puberty but can develop at any time.

It was no wonder Wendy came down with this. Amidst parents demands of, "Do *better* than your best," and pushing us always to be number one in everything we attempted, Wendy's way of controlling her life in the midst of all the tumult was to control her weight. They never seemed happy with our bounty of successes. The youngest, she was the only child left in the house when her siblings grew up, and she alone had to suffer the brunt of my father's narcissism and verbal abuse. Too often I heard her pain about being called an idiot, and as often as I could I tried to boost her sagging morale. I always ached when she shared her struggles.

After college, Wendy came to Los Angeles to be with me, but those struggles forced her back to the east coast to finally get a handle on it all. I tried to give her all the nourishment she needed, but in those days, my own skills were not as sharp, and my awareness was a bit oblique. I'd heard so much of it through my parents, who had a tough time facing up to their contribution to her problems. It still hurts to know how hard she works to keep things together.

Wendy fought the good fight and got the disease under control. Like alcoholism or drugs, using food to control her life would always be with her but she got through it and has managed to maintain her sanity. She graduated from Duke University and became a successful attorney and practiced for years, until she had enough of the legal world. When her husband Jack got an offer to work for the Norfolk Tides minor league baseball team, they jumped at the chance to leave Stuart, Florida, behind.

Wendy was about to celebrate her sixty-fifth birthday, so it was important for me to be with her. I couldn't say no to her husband when he suggested it and I was excited to surprise her and hang out a bit with her and Jack.

The Uber driver was a nice fortyish African American woman who had just moved to Norfolk from Houston. We had an interesting forty minutes or so gabbing about Houston, as well as Wilmington where she had also lived, working for the government. We agreed Houston was not the place to be, but she raved on about North Carolina and Wilmington as "just a *fine* place" to live.

As the car pulled up, I saw Wendy on her terrace balcony arranging some chairs. I rolled down the window.

"Excuse me, Ma'am," I said. Wendy looked directly at me but didn't recognize me until I spoke again. "Could you please tell me where Wendy Young lives?"

"Rob? Oh, my God!" And she ran off the terrace.

I thanked my driver and got my bags out of the trunk. Wendy came out of her house, and we hugged tight.

"Surprise! I didn't want to miss the sixty-fifth celebration!"

She was speechless. I held her a bit longer, then we went inside.

Wendy took me up to the guest room. Well, not exactly a real guest room, more like an extra room with baseball and theater memorabilia all over the walls with a small leather couch. It was going to be a long week sleeping on that couch.

Jack is an avid collector of baseball and theater memorabilia. He has hundreds of autographed baseballs, bats, and pictures with many of the players he has known over his years of working in the industry as a clubhouse manager. He started in the clubhouse for the Atlanta Braves, and then for the New York Mets in Port St. Lucie. I met Gary Carter and others through him. Gary managed our Orange County Flyers independent baseball team and won us a championship a few years before he suddenly passed from brain cancer. His funeral, with Wendy and Jack also in attendance, was an outpouring of love and deep affection for a man who left too soon.

Jack's other passion was Broadway, and the evidence was visible throughout their modern and trendy townhome decorated with framed and autographed Playbills from almost every show you can think of.

After I unpacked I went downstairs to find out how my sister was faring. She looked tired and I was concerned. "How are you?" I asked. "How are things going?"

"I'm okay." She was cutting up some chicken to make herself a sandwich. "I've been trying to eat only certain foods to battle my cholesterol."

"Is that so wise? You look tired. Are you okay? Forget pinching on the food. Get your doctor to put you on statins already!"

"I know. I am. He says not until I go through this diet regimen."

"Well, just be careful, please. Do you feel you're eating enough?"

"I'm okay," she insisted. "I'm taking good care of myself so no need to worry."

"I will, but be careful, please."

I didn't want to push the conversation any further. She had her life in control, she was pursuing her passions of dancing and swimming, doing what she wanted to do now that she was retired. I was happy for her. Besides, even being her brother, I was a guest and had to respect her boundaries and not tread where I shouldn't. Still, I was concerned. She looked tired and thin.

I didn't inquire too vigorously for fear of upsetting her and stepping over a line. Her illness had defined our relationship that way. I was keen to be loving and supportive without criticizing or digging too deep, even if it was to be constructive. It was a boundary I did not cross for fear of hurting her. Even though our conversations over the years had become deeper and more intimate, for I felt her fragility because of the disease. It defined our relationship.

And, I am cognizant of my distress when I am not totally honest. I think I am "helping" her, even though with others I'm direct and effusive about everything and anything. Not being honest for fear of hurting another doesn't make me like myself. With my sister, I try to be more forthright, even when I know I'm dancing along the edge of that line. This time, I was hoping to do better with her.

Jack was going to be working until almost two a.m. The Tides were home, and he would be preoccupied until they went on the road again. But when they did, on Sunday, he was off to New York to see his beloved Mets and take in a few Broadway shows.

Wendy and I then spent a few days together, going out at dinner for Mexican food and other local fare. We went to the movies and saw *Yesterday*. Both the restaurant and the theater were in a shopping center, where all across America the same restaurants, same stores, and similar movie theaters are located. It was but another common denominator that welcomed me to but another city in the USA. New Orleans broke that mold, or at least Zeke and Martha hadn't taken me to any, and I didn't see one in Roswell. Comfort comes at a cost.

On Wendy's birthday, we went down to the beach to walk and smell the salt air and, at least for me, to see Virginia Beach. It was a warm, sunny day and the beach was filled, the boardwalk crowded. Virginia Beach had a different feel than Wilmington. It was a bit more harried, more traffic and more crowded than what I'd experienced in the Outer Banks and Wilmington in North Carolina.

As we talked, I learned more about my little sister and heard how she had her life in control. She confessed she had not seen much of Virginia Beach and the surrounding environs, going where only she needed to go to do what she wanted to do. In the three years she had lived here, this was only the second time she had been to the beach. I was surprised but couldn't argue with that, especially, after hearing her happy and pleased. She had come a long way and her thoughts showed an evolved and aware soul. I knew it was the disease that she still battled, but she became functioning, succeeding and contributing, and touching many others. Her stories of her dancing were proof.

Wendy had gone for her Master's in Dance. She had been a brilliant young pianist, able to play a song without even reading the music sheets, and that was before the age of five. I recall discussion between my parents about her skipping a grade in elementary school, but they decided against it. She excelled in dancing and even today, at sixty-five, whether it's ballet, tap, jazz, modern or ballroom, she excels, performing as well or even better than the teenage girls in her class. To her elder dance mates, she is a hero. She glowed when she shared with me stories about her dancing, the compliments her teachers paid her, and just being, finally, who she was. I knew what she meant. I had seen her steal the show when, a few years before, she had performed one of the leads in *The Nutcracker Suite*.

The beach was fun. A huge brass statue of Neptune, King of the Sea Underworld, stood twenty feet tall on the boardwalk. We walked and talked, laughed and reminisced, sharing our familial bonds. We even stopped to get a bite. After all, it was her birthday. I insisted that we have a piece of birthday cake and some ice cream. It was a good day. I was glad to have made it in time to be with her, on her day. Besides, I got to see another tribute to aviation. This time, at the beach, was a memorial to Naval Aviation centered in nearby Norfolk.

Wendy seemed happy, as her life was. She had her routine. Sleep, breakfast, dancing, swimming, biking, or whatever else she wanted to do. Our father's riches had provided for her and she was enjoying the fruits of his labors. Me? I invested my inheritance and lost it all in minor league baseball.

But how do you measure present happiness against all of life's past experiences?

Jack returned from New York on Wednesday. The next day I went with him to the stadium in Norfolk. He took me on a tour of his dominion, including the visitor's locker room, as well as the under-bowels of the facility, from which we walked up and onto the field.

There is a certain magic about seeing a ballpark and its grass playing field. To many, myself included, it's like walking into church or the synagogue, and stepping onto holy ground.

The very first time I experienced it was when my mom was teaching a summer day camp for the village of Rockville Centre and took me there every day to keep me occupied. I was no more than three or four years old. We went on a field trip to a baseball game at Ebbets Field, home of the Brooklyn Dodgers before they moved to Los Angeles.

I still vividly recall walking into the stadium, going over a hanging ramp into the old park, and then seeing it. This magnificent, deep green, well-cut grass baseball field and infield diamond stood out and grabbed me. Today, whatever stadium I visit, that feeling always comes back when I see the field for the first time.

Hallowed ground, indeed.

I was planning to go by the weekend but the weather turned and it wouldn't be until early the following week that I would depart. But I sensed I was wearing out my welcome. Wendy would go off to her room without seeking my participation in her day, and she and Jack did not include me in their evening activities. I felt isolated and sensed I was intruding on my sister's daily routine, and my presence was wearing on her. I decided to take a motel room down the road for a few nights.

Wendy seemed relieved. I had read the situation correctly. Besides, after sleeping on that leather couch, I needed a good night's rest. Jack took me to a nearby Quality Inn the next morning. It wasn't the Ritz but it would do.

After nine barely tolerable nights on the small guest room couch, I relished stretching out on the bed. I spent the day writing and taking it easy and ordered in some dinner from a local hamburger joint. I had such a craving for a hamburger and hot dog that the Uber Eats fare from Five Guys in Norfolk had me salivating.

While I was waiting for dinner, I checked on the weather. There was a line of storms coming but Flight Service had informed me on Friday that they wouldn't pass through Norfolk until Tuesday, so I was planning a Wednesday departure. My Radar confirmed the prognosis.

But now, on Monday evening, the weather advisor said it was moving more quickly than previously predicted, so I would be good to go in the morning.

Apparently, the low front that was causing havoc for a few days now, pushing eastward, with a high pressure front from Canada settling in over New York and New England, was pushing the low southward. Now, the prediction for rain for Norfolk on Tuesday was revised, as the high pressure was doing a better job and

Norfolk would be clear, as the low was being pushed more quickly into the Carolinas.

I was stoked. The end of the eastward portion of my journey was now before me. While I waited for my food delivery, I made a To Do list for after dinner. Didn't want to leave anything behind, and doing the list made me focus on the upcoming task.

I took a nice deep breath and smiled. "Chill, dude. Get ready. Be prepared."

That hamburger and Hebrew National dog tasted even more delicious.

The finish line was right ahead of me.

CHAPTER XIX

———————————————————————————→

LEG TEN
PART 1
ORF-CDW

July 9, 2019 ORF-CDW-DXR

Norfolk International Airport, Norfolk, VA to Cadwell Municipal Airport aka Essex County Airport, Caldwell, NJ to Danbury
Municipal Airport, Danbury, CT

Distance: 255 nm ORF-CDW.

47 nm CDW-DXR.

Total: 302 nm.

Route: ORF-CDW Direct.

CDW-DXR Direct.

Start time (ORF): 7:52:17 a.m. Wheels up: 8:04:41 a.m.

Wheels down: 10:17:12 a.m.

Shut-Down time (CDW): 10:21:24 a.m.

Logged Time: 2.7 hrs. Flight Time: 2.7 hrs.

After 4 days of showers, all clear to go. 3,500' smooth. OMG! NY
Skyline!! Dir CDW but didn't x Del Bay until narrwst pt. NY Approach Controller rapid instructions & thnk u!

The excitement of the upcoming day had me up bright and early. I checked the weather as soon as I woke up, forty-five minutes before the alarm was set to wake me at five, and I used the extra time to call Flight Service again. The news was even better. The weather was clear—no lingering clouds or precipitation. The high-pressure trough was doing its magic, pushing that low into the Carolinas as predicted.

I couldn't sleep and I gave up pretending I could. My heart was beating too fast and too strong. And here we were, ready to complete the eastward journey, rest up in New York for a bit and take time to see friends and the old stomping grounds.

There was no coffee machine in this Extended Stay America in Chesapeake, Virginia.

The room was old but heck, not even free coffee? I needed my caffeine but it was not to be. When I called the Front Desk to inquire, as the printed brochure indicated you had to ask, I gave up after being left on hold for far too long. I figured I'd get up and out early and have a few sips before I got airborne, hoping the brief ingestion would get the motor running.

Despite my interrupted morning coffee routine, I was energized. I showered, shaved, got dressed and called Uber. A ride was six minutes away so I packed up my last few things, did a last walk-around to make sure I didn't forget anything, and went outside to wait.

A big white Chrysler 300 pulled into the motel courtyard and I waved. Kia was a pretty African American woman who had just started driving for Uber. She had moved to Virginia Beach from Charleston, SC, and was a consultant to the government on staffing health care facilities. Her company had lost a contract so she was now part-time with them and she needed the extra income. That seemed to be a familiar refrain amongst all the Uber drivers I had experienced over this journey and her story rang a bell with me. I sat in the back seat and gabbed with her about my trip and my life, and listened to hers.

We all seem so alike, in some fascinating way. Everyone is just trying to make it work, to keep it all going amidst the crumbling dream of America. I started to wax philosophically about the times be a changin' and we briefly got into a discussion of the political maelstrom into which we have all been sucked. She pulled up to the Signature FBO at Norfolk International Airport just after 6:30 a.m. I got my bags out of the trunk and bid her farewell, handing her a five-dollar bill, also making sure to tip her on the Uber App.

It was a glorious, sunshine-filled day and I anticipated a good flight up the coast into the New York metropolitan area. I could stretch and make it to Danbury, my final destination, but I would have less than three gallons of fuel for my reserves. My rule was set and hard: If not five gallons left, as predicted by Foreflight (which met the fuel requirements for VFR flight with half an hour of flying time left) a fuel stop was required. So I had set up a lunch date with a dear high school friend, Amy, and would stop near her home at Caldwell Municipal Airport (CDW), now known as Essex County Airport. It had a bit of notoriety, but not of the good kind. It was the airport John F. Kennedy, Jr. flew out of on his fateful last day.

Everyone asks me about that incident. Sadly, as all pilots know, it was pilot error. His death was tragic and should have been avoided but he didn't counter back at the steady stream of unfolding events and factors. Clearly, he was not aware of or paid no heed to them. Or, perhaps he thought he was quite capable as a pilot could handle them. We will never know.

He was a relatively new pilot with less than two hundred hours of flying time. He chose to fly a Piper Saratoga, an airplane that was too sophisticated for a new pilot with so little experience. A six-seater, 350 horsepower airplane, it was a "complex" airplane with a retractable landing gear and an adjustable propeller. I didn't learn to fly a "complex" airplane until I received my commercial license, which I got with almost fifteen hundred hours of flying time. One cannot obtain a commercial license until he or she garners a minimum of two hundred hours of pilot-in-command time.

Worse, he left late, at dusk, in deteriorating weather conditions, and he lacked an instrument rating to navigate at night in adverse conditions. Throw in the fact that the Saratoga aircraft had an auto pilot, which could have saved his hide. These deficiencies added up to a series of cascading factors that made the crash inevitable. A low-time pilot rushing to a destination, not instrument rated, over water, at night and in instrument conditions, spelled this disaster.

There but for the grace of God go I.

I paid my bill with Signature and grabbed a baggage cart. But before I went out to Two Niner Lima, I made myself a cup of coffee and went over this last leg one more time.

Signature is the FBO that always has good snacks and refreshments, as well as accommodations for pilots, who really enjoy the first cabin treatment. Preferring not to be stuck on the freeway for hours, I often used them for meetings in Southern California. I made it a regular habit after attending a meeting in Orange County years ago. On my way back, a fuel tanker overturned, closing the 405 Freeway near Long Beach and blocking my nearest exit. Six hours stranded behind that calamity made me vow to fly to my meeting, even if a thirty-minute trip down the coast to John Wayne Airport seemed a bit insipid.

The coffee tasted especially good, as it should, since it was Starbucks. I took an apple from the basket on the counter and grabbed some napkins. My small breakfast would give me energy for the upcoming flight while I reviewed my flight plan on Foreflight.

The route would take me out and over Norfolk Bay, then up through Delaware and over the Delaware Bay. It was a lot of water to cross there, so I decided not to be too bold. I would cross nearer Philadelphia, where the Bay is narrow. That point appeared on the Foreflight Sectional map on my iPad. The direct route projected us at two hours and one minute. A few more minutes to give myself more of a safety margin if the engine quit over this narrow band of water wouldn't be so bad. If that happened over the full stretch of the Bay—well, then we would be in big poop.

I walked out just before seven thirty, pushing the loaded baggage cart. Two Niner Lima, not too far away, was sitting patiently on the tarmac.

Stopping for a moment to talk with her, I patted her on the nose. With all the excitement that our Journey Across America was on its last eastward leg and we would be getting a much needed rest, I was, as always, apprehensive. I wanted to make sure she was good to go.

"Only a few more hours and we make it. Let's do it, girl! No time to mess up now." I could have sworn she smiled back at me.

"Got it, Captain B!"

Hugging her, I held her red cone proboscis a bit longer than my usual perfunctory tap. My reliance on this machine for so many years had led me to this point. I had developed a conscious relationship with her over the years, engaging in conversation and treating her like the good girl friend she was to me. She had been my magic carpet–for twenty-five years now. My life was in her hands. Since I had become a big *Terminator: Judgment Day* fan, I always personalize machines, be it my toaster, dishwasher, oven or refrigerator. I guess I fear the day they become aware, and I want to make sure they consider me a friend. With Two Niner Lima, our love affair went much deeper.

I have been flying Two Niner Lima since 1994. I am in sync with her and notice every sound and every little nuance of my partner. From the cockpit to her air frame, I can tell if something is amiss, or if the engine sounds different, or a part is not moving correctly. She has served me so well for so long, I knew my affectionate gesture to her now encouraged her to make sure we finished this last leg safely and proudly.

I got settled into the left seat, adjusted all the equipment as usual. Two Niner Lima fired up after a bunch of turns of the prop, reflecting her ten-day rest. We got clearance and flight following for thirty-five hundred feet up to CDW and after a lengthy taxi and the necessary run-up going through the checklist, off we went on a straight-out departure from Runway 23.

We were out over the Chesapeake Bay for longer than I wanted, and after my request to resume my own navigation, Norfolk Approach complied and we turned left and north, up the coast of Virginia, over the Delaware Bay—and not at its widest point, thank you, of over forty-plus miles. Instead, I took a slight northwest detour and crossed the Delaware River at a lesser point of only ten or so miles wide.

The same familiar farms and towns I had seen all across the country were appearing less and less frequently. Philadelphia was about thirty miles in the haze to my west (and left), and the northeast corridor began to reveal its congested, crowded self.

It was so cool to be speaking with Philly Approach but when they handed me off to New York Approach, well, I was just so tickled. Wow! And, when I saw New York City sticking upward and out of the haze, I was just amazed. All the familiar sites I have seen from approaches and departures in airliners for so many years were now mine in dear Two Niner Lima.

"Never thought I'd see us here," I said out loud to her.

New York Approach was barking out its instructions. Three major airports certainly would keep any controller hopping and mine, handling this initial sector in mid-New Jersey, was no exception. Pilots were stepping on each other, all trying to talk at the same time.

"Listen up, all of you" the controller barked. "No more talking. I have too many planes here. I will tell you what to do and when. Got it? I've got a traffic alert to deal with!" Things got real quiet real quick.

"Jet Blue 361. Stop your descent immediately. Traffic alert. Traffic two o'clock, four miles. Fifty-five hundred feet. Let me know if you have him. Now, Delta 447—descend and maintain four thousand. American 55—climb and maintain ten thousand feet. Jet Blue 512—climb and maintain eight thousand feet."

You could hear a pin drop. The next voice I heard was a new controller. Obviously, the supervisor must have seen one of the controllers losing his grip.

"Grumman Two Niner Lima, thanks for your help. Cleared into Class Bravo, descend and maintain twenty-five hundred feet, direct Caldwell. Contact Newark Departure 119.2."

Newark took me right up to Caldwell, where I spotted the airport. It was more difficult to see airports here in the east, surrounded as they are by forests, with towns, fields and farms sprinkled throughout the dark green blanket. Not at all like the tan southern California sprawl.

I was concentrating now. No room for error with these last legs. Calm winds and a good descent in the smooth morning air greeted my good landing on Runway 22. I taxied to Airbound Aviation, the only FBO at CDW, and followed the linesman's instructions, bringing Two Niner Lima to a stop a few feet from the front door of this FBO.

Sliding the canopy open, I accepted the lineman's offer to refuel Two Niner Lima then and there. I took the iPad out of its cradle, removed the Stratus from the glareshield, and put them both on the floor of the copilot's seat, outside of the glare of the sun. There was no need to to put on Lima's cover as I'd be but a few hours with Amy before taking off on the last leg to Danbury, a short afternoon hop. Before I got out of the plane, I texted her and she replied she would be there in twenty minutes.

Forty-seven nautical miles and twenty-three minutes flying time was left to go before crossing the finish line of our journey across America at Danbury, Connecticut.

I was stoked!

LEG TEN
PART 2
CDW-DXR

July 9, 2019 CDW-DXR
Cadwell Municipal Airport aka Essex County Airport, Caldwell,
NJ to Danbury Municipal Airport, Danbury, CT
Distance: 47 nm CDW-DXR.
Route: CDW-DXR Direct.
Start time (CDW): 2:09:51 p.m. Wheels up: 2:16: p.m.
Wheels down: 2:48:15 p.m.
Shut down time (DXR): 2:52:11 p.m.

Log Entry: CDW-DXR: 47 nm 0.8 hrs. Flight time: 0:36 hrs.
Hop up to DXR after lunch with Amy Leffert. Fun! 3,500′ light
Turbulence. NYC. Wow! Two Niner Lima is here! So exciting!
DXR hills on dwnwnd + final/High/Slipped/Good ldg.

Amy just had to come and see Two Niner Lima in person. I was
waiting outside when she pulled up in her white Accord, rolled
down the passenger window and told me her wish. She parked
and we hugged a warm hello. It was good to see her friendly, loving face.

As we walked into Airbound Aviation, I shared with her the
goings-on, and we walked out onto the tarmac for her to visit with
Two Niner Lima. She asked some good questions, and touched by
my friend's interest, I explained the instrumentation and avionics.

The commemorative photos I took show the warmth between old friends.

We went to her beautiful home and had a delicious lunch while we shared our life stories, catching each other up on all the adventures we'd had. Before we knew it, it was time to go. My ETA at DXR was between three and three-thirty p.m.

With another big hug and a promise to see her again soon, I took care of the fuel bill and headed out to Two Niner Lima. It would be a short trip, less than a half-hour flying time to Danbury.

When I angled up to Connecticut across northern Westchester County on a heading of 060 degrees, I was hoping to take some good pictures of New York City, so I put my phone next to me instead of setting it in its holder on the glareshield.

Start-up was per usual, run-up as well. I notified Tower and the air traffic controller cleared us for takeoff. We took off on Runway 22, up and over the tree line where the winds were more noticeable—and noticeably buffeting us. Then we climbed out on a right downwind departure up to thirty-five hundred feet.

It was light to moderate turbulence at that altitude, so I requested fifty-five hundred feet to get over the haze layer. I was just at the bottom of it, and the mix of differences in air temperature was causing Two Niner Lima, almost at its gross weight of sixteen hundred seventy-five pounds plus, to be jostled a bit more for my liking.

But control came back to me. "Sorry, Two Niner Lima—got to keep you at thirty-five hundred because traffic in Newark will be passing right over you at four thousand feet."

As he said that, with me still staring out to my right, eastward at New York City and heading right for the new Tappan Zee Bridge, I saw out of the corner of my eye what he meant. A Jet Blue A-320 was passing right in front and over Two Niner Lima, a mere five hundred feet above us. I quickly calculated the wind direction, bracing for any wake turbulence to come drifting down at us. Fortunately, it blew south and past me, away from our flight path.

I tuned in the ATIS at about thirty-five miles out but could not pick up the weather and runway landing information. I had it set up on Comm 2, so I would still hear New York approach on Comm 1. With good reason, we have multiple radios in our planes. Finally, I confirmed with the controller that the ATIS frequency of DXR to which I was listening was correct.

"But I'm unable to hear it," I advised him.

"So you want it from me?" he asked kindly.

"Affirmative and thank you!"

"Grumman Two Niner Lima, advise when you have the airport in sight." "Roger," I replied.

I thought I saw it amidst the trees and forests blanketing much of Connecticut. I was at least twenty-five miles out but as I got closer and closer, I still couldn't see the runways through the haze.

At twelve miles out, I knew I needed to descend soon to the pattern altitude of seventeen hundred feet, and I had to slow down and get down.

"New York, Grumman Two Niner Lima. I think I have the airport in sight," I advised, although I still wasn't certain, even though it matched up on my Foreflight moving map.

"You think?" the controller replied sarcastically.

"Roger, New York. First time in this airspace. I'm from Los Angeles, just finishing a long trip."

I heard him chuckle. "Okay then, Two Niner Lima. Danbury is right on your nose, seven miles ahead. Contact Danbury Tower 119.4. Welcome to New York."

"Over to Danbury Tower 119.4. Grumman Two Niner Lima.

And thanks for your patience and help today."

I clicked the microphone push-to-talk button twice, a silent way to acknowledge him and express my gratitude.

We were almost there, but landing was going to be a challenge. There were hills surrounding DXR, and as I turned onto the downwind leg, there right in front of me stood a pretty high radio tower. It was located at about where I wanted to turn and descend onto my base leg. I decided to turn sooner than that; no need to mess with it. Just like the Godzilla tower at FFA.

The hills, blanketed in trees, were disconcerting to me, as they had been at Mendocino when I flew up to Oregon a few summers ago, as well as all the airports I had encountered on this trip. Not like in the west.

But these hills were another matter. The trees seemed too close for my liking.

I descended on the downwind, turned before that tower onto a very brief base leg, and overshot the extended runway centerline by a drop as I rolled out onto final.

I found myself too fast and too high—no problem in a Grumman—as I slipped Two Niner Lima a couple of times, got on the glide slope as confirmed by the VASI lights (red over white, just right!) and bled off my air speed, looking down at the end of the runway. The wheels kissed the ground.

I was ecstatic.

I did it! I flew cross-country in Two Niner Lima.

We did it! She performed magnificently, without a hitch.

I taxied into West Conn Aviation, where my dear Enid had arranged with her boss to allow me to hangar Two Niner Lima while I stayed in New York and visited with friends. Mike, his assistant and the FBO's flight instructor, was the linesman, and he directed me to a final stop with the same ground signals—but, this time, batonless. I saw Enid, her camera up to her eye, videoing the arrival.

I went back into the cockpit and shut things down. Enid came up to the plane, smiling and still filming.

"Wow!" I greeted her. "I can't believe I did it!" I was deliriously exhausted and so damned pleased.

Wow, indeed!

Journey Across America, Part One. *Finis*.

I was tired and so very proud of us both.

Two Niner Lima and I were in need of a well- deserved rest.

CHAPTER XX

—————————————————————→✈

INTERMISSION

SUMMER BREAK

All I wanted to do was sleep for a few days. I was just plain beat. Despite the emotional and physical exhaustion hitting me as we drove back to Enid's apartment in Larchmont, the sense of accomplishment was flooding over me, as well as personal satisfaction.

All my life I've been compared to a big brother and despite my many accomplishments and prowess, I've always felt I never measured up to him on the athletic field. Never able to prove to my father that I was just as good as his firstborn son (and thus, not worthy of his love for which I was desperate), this carried over into my sense of Self.

It has taken me so long on my life journey to overcome that sense of not being worthy and loved.

Flying was my antidote to that denigration of my spirit. I had mastered a skill few are able. I mastered it well, achieving my private and commercial licenses and an instrument rating to pilot sin-

gle and multi-engine airplanes through the skies. Few experience
this mastery and the perspective from sitting in the left seat.

But I did.

I will never forget when I flew out to the desert to see my parents who were staying at the family condo in Palm Desert. My
Father was waiting for me when I landed at Bermuda Dunes. He
couldn't believe I could fly that machine and had arrived from Santa Monica in an hour. He was beaming and appeared unusually
proud of me. At last, I felt the love for which I had been longing. As
we grew closer in his older years, we were finally respecting one
another, adult to adult, as friends.

But this Journey Across America — well, this was special. I had
done it. I had crossed the USA in a two-seat aircraft, a training aircraft at that. I had met new weather and aviation challenges. I had
used my skills, honed and proficient after 40 years of flying, and I
had employed the judgment and discipline learned.

And I had succeeded.

I had taken off over the Pacific Ocean, then crossed the entire
massive country, all the way to the Atlantic Ocean. I had flown Two
Niner Lima all the way up the east coast into the famed New York
airspace, where the infamous controllers alternately praised and
barked at me. And I landed safely at my destination.

My beloved Two Niner Lima performed so well, never missing
a beat. She gave me confidence for the return trip, although at that
moment, after this eastbound accomplishment, I wasn't planning
to fly her back for a long while.

Or not at all, I thought. *What more do I possibly need to do as a pilot?*
I flew across America!

And as the car hummed along I-684 heading south from DXR,
I sensed I was feeling better about Me. I'd been so loved and nour-

ished along the way, every one of my friends extending themselves beyond what I could ever imagine, showing their love and compassion over and over. I was humbled.

I settled in and enjoyed the summer respite on the east coast. I rested. I wrote more. I started my daily power walk and lifted some weights in a regular routine. Dinners with friends filled my time, but soon, I was getting anxious to get back to SoCal. I had unfinished business there, as well as some business opportunities. I wanted to see if I could create something positive out of them and recover from the difficulties of last spring.

As for where to live, I had many choices, and I was considering some of the wonderful places I had been, but first I needed to get back to Los Angeles and have my torn meniscus repaired and make sure my heart was still good. I felt better about Me and for the first time in over a year, I felt ready to go toe-to-toe and take it all on. I was ready to get back in the ring. I was no longer in retreat.

The biggest decision I had before me, however, was whether I should fly Two Niner Lima back home now, or go back to L. A. on Jet Blue, then return to DXR in a few months to fly her back.

I realized how much I love flying, and after almost eight weeks away from the left seat, I knew I couldn't part with Two Niner Lima yet. She was a part of me, as was flying. It nourished and sustained me. The trip had been the perfect tonic for my wounded psyche.

I wasn't so down anymore. My spirits were positive. I wasn't beating Me up anymore, feeling sorry for my plight, so beaten I just wanted to escape to somewhere and chill. But now, with August quickly rolling by, my energy was picking up and my optimism was growing. I realized I needed to fly back to the west coast for this Journey Across America to be complete.

For myself.

For Two Niner Lima.

We needed to get back home. Yes, in a sense, to come full circle.

However, I was feeling a little anxious. It wasn't the same apprehension I'd felt when leaving Santa Monica to begin the eastward trek. Then, I was flying into the unknown.

Unknown places. Different weather. There were no mountains to contend with, but with the daily summer heat and convective activity I'd been constantly concerned. Checking the weather diligently before any trip became an obsession. Never relaxing my guard, I'd watched the trends, checked the prognosis charts, and diligently called Flight Service.

And I'd done it. I made it.

Now, facing the westward journey, it was more about getting home. I planned to stop and see a few old friends, as I did before, but I had set up only a three-week window to do so. Going eastward, I'd had no timetable. I was footloose and fancy free.

But now I had medical appointments made months ago. I wanted to deal with my knee and confirm my health status, and then decide what was next, after seeing what I could accomplish. There would not be much time to dawdle and making allowances for weather, I felt the pressure building to get going.

Get home-itis was staring right at me, in my face as close as it could get. The Dark Beast. I was ever so conscious of rushing but feeling this pressure made me stop and think further.

I would do my best, not push the weather, and not succumb to this bogey man.

I was, however, still concerned about Two Niner Lima. She seemed to be burning more oil toward the end of the eastward sojourn. Despite her age on her airframe, she was a relatively young girl, with less than seven hundred hours on a new engine installed in 2003, but one never knows when and if. Being vigilant about your aircraft never ceases. She wasn't the newest car off the lot so I was even more anxious that she would continue to purr without any hiccups, and get us home safely. No serious malfunction to put us in harm's way, please and thank you.

I was far less anxious about whether I could make it. Flying eastward, I had been nominally concerned even though I was flying into new places and crossing the country on new and unfamiliar routes. But this time going westbound, I had more confidence.

It had been a few weeks since I'd seen Two Niner Lima and had been in the left seat, so I scheduled a day with her and started contacting friends I hoped to stay with along the way.

The air was getting cooler, and it told me to get a move on before early winter weather came to the northern states. I was planning my route that way—westward to the Rockies, then down to New Mexico, over to Arizona and into southern California—the reverse of the trip east on this journey.

I would go to Pittsburgh, then Detroit, then up to Sioux City and over to Rapid City, South Dakota (to see Mount Rushmore), then down to Denver, and back to Tucson before returning home. At any rate, that was the plan.

Rain came and pushed back my schedule, but finally the sun was shining and I was off to DXR on a bright Monday morning. I was planning to leave at the end of the week, depending on the weather prognosis, which indicated Thursday would be the day.

I had requested Two Niner Lima be put outside her comfy hangar where she had rested for the summer, and decided to start her up and do some takeoffs and landings, to get the rust off me. As it was almost seven weeks since we had arrived at DXR I was concerned the battery would be down too low for her to start.

My baby was a sight for sore eyes. Sitting outside, her cover still on, she looked contently and exquisitely serene at her Captain.

She was so regal and poised. The vista of her there, set against the hills surrounding DXR, just took me back. As I approached her, I saw that smile still on her and patted her on the nose.

"Time to get ready to go home!"

Taking her cover off, I unlocked the canopy, took out the gust lock, and sat down inside her. Since I didn't have to load my bags today, I took some extra time looking about the cramped quarters. I stacked my stash of sectional maps, strewn about on the right seat, into an orderly pile and tidied up the floor and in the baggage area, then I went out on the wing walk. Leaning back, I took the fuel sampler to assist in my walk-around.

Two Niner Lima looked good. Cleaned up by the recent week of rain, but for a few green dots still remaining near the GPS antenna on top of the fuselage from her lengthy stay in New Orleans, she appeared in good shape.

My walk-around detected no issues, but her oil capacity was down below the six-quart line, resting at five and a half quarts. I made a note to add another quart of oil when I ordered fuel before I left.

I was rusty in my pre-flight routines, as is always the case when not flying regularly. I was not concerned as I knew that like any regimen practiced and mastered for so long, it would come back to me as I went.

Primer, mixture rich, carb heat off, fuel pressure on, then off. It was time.

"Clear prop!" I shouted outside the open canopy to make sure no one was walking by that I didn't see.

Ignition. The prop did not move. Ugh. Maybe I was right about the battery.

I looked down again. Of course! I hadn't turned the key all the way to "On." Rusty I was.

I pressed the ignition.

Two strong turns of the prop, and Two Niner Lima fired right up. I let her run a bit to warm up, to get the oil flowing after being inactive for so long. After about ten minutes I decided to check the ATIS and do some air work in the pattern. Then we taxied out for takeoff to Runway 08, opposite of Runway 36 on which I had landed upon arrival. This time I wouldn't have that tower to deal with.

Two Niner Lima had no problem at all with the practice run. I did, however, showing my rust but by my third and final landing, I nailed it.

A good landing is always about maintaining a constant final approach speed. For Two Niner Lima, it is between eighty-five and ninety knots, and then flaring while looking down at the end of the runway for the correct perspective.

She climbed briskly and rolled out smoothly as we completed the first two touch-and-go's. This flying practice routine is where you make the landing, roll out, clean up the airplane, and then take off. We do this rather than come to a full stop and taxi off the runway and back to take off. It's a quicker way to practice, saves fuel and time, and having been in Two Niner Lima for so many years, I could do it quickly: Flaps up, trim to takeoff position, then apply full power, all the while rolling out and maintaining direction down the runway.

My pattern work at this new airport got better with each takeoff and landing, as I got familiar with flying over the wooded hills and the perspective on each leg. I felt the rust fading away as I let Two Niner Lima slow down to taxi speed and got ready to turn back to West Conn Aviation after my third and last landing.

I applied the brakes and made the right turn off Runway 8. Two Niner Lima has differential braking for turning, meaning you apply the brake on the side in the direction you want to turn. Rolling out, I didn't notice anything amiss, nor on making the right turn onto Taxiway B(ravo). But after I made that turn, I started to straighten out Two Niner Lima to proceed down the taxiway.

Feeling a moment of panic, I realized my left brake wasn't working and I couldn't straighten Two Niner Lima out. I pushed the pedal down to the floor, hoping I would get some response, but she kept turning right and I was about to run off the taxiway into a taxiway light. It seemed we were about to go in a circle. With my one working brake, I made an abrupt stop. Two Niner Lima's tail was jutting out onto the runway.

I advised ground control and before I shut down, I heard the controller tell the gentleman mowing the grass between Runways 8-36 and 17-35 to head over to me and see if he could help. Quickly, I jumped out and pulled Two Niner Lima off the runway so I wouldn't be the cause of the airport shutting down. The kind lawn mower man joined me and we pulled Two Niner Lima right into her tie-down space at West Conn Aviation.

When I advised ground control that we were okay, he chastised me for jumping out and pulling the plane off the active runway. Apologizing profusely, I replied that I hadn't wanted to interrupt operations. He made no further comment so I clicked off my radios and shut Two Niner Lima down, clicking off the battery power.

During my life with Two Niner Lima, this was a common experience. There can be a small leak in the hydraulic line to the brakes, or air gets inside it from infrequent use, and a brake failure occurs. For whatever reason, it has only always happened with the left brake. Nonetheless, I was not concerned and glad it happened before I planned to depart.

This was exactly why I took Two Niner Lima for a warm-up before starting the long trip back to Southern California.

Hoping it would be an easy fix, I entrusted her to the West Conn mechanic. Bernie was a good looking, bespectacled, fit young man, almost Clark Kentish in appearance. I asked if he could take a look and make the needed repairs before I left at the end of the week.

Bernie owned and ran U.S. Flight Aircraft Maintenance, the official Cirrus Authorized Service Center, which was based at DXR. He reminded me not to leave the hand brake on so he could move the plane into the hangar. He thought there would be no problem with that left brake, suspecting the long period of non-use was the culprit. He said he'd have Two Niner Lima ready to go in a few days.

I breathed a big sigh of relief, then spoke with Mike again and got the information on which FBO to call for fuel and oil. I thanked him for everything and asked him to convey my gratitude to Chris, the owner, for giving Two Niner Lima a summer home. Chris is Enid's boss, and she has been working with him for so many years, so it saved me a ton.

Another conversation with a Cirrus owner made me dream of the day I would fly bigger and faster, true cross-country aircraft.

I felt good about the practice in Two Niner Lima and was not too concerned about the brake issue, other than what Bernie would charge me to repair it. Later that night, I checked the weather. All was looking good for departure in a few days, with a high-pressure ridge settling in over the Ohio Valley and clearing the east coast all the way to Pittsburgh, my first destination. Giving myself on extra day to make sure the weather settled in and Bernie would have ample time to make the brake repair, I decided it would be Friday.

It was time to begin the Journey Back to SoCal.

CHAPTER XXI

———————————————————————————➤

BACK TO SOCAL
LEG ONE
DXR-AGC

August 3, 2019 DXR-AGC

Danbury Municipal Airport, Danbury, CT to Allegheny County

Airport, Pittsburgh, PA Distance: 292 nm

Route: DXR-AGC Direct.

Start time (DXR): 10:25:03 a.m. Wheels up: 10:40:19 a.m.

Wheels down: 1:06:11 p.m.

Shut-Down time (AGC): 1:08:23 p.m.

Log Entry: Time Logged: 2.9 hrs. Flight Time: 2:26 hrs.

Back to SoCal! Leg 1. Good flight @4500'. Lt to mod trblnc over

Allghny Mtns. Slight hdwd. Good ldg.

Of course, I was up early. Sleep was slow to come by, then intermittent, as I "flew" the flight a few times before I finally drifted
off, rehearsing my departure from DXR. I had often used visualiza-
tion to make myself feel more comfortable with an upcoming task,

and not having flown into new territory since my arrival at DXR (almost two months before) nor been in the left seat, I was anxious and a bit apprehensive.

After all, this wasn't like hopping into the car for a Sunday drive. It was putting myself into a critical situation where any mistake could be a deadly one. So, as always, I did my pilot preparation with a somber reflection. Again, thank you, Bill Beecher, my first instructor, who had taught me so well. I remember him saying once, another lesson now ingrained, "Do you think I want to break my bones up here?"

I was not in a rush to depart early and beat the weather because of the lack of anticipated convective activity. Flight Service had advised that the high-pressure ridge had, indeed, stabilized and it would be a good day for flying. When I awoke, I checked Foreflight and My Radar while sipping my first cup of coffee and confirmed it. The favorable and positive weather reports over the last few days had me confident I would be able to get to Pittsburgh, then on to Detroit, over the next four days.

Earlier in the day I had called Reliant Aircraft Service for fuel, and requested they top off all four tanks on Two Niner Lima, both the Main and Aux fuel tanks. I also requested they add one quart of oil. I left a check with Enid to deliver to West Conn to cover the charges along with a note to her boss Chris, thanking him for allowing Two Niner Lima to rest inside his hangar for her entire stay on the east coast during our summer respite.

Bernie had called me in the afternoon the day before and told me all was good to go. He had repaired the leak in the left brake and replenished the brake reservoir with hydraulic fluid.

"How much do I owe you?" I asked, waiting for the few-hundred-dollar answer. I had been worrying how I would manage to get back with my funds running low. I was at the budgeted point of uh-oh.

"Sixty-five dollars," he replied.

"That's all? Wow! Thanks, man. Can I bring you a check tomorrow before I leave?"

"Oh, no problem. It took me only a few minutes to confirm the problem and fix it, Bob. Sure—just drop it in the hangar mailbox by the back door."

"Wilco, Bernie. And, again, thanks for taking care of it right away. Hope I'll be back soon."

When I hung up, I smiled. Here was another fine person in the aviation community I'd met on this adventure. From Robert in Deming to the pilot at Abilene who told me how to transit the DFW airspace to get into Addison, to the New York controller who welcomed me to New York, pointing out Danbury for this wayward traveler, they had all nourished my pilot soul, making the Journey even more rewarding than I ever imagined.

But I was a bit melancholy now, getting ready to leave. I had felt safe and secure with my childhood friends on the east coast and found the refuge comforting. Despite that, I knew it was time to go, and go I must.

I had to complete the Journey Across America with Two Niner Lima to hopefully find the new Me and begin anew.

Yes. Back to SoCal, indeed.

I arrived at DXR and West Conn Aviation with all my bags, again ready to board Two Niner Lima. Enid drove me right onto the tarmac and up to Two Niner Lima where I had parked her the other day. I unloaded the bags from the trunk and put them on the wing walk on the pilot's side.

Doing my walk around, I removed the chocks and unsnapped

the ties on the two straps fore and aft. Bruce's cover had lasted me a long time, holding up against the new weather elements we encountered on our journey east, besides warding off the ocean dampness at Santa Monica for years. It had lasted far longer than the previous cover I'd bought back in 1994. This one was going on sixteen years, and still doing a fine job of keeping the cockpit dry and the avionics cool, away from the beating sun.

I loaded up the bags and got out the Stratus, my iPad and my phone, then I grabbed the fuel strainer from the back pocket behind the pilot's seat and scampered down to start my walk-around. The routine was coming back to me and despite the building excitement I slowed myself down, making my inspection of Two Niner Lima slow and steady, meticulous in every way to ensure we were both back in our elements and ready to go. She in the air, me in her left seat.

Reliant had already loaded the fuel and Two Niner Lima now had over six quarts of oil. I was pleased and needed to now wash off the grime before bidding the east coast adieu.

I said my farewells to Mike and Enid, walked out to Two Niner Lima and climbed aboard. I slid the Stratus into its holder on the glareshield, placed the iPad and phone into their holders. Next, I plugged in the communications connection to the phone. After fastening and adjusting my seat belt and harness, I placed my ANR (Active Noise Reduction) Bose headset over my ears, turned it on, and adjusted the snug fit. They really lessened the noise environment, making it far more pleasant to be in this piston aircraft, especially when the power came on and they muted the outside sounds.

Each step awakened my pilot routine pre-engine start.

We were all set. I pulled the checklist and my writing pad, secured in a metal lap tray with clips, over from the right seat and placed it on my knees. But, before I started, I took a deep breath.

The butterflies in my stomach were flapping mightily and I wanted to feel grounded and centered, as I began again. Taking another deep breath, I let it out with a sigh, a Life Spring technique I learned from that self-improvement training from many years ago. I often use it to slow things down and rid tension from the clenching muscles. I closed my eyes.

"God, I am going now. I don't know what you have in store for me. Whatever it is, I ask for your courage and strength to keep going and get home safely."

I recited the Hebrew prayer.

"Shma Yisoroael,

Adonai Elohenu,

Adonai Echad."

"Here, Oh, Israel,

The Lord our God,

The Lord is One."

I am not that religious, but I am spiritual. I have always prayed, and tried over many years now, to make it a daily habit. I do believe in reincarnation, in an afterlife, and that we keep evolving, our souls learning our lessons that we practice and experience over and over until we get it right.

Faith was hard to maintain after all I had gone through, but never once did I not stop believing everything would turn out all right. The Universe never lets you down and I still believed it. My foolish optimism, I guess.

But God, or the Universe, or whatever, or whomever it is, I was feeling blessed and fortunate to still be alive and having this incredible adventure every day. Life's forces seem so amazing, nature so beautiful, people so interesting, it was hard for me to dismiss the thought that a higher power was not somehow involved.

Anyway, that was my prayer. Not to ask for something. Only for the strength and courage to keep on going. After all, everything had always seemed to work out, so if I kept that Faith, despite the setbacks, despite the pain, what else did I need to keep on going?

Perhaps each of us have some notion of a higher power as we go through our struggles and pains. Religion is a strange thing, faith even more difficult, but I always felt some connection and had tried to maintain it, more so as I aged.

I took another deep breath, opened my eyes, and began going through the check list.

Primer, seven squirts, as I always did, mixture rich, master switch on, fuel pump on, fuel pressure checked, fuel pump off.

"Clear prop!" I shouted through the slightly opened canopy.

Mike and Enid were now standing in front of West Conn Aviation, Enid holding her phone up to her eyes, videoing the departure as I had requested, as she had on my arrival.

Ignition on both magnetos. Starter engaged.

I pushed the starter and Two Niner Lima turned right over on the very first blade of its prop turning. She was obviously ready and raring to go.

Radios on. I got the ATIS. Then, briefly did a video, speaking to all my Facebook friends with whom I had been sharing my Journey.

I contacted ground control and requested Flight Following to Allegheny County Airport (AGC) in Pittsburgh. I was cleared to taxi to Runway 35 via Taxiway C(harlie) then B(ravo).

I began to pull out of the tie-down space, turned onto C(harlie), waved to Enid and Mike standing in front of West Conn, and slowly taxied for take-off.

Run-up complete, I was ready to go. I had my clearance for Flight Following and put in my squawk code of 2727, with New

York departure control's frequency of 126.4 set up on stand-by in Comm 1.

"Danbury Tower, Grumman Two Niner Lima, ready to go, Runway 35, request left downwind departure."

It was a quiet morning at DXR and I was number one for departure, with no other aircraft in the pattern for either runway.

"Grumman Two Niner Lima, Runway 35, cleared for take-off," came from the tower, and I acknowledged:

"Grumman Two Niner Lima, cleared for take-off, Runway 35."

I eased the throttle forward and turned on to Runway 35, lining us up, and stopped. This was a shorter runway then Runway 8-26, almost one thousand three hundred feet shorter. I decided to hold the brakes and let the power build up as I was still concerned about our gross weight, worried that my bags would affect Two Niner Lima's performance, even though she'd exhibited no problems the entire journey.

I pushed the throttle all the way to its stop. Two Niner Lima strained against the brakes and then I let her go. She accelerated rapidly as soon as I took my feet off the brakes. At seventy knots, I slowly pulled the yoke toward me and she sprung into the air. I straightened her out and out we climbed.

We were on our way. I corrected for a slight right cross wind and when we reached a thousand feet above ground level, I turned upwind, still climbing. Once I was wide enough from Runway 35, I turned downwind for just a few seconds before departing the traffic pattern, now above one thousand seven hundred feet, heading on a course of 268 degrees direct to Allegheny County Airport in greater Pittsburgh.

For the first time this Journey I was heading westbound.

Danbury Tower advised me to contact New York departure and I checked in.

Things were going smoothly. I was with Departure, so I had another set of eyes looking out for me. I continued our climb to four thousand five hundred feet and leveled off. At this lower altitude, I had a closer view of the landscape passing beneath me.

We were approaching the Hudson River. It was quite wide at this point far north of New York City. West Point was visible through the morning haze, sitting on its promontory above the river. I recalled my visits there, my mind wandering to a trip as a young boy to see an Army football game in Michie Stadium when Pete Dawkins ran wild, to my visits there playing college soccer at Brown. I grimaced when I thought of our game my Senior year, when my coach was so angry because I'd tried to beat the goalkeeper near side on an almost impossible angle with a close-in blast instead of passing across the crease to a wide-open player.

New York departure interrupted the memory of my retort to Coach Stevenson's criticism.

"Grumman Two Niner Lima, Traffic eleven o'clock, two miles, same altitude, an Aerostar, also heading to Allegheny County Airport."

I looked at my eleven o'clock position and despite the haze, easily picked out the twin-engine aircraft slightly ahead of me.

"Contact. Grumman Two Niner Lima has the traffic."

For the next fifteen minutes or so, I watched the Aerostar slowly pull away from me probably a good 50-60 knots faster than we were going, obviously so, as this model was one of the speediest twin engine piston planes flying. Designed by legendary aircraft designer Ted Smith, it had a wing positioned in the middle of its fuselage, designed eventually to be a small jet. I guessed it was doing 170-180 knots.

As we moved across the Hudson, I was showing a ground speed of one hundred twenty knots plus. I took a glance down south, toward New York City, and saw the new Tappan Zee Bridge in the foreground and skyscrapers faint in the distance.

I was smiling, thinking of July, and the first time I saw the city in Two Niner Lima.

Now, I bid it farewell.

The Delaware River was the next milestone. I had an affinity for this river, having canoed down it multiple times when I attended Camp High Lake in the Poconos and had to swim the lake, a few miles across. At ten years old, I couldn't swim a lick, but then one night at dinner they announced that little Freddie, a freckled eight-year-old redhead with an infectious smile, had done it. I was determined to make that canoe trip down the Delaware, even if I had to do the side stroke the entire way across the lake to meet the stringent requirements.

Glancing down, I reveled in the deep, verdant green of the topography. As we droned on westward, the forests in western New Jersey gave way to many farms in eastern Pennsylvania, where the Pennsylvania Dutch first settled, and, as across the country, the farms were frequent, interrupting the carpet of forested land. It is still astounding to me how huge the country is, so many farms, so vast and expansive.

The sight of two nuclear power plants took me back. I wasn't aware that they were here in Pennsylvania or most places anywhere in our country. College Park and Penn State passed by on our right side. Set amidst the rolling green farms, the university looked idyllic, the brick buildings of a campus evident, the famed football stadium visible. The air was smooth, with hardly any ripples. A most pleasant flying morning.

College Park had its own airport and, as I drifted by, I played a game Bill Beecher had taught me:

"If the engine quit now, where would you go?"

At forty-five hundred feet, I had a radius of approximately eight miles to find a place to put Two Niner Lima down, if needed. I wouldn't make it to nearby KCGS (College Park Airport) so it would have had to be a field or road. I scanned and saw many choices. Thank you, Bill. Another lesson learned well.

After College Park, the terrain rose a bit, and I surmised correctly these were the Allegheny Mountains. Not very high, not even as high as the Santa Monica Mountains, and I was puzzled by their designation. Mountains? These are teeny, itty-bitty hills. Two Niner Lima had ample room above ground level and we felt a few bumps of some light turbulence as we crossed over. We were traveling against a slight headwind varying between six to ten knots over the few hours of flying. The "mountains" gave way to a hilly topography and before I knew it, Pittsburgh was coming up.

I was excited to be getting there. I was going to stay with my second wife, Lynn, who re-married a long time ago to Sal. They had moved back to their hometown where Sal worked with his dad in the family barbershop, then took it over when his father retired shortly before his death a few years ago. I had been close with them in Los Angeles for many years. Lynn and I realized we were better friends than spouses and we still shared a sweet and enduring friendship. I had not seen either of them in thirteen years and I was looking forward to spending time with them.

Now, in the distance, I could see downtown. AGC was on the south shore of the Monongohela River dotted with barges and boats. I could see the Monongohela and the Allegheny River merging into it and surrounding the skyscrapers of this metropolis. Bridges crossed it, connecting people on both shores. I was thrilled!

A city I had read and heard so much about, and here I was, with Pittsburgh Approach handing me off to Allegheny County Airport Tower.

Two Niner Lima and I were directed to descend down to three thousand feet and follow the Monongohela to the airport.

I entered the airport traffic pattern on the forty-five degree approach, descending to the pattern altitude for landing on Runway 10. I could now see all the hills about Pittsburgh, and parts of the city poking out from its forested cover, sandwiched between the rivers that built this legendary city. The Pirates, the Steelers, the Penguins. So much history here of us all pushing westward toward our Manifest Destiny.

I was excited.

Taking a deep breath, I slowed myself and Two Niner Lima down to its one hundred five knots for the downwind landing leg. After checking in with the tower when I came up abeam, I was cleared to land. I made a right base turn, descending at 95 knots. I turned final and was right on the money, the VASI lights confirming I was on the correct glide slope. I slowed to 90 knots and came over the fence, where I greased the landing and rolled out down the runway, exiting at Taxiway C(harlie) and on to Taxiway A(lpha), to the old art deco terminal adjacent to Corporate Air.

I had made arrangements with Lynn and Sal that Sal would be picking me up. I clambered out of Two Niner Lima, got the linesman to bring me a baggage cart, and loaded up my bags, then texted Sal. Sure enough, he was on his way and would be there in twenty minutes or so.

Pittsburgh, PA. Oh, my.

Leg One Back to SoCal was in the books.

CHAPTER XXII

————————————————————————————————→

BACK TO SOCAL
LEG ONE

FRIENDS

Mistaking the linesman's instructions, I had managed to taxi Two Niner Lima quite close to the hangar right next to Corporate Air. As I came facing him, I realized he had wanted me to come down the aisle in front of the FBO, not from the other side. I still had enough room to slip into the spot on the tarmac closest to the door, my left wing just able to squeeze past the hangar by a good three feet plus. So, it was but a short walk into the FBO after apologizing to the linesman, then securing my luggage and flying gear, locking the canopy, and putting the cover over Two Niner Lima.

The FBO and AGC had a 1960s feel, worn but welcoming. The airport tower was of that vintage, sticking out above a building, not stand-alone nor as high as they are built today. I speculated that this airport was probably built in the early years of aviation, and I checked later that evening which confirmed my hunch. Located seven miles from downtown Pittsburgh, it was the third

largest airport in the country when it opened in 1931. It served as
the gateway to the city until Pittsburgh International Airport (PIT)
opened in 1952.

As per my usual, I checked in with the front desk and went to
wash up and refresh myself before Sal arrived. I was sipping on a
complimentary bottle of water when he walked in, his big warm
smile greeting me after all those years. Sal was just a good, decent
soul, and although I was the ex-husband, he was always gracious
and friendly.

We hugged hello. He helped me shlep my bags out to his car,
and we were off, gabbing away, catching up on the years. When
we got to their home, I saw how wise they were in preparing for a
simpler life. They had sold their house after Sal's parents died and
decided to renovate the upstairs apartment above the barber shop
and another store they owned.

Sal took me through Sal's Barber Shop where he did his thing
and I was startled by how he had decorated it. It was right out of
the 1950s and earlier, with a wall of antique shaving mugs and lo-
tions, only one barber's chair and a bunch of seats for his waiting
patrons.

Sal told me he was busy all day, with people lined up waiting,
and he accepted no appointments. It was all first come, first served.
We discussed the business aspects of the shop, what he charged, how
he advertised and promoted his business and other tidbits. I was so
impressed because he charged only a reasonable amount for a haircut (thirteen dollars). I couldn't help but remind him how different
it was from Capelli's, the shop he owned in Westwood, where, like
any hair salon in Los Angeles, a haircut cost a small fortune.

"Why do I need to charge more?" he responded to my incredulous, "That's all?"

"I am busy all the time," he went on. "I make plenty. We live well. Everyone is so astonished that I make more in tips!"

I smiled.

"Hey, come on—sit down now. You need a haircut!"

"Sal, you are the best! But we have plenty of time for that over the next few days. Let me get settled since Lynnie is going to be home soon. We can do that another day!"

That was Sal. Generous and concerned always. Lynn did good marrying him.

We walked up the stairs to their apartment which was connected to the shop. I was quite impressed with the immediate warmth and decor. It was smartly appointed, lots reminding me of Lynn's good taste. There was even some furniture I recalled from their home in Santa Monica. It was spacious and open, like a loft. Sal gave me a quick tour and shared with me how they built it out and why they gave up their home.

No more commuting to work. Just a walk down the stairs. They cut down on so many expenses. They owned the building outright so there was no mortgage, and they collected rent from tenants who had a store and an apartment in the building.

"It changed our lives," he explained. "We can walk to anything on the boulevard. It just made life so much simpler for us."

I couldn't argue.

I excused myself and put my bags down in the guest room. Just then, Lynn arrived. We hugged. It was so good to see her. She had just survived breast cancer, so she proudly sported a pink streak in her hair. She still had that cuteness to her, and she was her same loving, good self.

Lynn didn't feel like cooking that night. Of course, she proudly told me she had stocked up on Cheerios and bananas as well as some vegetables for me, but she and Sal wanted to take me to dinner at one of their favorite local Italian restaurants where we could catch up and they could "hear all about your adventure."

Cheerios and Lynn were always a special thing because years ago, I had hidden her engagement ring in the box of cereal. When she made us breakfast the morning I proposed, out it fell!

I unpacked a bit, freshened up, and off we went to dinner.

The restaurant was a short drive away, and the road we took meandered down a boulevard of sorts surrounded by hills. I was astonished that the city proper was built along and amongst these hills which, deeply forested, gave the "city" more of a suburban feel, like northern Long Island, with its hills and villages planted amidst the dense foliage.

When we arrived and walked in, I got it right away. Because he grew up here, everyone knew Sal, and now Lynn, as they had his father and the barber shop. It was so pleasant to see all the warm greetings to my old friends from the hostess and the wait staff. I was impressed.

We talked at great length about them going back to Pittsburgh where they were raised. Lynn had spent time there during her adolescence, far less than Sal, but enough to make her into a mad Steeler fan. She shared her fondness for the city in which she spent her formative years. For Sal, working with his dad, even if only for a few brief years before he passed, had been a dream come true. Named after his dad, Sal's Barbershop was a testament to Sal and his family.

I shared with them my plight and what had led me to begin my Journey Across America. I was now on my way back, so I was beginning to find Me again, and feeling more optimistic about things.

The love and nourishment from my many friends and people I'd met had impacted my fragile psyche, giving me the necessary resuscitation to begin healing. Lynn and Sal added more love to this soul, and we had a wonderful time together during my stay.

Dinner was divine. Real, family-style Italian food. "What else would you expect?!" crowed Sal as we laughed and enjoyed each other's company. It was as if no time had lapsed, despite the thirteen years we last broke bread together. Along with an assist from the bottle of Italian wine we leisurely consumed, we savored the excellent cuisine and company.

We had even more of a kick when Sal went "the long way home" and surprised both Lynn and I when he pulled into an empty shopping center parking lot. He pointed up to a billboard on the edge of the property, facing in the direction of a highway. There stood Sal in an advertisement for the hospital in which he was operated on for his colon cancer. The doctors managed to remove a huge mass which had not spread, so when they excised it, they got it all. He didn't even have to undergo chemotherapy or radiation, so he was one lucky guy.

Lynn told me how one day she got a call from the hospital's PR rep, who wanted to know if Sal would be willing to appear in some advertisements. She remembered saying, "Sure, fine, I'll sign the release," so they could use his likeness. She'd thought nothing of it, until a few weeks later when, all of a sudden their phones didn't stop ringing. Sal was on every billboard across the city, at bus stops on smaller posters, and on the very buses and light rail trains themselves. Everyone was recognizing him. Well, let me tell you—it was staggering to see my friend, so huge, grinning down at me. What a kick for him and Lynn.

"Being Sal's hospital is our most prestigious award. St. Clair

Hospital" was the text that accompanied a huge picture of Sal doing his thing, cutting hair and smiling, the barber pole right next
to him. Such a wonderful moment for a great guy. Although not
the way you want to have such notoriety as the result of the cancer
freaking you out at the time. But thank God, all's well that ends
well.

The next day Sal and Lynn took me on a tour of the city. I was
mightily impressed. Downtown was brand new, not the Pittsburgh
I heard about when I was growing up in New York. No more dirty
air all over, filled with soot and factory particulates from the belch-
ing chimneys of the steel factories.

No, Pittsburgh had become a modern city, cleaned up and no
longer dependent on the industry from which it rose. I marveled
at the skyscrapers wrapped in glass abounding downtown, all the
bridges crossing the rivers painted in Pirate-Steeler yellow. There
was a funky part of downtown and on this Saturday the streets
were bustling, filled with markets and open-air restaurants and
people dining on this warm summer day.

We drove by PNC Park, home of the Pirates, then Sal navigated
through the busy downtown streets and we crossed a bridge to get
a better view of the city, which seemed to be young and vibrant
and full of positive energy.

Up a hill we climbed, then pulled over. Downtown was right
across the river and I could see exactly why Pittsburgh had its ro-
bust growth as the gateway to the Ohio Valley when the country
moved westward. From this viewpoint, I had a much better picture
of PNC Park. It was nestled right up against the river, as was Heinz
Field, the home of the Steelers, its seats painted proudly in Steeler
Gold, sitting next to the Carnegie Science Center. All the names of
the Pittsburgh greats were everywhere. Carnegie. Mellon. Heinz.

Atop this promontory was an eye-opening memorial consisting of a bronze statue, designed and built by James A. West in 2006, called *Points of View*. It depicted a meeting in October 1770 between George Washington and Seneca leader Guyasuta. This homage to our past fascinated me.

These historical figures first met in 1753, when Guyasuta guided Washington up the Allegheny River to Fort LeBoeuf to deliver a message to the French. Washington requested they leave the region so the British could trade with the area's indigenous people. The attempt failed, the French remained, and the French and Indian War erupted soon after in 1754.

First allies, then opposing sides in that war, these two leaders met again seventeen years later when Washington was on a surveying mission on the Ohio River. They sat overnight at a council fire where they revisited their past and debated the future of this highly prized region. Though they held very different ideas about the fate of this area, they parted on friendly terms. *Points of View*, the work of local sculptor James A. West, captures a moment in time between two formidable men whose actions had a huge impact on Pittsburgh, southwestern Pennsylvania, and the country that would become the United States of America.

This was a reminder of the father of our country's exploits and the breadth of his experiences, as well as the Native Americans' plight against the push of our Manifest Destiny. I had recently seen maps of what we had done to this race—the genocide we undertook in our rush to conquer the land.

As I had done in my own personal journey in this incarnation, I always felt and strongly advocated that unless we deal with our past, revisit it, acknowledge what we did, accept the responsibility and blame (the shame and horror of it all) we will never evolve and mature, as a people or a country. I don't think it will ever be possible to move past it—nor should we.

I stared at the statue of Guyasuta, imagining his plight, his family, and the horrors that befell them. His one lone feather stood upright, in his headband, behind his head. The sculptor captured him and the President-to-be Washington, leaning in and eye-to-eye to each other.

You could feel the strength and bravery of each strong soul, men from such different cultures now trying to find a way to co-exist, both knowing the inevitable, and both committed to fight and sacrifice to the end.

I was deeply moved. And, when I recalled looking down from Two Niner Lima upon my arrival at the point where all three rivers merged, I understood the importance of that meeting here, at the gateway to the new frontier.

Lynn threw some chicken and a salad together for a quiet dinner at home that Sunday night. We watched some TV and unwound. Sal would take me to the airport early the next day, as I wanted to get to Detroit by noon or so. The weather would be holding for another day before some more midwest storms would be reaching the Great Lakes and then coming down to Pittsburgh as they moved east.

I hesitated about going, thinking about it some more, but then had to put aside feeling so comfortable and loved in the cocoon of my dear old friends' home. I could have stayed for a week just hanging out, laughing and enjoying their good company, but I wanted to try and get home by mid-September. Time was pushing me.

Now I was on alert against Get Home-itis. It was right there in front of me, a lesson of long ago ingrained. I reminded myself to call Flight Service for the weather, go over my flight planning before I went to bed, and get a good night's rest, despite wanting to stay up a bit late with Sal and gab some more.

Apprehension has always been with this pilot. There never is enough preparation, enough thought, to make the safest and best choice, using your personal judgment on a "go or no go" decision. Even after all my years of flying, and flying Two Niner Lima, I never took the discipline of flying a small plane lightly.

Because you never know.

CHAPTER XXIII

———————————————————————————➤

BACK TO SOCAL
LEG TWO
AGC-VLL

September 3, 2019
AGC-VLL
Allegheny County Airport, Pittsburgh, PA to Oakland/
Troy Airport aka Vance Brand Airport, Troy, MI
Distance: 255 nm Route: AGC-TOL-VLL.
Start time (AGC): 10:12:51 a.m. Wheels up: 10:26:44 a.m. Wheels
down: 12:18:23 p.m.
Shut-Down time (VLL): 12:24:28 p.m.

Log Entry: Time Logged: 2.2 hrs. Flight Time: 1.9 hrs.
Spcl VFR departure remain clear of Pittsburgh Class B. 3,000' up
to 4,500'. Lake Erie. SIGMET brought nasty winds. Difficult ldg.
Almost 24 kts x-wind.

I had a small window of good weather to get out of Pittsburgh
and up and into Detroit before some afternoon thunderstorms

came my way. Sal volunteered to get up early and take me out to AGC for a mid-morning departure which would get me into Detroit between noon and one p.m.

I planned the two-hour flight to go by Lake Erie direct to Toledo, then up into the Oakland/Troy Airport, or Vance Brand Airport as it was known (VLL) in Troy, just north of Detroit.

It was a short drive. Sal dropped me off at Corporate Air and I took care of business, paid for our fuel and loaded up Two Niner Lima.

I was looking forward to spending time with Alan, his wife Meredith and his precious daughter Joey, now nearing five years old. I'd seen them in Brooklyn a few years before and was interested in seeing how my friend was doing.

Two Niner Lima fired right up, and after my brief video to the fans on Facebook, we called Ground Control, requested Flight Following to VLL, and were cleared to taxi out to Runway 28 for take-off via Taxiway A(lpha).

Runup was normal, all systems were go.

The airport was quiet this morning, with some dense fog lingering. By the time I was ready to go, most of it had dissipated but for a patch at the departure end of Runway 28. I requested a Special VFR clearance, thinking I could remain clear of the fog bank and climb above it, but I wasn't certain I could top it quickly where it sat. Peering out, I saw it wasn't that wide and figured I could side-step it to avoid penetrating the clouds.

I was immediately cleared for takeoff on a straight-out departure onto my heading of 302 degrees direct to Toledo. The dissipating fog bank was no longer an issue in the morning sun, and we easily topped it climbing out.

Next, I contacted departure. The controller kept me at three

thousand feet all the way until the end of the Terminal Control Area
for the Pittsburgh Class B(ravo) airspace. We then climbed quickly
up to forty-five hundred feet for our leisurely flight westward.

The scenery across the small remainder of western Pennsylvania, and then through Ohio, was the same farmland and lush
verdant green of forest and farmhouses, sprinkled all over and re-
peating. The sunny weather in western Pennsylvania gave way to
a hazy and darker sky as we got closer to Toledo, flying alongside
Lake Erie. Small puffs of clouds started to dot the sky below me.
Toward my west, a deep grey of ominous cirrus clouds boded bad
weather, and I was glad I'd been wise enough to pay heed to Flight
Service's warning about the weather.

I didn't have an inkling of what was to come.

Seeing Lake Erie for the first time in my life, for whatever reason, really jazzed me, especially from my perspective of forty-five
hundred feet. So many other new sights had also given me a boost
on this Journey, some I had read and studied about for years. And
although I had flown over Lake Michigan many times in airliners
as a passenger, I had never seen the Great Lakes up close. Smiling and recognizing the curve of shore along northern Ohio, I was
a bit flabbergasted by how accurate the maps were. They clearly
matched what I was seeing.

With a brief video, I shared my excitement with my friends.

Seeing Toledo in the distance I decided to cut off this leg by
heading up, far from the east side of the city. As I angled north-
westward, I got my first hint something was amiss. My ground
speed increased dramatically, from a respectable one hundred
thirty-two knots all the way up to one hundred sixty-three.

I just chalked it up to the storm, I saw in the distance to my left,
the counter clockwise winds of that low pressure rotating south,

then northward, darkening the western sky. It appeared to be over fifty miles away. Little did I think I would soon encounter its enormous strength.

ATC confirmed my suspicions when they advised that very thunderstorm would provide significant precipitation, and there were tornado warnings. It was still forty miles away from Detroit Metropolitan Airport, traveling at seven knots and moving east.

Detroit Approach requested I descend to twenty-five hundred feet and get away from the airport, instructing me to fly up the Detroit River and stay as far east as the river allowed. As I descended, the turbulence began. I was having quite a bumpy ride down so low.

Detroit Approach rattled me some more.

"Grumman Two Niner Lima, Radar services terminated. Squawk VFR."

"Detroit, Grumman Two Niner Lima, request vectors to Vance Brand."

"Unable," came the terse reply.

I didn't argue any more as his tone made it clear he'd had enough of us for his shift.

I had been following my flight path on Foreflight and thought I should make a left turn for a long straight-in approach into VLL, but the airport seemed way too close on the iPad map. I hesitated, looking desperately for the field.

Admittedly, I was lost.

"Shit. Okay. Breathe. It's got to be there!"

I was still at twenty-five hundred feet.

Pattern altitude for VLL was seventeen hundred twenty-seven feet so I didn't have to descend much more. I kept on looking. Finally, I saw the airport but wasn't set up properly for the established forty-five degree entry into the pattern. Coming right up to the airport mid-field, I was too close to set up for pattern entry.

Quickly I decided to head out and back in on a forty-five and get set up for a left-hand pattern to land on Runway 28.

I had been remiss in studying this airport's layout beforehand. Foreflight even has a 3D view of the airport and its surrounding terrain. Now I was upset, kicking myself for not being more thorough in my pre-flight preparations. When I saw how small this uncontrolled airport was—an airport without a tower and with a short runway—the butterflies were screaming.

I knew what I needed to do to salvage that lack of preparation. Announcing my intentions, I headed out and away from the field. No one was in the pattern and when I heard the AWOS, which I had checked in with a few minutes before, I understood why. The winds from that storm were blowing on an almost direct crosswind of one hundred ninety degrees at eighteen knots, gusting to twenty-five knots. Two Niner Lima's maximum crosswind component at ninety degrees was not to exceed twenty knots. This was going to be some ride!

Sitting up a lot straighter, I began my descent to the pattern altitude, turning to my left, right into that crosswind and back one hundred eighty degrees, preparing for entry onto Runway 28. As I did, all things seemed to go to hell in a hand basket.

Two Niner Lima was difficult to control. She was bucking like a bronco, with different forces of yaw and pitch and roll all acting up, fighting amongst each other from the fierce, conflicting winds.

I pushed and pulled and wrestled Two Niner Lima onto the downwind, then pulled power to begin my descent from pattern altitude. As I dipped the left wing down to make the turn, the wrestling and bucking got worse.

"Fly the airplane!" I heard Bill Beecher's shout.

I was now on final, and Two Niner Lima was getting tossed about. I was trying to slow her down. Despite the strength of the wind, I put out full flaps. Their effect on this Grumman model was negligible.

We were high and too fast. I had kept power in because of the winds and now I had to get her down. Or go around. My approach was horrible, my final approach not at all stabilized, and here we were, coming up and over the fence, still way too high.

Go around, I thought.

I saw I had plenty of runway left and I knew my girl.

Pulling the power back to idle, I bled off airspeed. I had been crabbing on an angle into the wind, at twenty-plus degrees or abouts. I held it for a few more seconds as we descended. We were now into the first third of the runway and I realized—it's now or never, or go-around.

I kicked in right rudder and as I bled the airspeed down past ninety knots and we descended a bit more, reaching for the runway, the winds—for whatever reason, thank you, God—dissipated to a whisper. After all that tumult, we landed uneventfully.

Whew!

I caught my breath as we rolled out down the runway. Turning off this narrowest of runways we taxied toward the small terminal at mid-field. I saw the Stars and Stripes waving straight out, almost perpendicular to Runway 28, and now understood what happened.

All the tall trees lining the airport and runway were the difference for us when we descended. They must have acted as a wind block of sorts, which is why, all of a sudden, everything seemed to stop, and the air became smoother. Which is why I was able to get through the wildly windy difficulties on my final approach. But it didn't explain the ferocity of the winds or the different forces I experienced wrestling with Two Niner Lima.

In all my years of flying, I had never experienced such forces. It was like I was riding a bucking bronco. Pushing and pulling, turning and coaxing her to get her to go where I wanted to go and how I wanted to go, so un-Two Niner Lima like. Power seemed so necessary, not like on a calm day, when the descent after pulling back on the throttle results in a steady decrease in airspeed.

Today was something new and still puzzling. Multiple wind directions, wind shear, fighting and pushing Two Niner Lima as I had was not only a bit frightening in retrospect, but still puzzling. I put it on that advancing thunderstorm, the one with tornado warnings—very unstable and erratic air. Something small planes clearly need to avoid.

I still don't understand exactly what happened, but *I flew the airplane* that day.

Just as I taxied in and shut down adjacent to the terminal, the wind seemed to get stronger. An elderly gentleman sauntered out, holding some chocks in his hand, and approached Two Niner Lima.

Coming up to the right side of the cockpit, he asked, "Need these?" He held up the blue painted wheel chocks, with the letters VLL stenciled in white.

"Why, yes, thank you, kind sir." I exhaled, realizing I could stop holding my breath. "Boy, that wind was fierce!"

"Do you have tie-down ropes? It's going to get a lot worse"

"No," I replied. "Do you have any?"

"Sure. I'll leave you these and get some." He put the chocks down in front of the airplane and went back into the terminal.

Right away, I began unloading Two Niner Lima, sensing from

the winds and darkening sky that it was going to start raining soon. I texted Alan I had landed and he replied he would see me soon. He was about half an hour away.

I was still beating myself up a bit for not leaving sooner. If I had honored my practice of getting airborne early, I wouldn't have encountered the fiasco I just had flown into landing. Buoyed by the routine of the Danbury-Pittsburgh leg a few days before, I had relaxed my guard, thinking it would be an easy, routine two-hour flight.

A few more seconds of rational thought had me dismiss my harsh debriefing as too much second guessing. I counted my blessings. We had landed safely and I had flown the airplane.

John, as he told me his name was, came out of the terminal with two yellow nylon ropes in his hands. He helped me affix them to the tie-down rings on Two Niner Lima, one each on the bottom of the wing at the wing tip, and one underneath the end of the fuselage at the tail. Aloud, I marveled at how he tied the perfect loop knot, strong and secure.

"From my boy scout days," he explained.

I locked Two Niner Lima up, put on her cover and, as was my custom, affectionately patted her on her snout.

"Great job, Girl!"

She knew it.

Noting the pitter patter of rain drops now arriving in Troy, I carried my stuff in. After refreshing myself in the men's room, I went into John's office, introduced myself and thanked him for his aid and kindness.

John explained that he was a former flyer, employed by the county in the Parks Department, when they asked him if he would like to manage the airport facility. Seems they knew he was then a flyer, and he accepted the invite. The terminal was shiny and clean—small but with the requisite pilot's briefing room, vending machines and waiting room.

"I had to stop flying when the old ticker started acting up on me," John told me. "I have two stents in me and the missus said, 'Enough.' Happy wife, happy life—but I sure do miss it. This makes up for it."

"Just got three stents myself, a few years ago," I said. "It changed my thinking about things. About why I'm having this adventure, flying my plane across the country."

"Where have you been so far?"

Well, there I went, telling him of our Journey Across America and how I was now headed back to Santa Monica, after a few more stops along the way. We were fast becoming old friends when in walked Alan. I got up from the office chair and embraced my friend. The boy I met when he was thirteen was now a grown man, tall and almost fifty, but he still had a huge smile and a bear hug for his friend and mentor.

I introduced him to John and we said our goodbyes. Again, I thanked him for his kindness and assistance.

Alan grabbed a few of my bags, and I slipped the backpack on and grabbed the last one. Leg Two was done.

One more step westward, back to SoCal.

CHAPTER XXIV

—————————————————————————>

BACK TO SOCAL
LEG TWO

FRIENDS

Alan is a big teddy bear of a young man and a good decent soul. He's the son of my dearest friend, Patti, my high school girlfriend's older sister.

I met Patti when I was twelve years old in Lake Como, Pennsylvania, in the Poconos at Camp High Lake. She was attending the girl's camp, Camp Winona, across the lake. For a few summers, she had a summer boyfriend who was in my bunk and I got to know her when we were budding adolescents. Then, lo and behold, her family moved to Rockville Centre. When I was a sophomore, I ran into her and her younger sister, Sheri, at the high school.

Lightning struck and I was doomed. Sheri would break my young heart a few years later.

It was wonderful to see Alan, and as we drove from the airport to his home, we were gabbing away, catching up with as much information as we could cram into the twenty-five-minute ride. He was curious about my trip and wanted to know how life was treating me. I said the same, about his life, and told him I was proud of him. Now a dad, his daughter Joey was almost five.

Meredith arrived home from work a few hours after I got unpacked and settled in my own guest room.

I had intended to stay with Alan and Meredith for about a week, weather depending.

Once again, I had one eye looking at My Radar and Foreflight, figuring out when I might depart. I didn't like the Get Home-itis that was haunting me. I was feeling pressured to make plans and worrying about the next storm brewing over Lake Michigan and heading our way.

I kept busy getting back into a routine. Alan and Meredith went off to work and Joey to school, so I had time for me. Meredith made sure to ask what I needed from the supermarket and stocked the refrigerator with vegetables and fruit, and even made sure Cheerios were on hand. I resumed my walking and working out. I ate well and rested. I wrote often and kept in touch with friends here and there. I wasn't anxious to move on despite the pressing schedule, as the next few legs would be long and arduous. Besides, I was enjoying the respite with my friends.

I was hoping to get to Mount Rushmore next, after stopping in Sioux City to stay with a fellow Brown alumnus and Brown Bombers teammate. The Bombers were a coed softball team my good friend Alan and I had started years ago. It was a co-ed team in the Santa Monica Municipal Softball League.

Greg had invited me to stop by Sioux City where he and his wife had moved after some time in L.A. He was a talented actor and when I saw he had recently starred in a local production about Harry Truman, the subject of my Political Science Honors thesis at Brown, I was keen to talk to him about his role, and Harry.

Mount Rushmore, a few hours flight from Sioux City, Iowa, to Rapid City, South Dakota, would be the icing on the cake before I headed down to Longmont, Colorado, where I would see Jennifer, an old girlfriend, and her sister and mother. From there, I was planning to go to Tucson, and then back to Santa Monica. Going full circle was my thought. I didn't want to test Two Niner Lima and myself in the Rockies and felt it was better to fly south and back home the way I came.

Meredith was an avid runner. Besides keeping her figure in tip-top shape, as she told me, it was a way for her to get some good thinking time and keep herself sane. One day, she said she was going over to the Cranbrook School to run and suggested I join her and Joey, who she would push in a jogger's stroller. I could walk around the beautiful grounds, instead of through the streets of Southfield, Michigan, where I had set up a neighborhood course. Always up for new adventures, I readily agreed.

Cranbrook School was a part of the Cranbrook Educational Community established in Bloomfield Hills, Michigan, by the early Twentieth century newspaper mogul George Gough Booth. It is a sprawling three hundred nineteen-acre campus begun as a farm and named after the birthplace of the founder's father from Cranbrook, England. The Community is an education, research, and public museum complex designated a National Historic Landmark. The chief architect was Eliel Saarinen, and it is renowned for its architecture in the Arts and Crafts and Art Deco styles.

It was as beautiful and tranquil a campus as I have seen, spread wide amidst a tranquil, forested setting. We separated as Meredith and Joey began their eight-mile run while I walked my fast walk once around the lake, then sat in different locations, enjoying the day and the pastoral backdrop.

First I sat by a running brook, listening to the birds, cooling down after my walk on the hot and humid summer day. Thinking Meredith would be finished soon, I headed back toward the parking lot, stopping at what appeared to be the Administration Hall. It was a huge brick building that, although a different brick color, reminded me of University Hall at Brown but the Cranbrook House, with its gardens, is the centerpiece of the campus. Lying on the grass there, I made myself at home, watching the clouds go by and enjoying good thoughts and moments of reflection.

Content, I pondered Alan's invite to stay a few months and rest but knew I couldn't dally too long. Spurred on by renewed confidence from all the love and nourishment received during my Journey, I was pressing myself to get home. I needed to get home and begin anew, to what and how I wasn't sure, but I didn't want to impose too long on my friends.

I felt like that fellow in the movies, hitching up his pants after he put on his boots, then striding out the saloon door to where his favorite horse was waiting for him. Well, I had Two Niner Lima waiting and we needed to keep moving.

I laughed at myself. How curious (I said in my inner voice). Outbound you were not at all anxious to move on and you were enjoying lingering. Now, you have ants in your pants and *have* to go? What will serve you best? It was an interesting discussion battling back and forth. Money sure was a part of the equation and I needed to rectify that issue. And I was confident I would.

On the other hand, I was experiencing life very differently than the twelve-hour lawyer days I had been grinding for the past forty-five years. This new journey, this new style of living, appreciating every moment, was too appealing and enriching to ignore.

I walked back to the parking lot, but Meredith and Joey were not around. I had not brought my cell phone, so I was unable to do anything but wait. Sitting down on a rock along a pathway I observed some students, books in hand, coming down the hill from the forest. I decided to explore the area some more.

I came across an outdoor Greek Theatre adjacent to the parking lot at Cranbrook House.

Although a bit smaller, it reminded me of the Getty Villa's amphitheater in Malibu. I sat at the very top of the audience seats and looked down, imagining the play below, or an orator speaking his piece.

The politician in me moved me down to the stage, where I pretended giving The Speech I Want to Hear, an op-ed piece I'd written during the summer and which I had sent to many newspapers and candidates, urging their advocacy.

I had met so many kind, loving people on my Journey that when I turn on the TV lately and see all the anger, hate, and disconnect from what I was experiencing, I realized we are all a lot more the same than we are different. Yes, different areas of the country may have some different views, but we Americans are unique and special. We cannot afford to lose all that we have. And we do, indeed, need to appeal to our better angels.

A young couple came upon me giving my speech. I hadn't noticed them but now, embarrassed, I did. Their few rounds of applause interrupted me, reverberating about the empty theatre. I was sure they had come to this secluded spot to neck, and here was this guy speaking to an empty theatre.

"Pretty good, sir!" I heard the teenage boy say as he stepped onto the stage.

"Well, just some thoughts I'd been trying to get out there! What do you think about everything that's going on in our country?"

"We have lots of work to do to straighten things out!" the girl remarked with a confident smile. She was about thirteen or fourteen, dressed casually in jeans and a Detroit Tigers' t-shirt, her backpack over one shoulder and white air buds in her ears.

"That you do!" I started to leave, feeling a bit awkward and wanting them to have their alone time. Then I added, "It is all up to your generation now. Make it so. Have a great rest of your day!"

Shyly I went down the hill to the parking lot. In a few more minutes, Meredith and Joey appeared, wondering where I had been. We caught up and drove home.

That night we were off for dinner at Alan's sister's house. Beth was Patti's older child, a lawyer like Alan, and she had interned for me one summer in L.A. just like her brother had done. She was now married, had her own beautiful young daughter, Zoey, and she was General Counsel at Chrysler. Beth was as striking as her mom and I could see the resemblance in them all, right down to Zoey. I last saw her and her husband, James, at Alan and Mer's wedding. James is a Brit who had emigrated here when he met his match, and Zoey was their creation. We gabbed about my trip and made a date for them to see Two Niner Lima.

The weather was delaying my planned weekend departure. I had hoped to leave on Saturday or Sunday, but storms across the Dakotas and Minnesota were blowing through and across Lake Michigan, into Michigan and eastward. I texted Greg that I might not be able to make it, and would keep him posted. I realized with this weather delay, I would have to cut out Mount Rushmore and plan an alternate route.

The bad weather was moving eastward, but it was staying north. I would have to fly south to avoid it, then go west below it.

Kansas City seemed liked a good choice and I began to lay out my flight from VLL to Kansas City's downtown airport.

It would be a long day of flying—over seven hours plus two fuel stops—but the bad weather gave me no choice. It would be a few more days before it would clear enough for me to depart, so I set up the flights down to MKC and over to Longmont, Colorado, with a fuel stop in Oberlin, Kansas. As I was laying out the routes and seeing to where I would be flying, I have to admit I was still amazed that Two Niner Lima and I were crossing this huge country yet again.

After work on Friday in the mid-afternoon, Alan made some time to leave work early on Friday—mid-afternoon—so he could pick up Joey. We were meeting James and Zoey at VLL so the kids could sit in the plane, and I could get her ready to go. I was hoping to leave on Sunday, so I started her up, taxied over to the fuel pit and topped off all four tanks.

Both Zoey and Joey were smitten. I could swear Two Niner Lima planted the seed for these soon-to-be newbie girl pilots, and I got a terrific selfie of the entire group, capturing the love and joy we shared with Two Niner Lima. We topped off the day with a fun meal at a local brewery, and I dared to have a hamburger. Eating meat was a treat for Captain Bob, who had been good all along the journey—except for moments like this when I had to have a rare burger and some crispy French fries.

On Saturday, the rain let up and Alan and Mer insisted on taking me to Greenfield Village in Dearborn. Built by Henry Ford to replicate the early Twentieth century when Ford Motor Company was established, it was a nostalgic reminder of a time gone by. There was an antique auto display, and I enjoyed the replica of the Wright brothers' bicycle shop in Dayton, Ohio.

When we got home after a long day, I checked the weather with Flight Service and realized I was not going to be able to depart on Sunday. It looked like more bad weather from Canada was joining the eastward flow of storms already enroute. The earliest window for my departure would be on Tuesday.

I took a deep breath and told Greg I would have to skip Mount Rushmore and Sioux City. I also accepted the reality that I probably wouldn't make it back in time for my appointments, so, over a joint after dinner, Alan helped me chill. We talked of work we might be able to create together and sleep came easily after the long day and some cannabis.

It rained steadily on Sunday, but less on Monday, and Flight Service still maintained it would be clear Tuesday morning. The last remnant of the storm would be moving northeast, passing above Chicago, and I should be able to get past it before it crossed Lake Michigan into the Detroit area by mid-day. I planned accordingly, with an early morning departure, fuel stops in South Bend, then Peoria, and on to Downtown Wheeler Airport in Kansas City. Alan would drop me off bright and early on his way to work. I made sure to get a good night's rest, or at least try.

I was nostalgic leaving such a warm and loving home. Joey and I had a bit of a breakthrough after our visit to Two Niner Lima and she became more attentive to me. Alan was barking at me to stay a while and chill. I felt so appreciated, but I knew I had to get back to SoCal and Me. Maybe I would come back and hang out some more later, I told him, but it tugged at me. It was hard to say no.

Yet, I knew. It was time to keep moving. Close the circle.

Get back to SoCal.

CHAPTER XXV

———————————————————————————————→

BACK TO SOCAL
LEG THREE

September 10, 2019

Oakland/Troy Airport aka Vance Brand Airport, Troy, MI to South Bend, IN for fuel stop, to Peoria, IL, for fuel stop, to Wheeler Municipal Downtown Airport, Kansas City, MO.

VLL-SBN

Route: Direct Distance: 151 nm

SBN-PIA

Route: Direct Distance: 168 nm

PIA-MKC

Route: Direct

Distance: 247 nm

Total Distance: 566 nm.

Start time (VLL): 9:03:10 a.m. Wheels up: 9:12:24 a.m. Wheels down: 11:45:48 a.m.

Shut-Down time (SBN): 11:47:23 p.m.

Log Entry: Time Logged: 2.6 hrs. Flight Time: 2.7 hrs.
Wx broke. Lgt chop. Strong headwinds + 29 kts. GS 106-110 kts.
Start time (SBN): 11:49:16 a.m. Wheels up: 11:53:40 a.m. Wheels
down: 12:29:45 p.m. Shut-Down time (PIA): 12:31:45 p.m.

Log Entry: Time Logged: 1.9 hrs. Flight Time: 2.2 hrs.
With CHI center. Stopped at 4,000' Haze. Good straight-in ldg.
Start time (PIA): 1:28:41 p.m. Wheels up:
1:41:15 p.m. Wheels down: 3:49:10 p.m.
Shut-Down time (MKC): 3:50:08 p.m.
Log Entry: Time Logged: hrs. Flight Time: 2.1 hrs.
Haze. But clearer south. Smooth at 4,500'.

PART 1

VLL-SBN

As usual for a flying day, I was up bright and early. I made my-self a cup of coffee from the Espresso machine as quietly as I could, then I grabbed a bowl of Cheerios and a piece of bread and cheese with which to fortify Captain Bob for the long day coming up. It was just past five a.m. and I sat at the kitchen table, the morning still the dark of night, thinking about my day ahead and leaving my friends behind.

There is something about years of friendship that transmute its status into almost family. After all, we don't get to choose our families, but we do choose our friends. Alan and Mer were testament to my almost life-long friendship with Alan's Mom. It impressed me that here I was, being taken care of by my friend's son, who I had taken care of years before when he was searching for himself and what to do. I became a father figure of sorts after he and his sister Beth were abandoned by their dad. Now he was looking out for me. Full circle.

I was deeply touched and proud of him and us, for fulfilling that need in our delicate and wounded souls. Our conversations were always intimate, open, and honest. I was so happy for him that he was a father now himself, and that he did it so well. He shared with me that it had given him a healthy new life perspective. He and Mer seemed a good match of two strong individuals who personified T-E-A-M.

As the sunrise began to slowly lift the dark curtain of night, I went outside to look at the sky. Clouds were still in the sky, but not as compact—partly cloudy, but I could get up and out. Foreflight still indicated that the TFA (Terminal Forecast Area) for Detroit and going south was VFR flying, so who was I to argue? I would go out and be ready to go and hope the forecasters got it right this time. Disappointed I hadn't been able to depart the day before, I was hoping the weather would be better today. But, once I got past the Chicago area, I would be free from the eastward push of that storm, and it should be smooth sailing past South Bend and the influence from Lake Michigan.

Alan arose early and, after my quick perfunctory morning shower, we both were ready to go by 8:00 a.m., just slightly behind my "schedule" that I wanted to keep. VLL was not too far away but Kansas City was, and with almost seven hours of flying ahead of me, I was anxious to get moving.

It was quiet at the airport, but John was there. I didn't think I'd see him again so it was a pleasant surprise to see a familiar face. We gabbed a bit and I handed him a check for the tie-down fees. I think I was a day short, all of $5, due to the weather delay. When I told him to let me know if I paid him correctly, he didn't seem too concerned.

I think he must have enjoyed this crazy cross-country traveler because when I asked if I could appropriate the tie-down ropes, he said, "What tie-down ropes? I don't see anything."

Thanking him profusely, I offered to pay whatever the nylon ropes cost but he pooh-poohed my concerns. Again, I was touched by another stranger's support and friendship.

Alan helped me load my bags onto Two Niner Lima. He placed them all on the wing-walk as I got her cover off, opened the canopy, and removed the gust lock. I did my walk around first, then hopped up on the wing-walk to position each luggage item—the suitcase in the middle, each small duffel bag on both sides of the suitcase, with the garment bag laid out, stretched to the rear bulkhead. Before placing the duffel bags, I took out the Stratus 3, iPad, and portable battery pack and laid them on the glareshield, along with my iPhone. I climbed in, hooked everything up, and got out to make one last bathroom stop and say goodbye to Alan and John, who had just strolled out to Two Niner Lima, parked right next to the small terminal building.

I was nervous, of course—my normal flying apprehension to be on my toes, my mind racing, as I made sure I was doing everything in its proper sequence. I forced myself to use a checklist, and do everything the same way over and over, just like when I fly on the airlines—ticket in the right pants pocket, receipts and phone in the left pants pocket, wallet in rear pocket—so I don't forget something. With Get Home-itis on my tail, I was extra vigilant this morning as I tried to slow things down and be measured and certain in my decision making.

It was more than the normal flying apprehension. I had tried to place it last night. Nothing had changed. This was but another cross-country flight, adding up to the Journey Across America and back, but the time deadlines of appointments and my eagerness to get myself back on my feet were manifesting with some anxiety. It was a different pressure, more I thought than my normal preflight jitters. Getting to Danbury, well, I couldn't believe I did it, that I had crossed the country. But now it wasn't about accomplishment, as much as it was to come full circle and be me again. It was almost as magical but seemed to be growing more essential.

The mind can be a powerful enemy if not well disciplined so when Get Home-itis kept haunting me, I paid heed, prodded by all the accident reports I've read. I was even more thorough in my preflight planning and preparation. Also, I think flying so much was making me worry more about dying in an aviation accident. The more I flew, the more the odds were against me. But Two Niner Lima kept on purring. Still, she was an old bird, and I was concerned about her.

I hugged Alan good-bye and, again, thanked John for his kindness. I climbed on board Two Niner Lima, fastened up, and got her started. Once again, Two Niner Lima was ready to go, turning over on a few downward turns of her propeller. I confirmed the AWOS with the Foreflight reporting, announced over the Unicom frequency my intentions to taxi, and then trundled down the taxiway to the departure end of Runway 27 to the run-up area. I waved good-bye to Alan and John who were on the infield grass. Alan had promised me he would video the departure.

This was a short runway, compared to most I had been flying in and out of, so I decided on the way down to the run-up area that I would hold the brakes and let the power reach its maximum before brake release. Although 3,549 feet was ample, and I should be airborne easily before I reached the half-way mark, I wasn't taking any chances at gross weight, fully fueled, with all my luggage to boot.

I took the runway and, with the brakes on, engaged full throttle. Holding her for a few seconds, I checked the directional gyro to match up to the Runway heading of 270 degrees, then released the brakes. Two Niner Lima gathered up speed and when I had exceeded 70 knots, I slowly pulled back and she leaped off the asphalt.

Alan and John had a hand-held portable transceiver and wished me good-bye and good-luck.

"Thanks, Al. Appreciate it. Talk soon!"

"You go, Bob!"

Later, I would see the video. The only thing I'd forgotten to do was rock my wings, the flyer's salute of gratitude upon departure. Next time.

We climbed up and straight out. I needed to stay below four thousand feet in this segment of the Terminal Control Area for the Detroit Class B(ravo) airspace, so I was following along on my iPad, watching my progress over the ground and comparing it with my altitude. I had contacted Detroit departure for flight following to my first fuel stop at Peoria, Illinois. They also made sure I would stop at four thousand feet, approving me only up to that altitude.

As I passed out of the segment restricting my altitude, Detroit Departure came right back to me, clearing us direct to Peoria.

I settled back in the left seat, my apprehension all gone. I was Captain Bob doing my thing and, other than a strong headwind keeping our ground speed at 106 knots, there was no significant turbulence, only some light intermittent chop making their way eastward. As I looked out to my right, I could see the hazy sky growing darker, further away than when I was coming into Detroit. Toward the southwest in front of me, it seemed lighter, which matched the weather depiction I was seeing on my iPad.

Sure enough, Flight Service had it right. The storm was just coming up to Lake Michigan, with its southernmost edge north of

Chicago. Once I got past South Bend down into Illinois to Peoria, there was no weather at all. In fact, the more we moved southwestward, the more the haze was diminishing, and the sun was getting brighter.

The headwinds did not abate and we would be too close to diminishing our reserves. I advised Detroit accordingly.

"Detroit Departure, Grumman Two Niner Lima amends its destination to South Bend, Indiana, for fuel stop. Two Niner Lima to Sierra-Bravo-November."

"Roger, Two Niner Lima. Understand destination South Bend."

I had no choice. "The Lord Giveth, and the Lord Taketh Away," was my favorite Bill Beecher saying about headwinds and tailwinds. Coming east the wind was usually behind me. Now, going west, I would be encountering those head winds.

Detroit handed me off to Chicago Center, and off to my right in the distance, about fifty to seventy-five miles through the haze and coming weather, I could make out the skyline and see the city around the southern end of Lake Michigan. It was interesting to see the suburbs extending and radiating in all directions, freeways evident now, snaking through the outlying populated areas to and from the city, wrapping around the southern tip of the Lake on both sides.

Western Michigan was filled with the same constant scenery I witnessed throughout the east. Deep green forests, interspersed with farms and small communities, an abundance of small lakes smattered about. But as we got into Indiana and looked northwest to Chicago, the farms were gone and the vast suburbs of the grand midwest city was painted well over fifty miles outward in every quadrant and around the Lake.

The ride smoothed out and, before I knew it, Chicago had handed me over to South Bend Approach.

I was tickled I would be landing at the airport of the hometown of the Fighting Irish.

For many years I had heard of South Bend and Notre Dame, the elite Catholic school with its football and basketball games on TV, and it had made quite the impression. But it wasn't until years later that I would recall what I bore witness to as a child, huddled in the winter, watching those games. Back in the 1980s my client and friend, Alan Mintz, had produced *Rudy*, the famous football movie, and I'd done the legal work for it. It was a great story of an underdog and I thought of Daniel "Rudy" Reutigger for a moment after contact with Approach. What a lesson there was for all of us in his story. And now, here I was coming to land at their home.

South Bend Approach had me set up for a straight-in approach to Runway 27. I lined up and timed my descent down to pattern altitude and across the threshold in fine fashion. Two Niner Lima kissed the ground and we taxied on into Atlantic Aviation to refuel, which was right off my right side as we rolled out after touchdown.

This was going to be a quick turnaround as I would spend a bit more time on the ground at Peoria, my next stop, where I planned to have lunch.

Refreshing myself, I ate the candy bar and apple I had, and sipped a bit of water.

PART 2

SBN-PIA

South Bend was quiet, and I was cleared for takeoff quickly. It was a short respite, just over a half-hour after landing when I climbed back into Two Niner Lima.

As before, away from the cities, farmland and fields were prominent, although not as much as the land adorning the hills back east. Things appeared flatter here—more fields, lots of green ones at that. Having driven through these parts a few times, I concluded it was all the corn. If you've ever driven through the midwest, you will have seen corn, corn, everywhere corn. Now, I had a different perspective and noticed that the green of corn stalks was not like the dark forest, but a noticeable lighter color and smoother terrain.

South Bend Approach followed with me for a bit then handed me back to Chicago Center for most of the ride, then they handed me off to Peoria Approach. I had been at four thousand feet and when Chicago finally cleared me up to forty-five hundred feet by the controller's advice of "Altitude at your discretion," I requested to remain at four thousand feet, even if it wasn't the correct altitude for a VFR flight.

Control granted my request.

The air was smooth, and I didn't feel the need to climb and change anything up. The sun was shining brightly, and the storm approaching the Lake area was receding behind us. Small, puffy convective clouds were building above me and I didn't want to risk climbing over them and into rising air. We were crossing through more of Indiana into Peoria in southern Illinois. Still encountering strong headwinds, our ground speed was averaging at one hundred four knots.

It was my only bitch about Two Niner Lima. She has been such a champion for as long as I have owned and operated her. On this entire Journey she has been flawless, but her range and fuel capacity were noticeably limiting. I didn't notice it going eastward because I had no schedule. Now, going back, I was thinking if only I had more fuel. I had no choice now but to refuel again for the longest leg to Kansas City. Most piston planes have a good four-to-five-hour fuel supply. With Two Niner Lima, I had three hours.

I had to chuckle. Despite that limitation she was like the Little Engine that could. For most of my flying around Southern California all these years, she was perfect. But being a trainer and not a real cross-country airplane was evident now. I couldn't have been more pleased with this amazing flying machine with which I was so blessed. Any time I thought of buying another plane, I always came back to Two Niner Lima, and how she has taken such good care of me. It was that kind of love relationship.

Peoria's General Downing Airport is southwest of the city, sitting off the Illinois River. Peoria Approach brought us down and into the pattern for a right traffic approach to Runway 4 and we touched down with no problem just under two more hours of flying time. I was hungry and felt the strain of my early morning departure, now with two legs behind me. I would take a deep breath and chill for an hour or so before the last leg down to KC.

I taxied Two Niner Lima into Byerly Aviation, the only FBO on the field, and followed the linesman's directions to a space right next to the building, with its glass door entry and proud blue signage.

"Welcome to Peoria" it said.

Peoria, Illinois.

How 'bout that?

PART 3

PIA-MKC

It was a small, quiet FBO—late morning, and not too much going on. I instructed the lineman to fill Two Niner Lima up—all four tanks—and walked inside. A nice middle-aged lady whose name tag said Wendy greeted me warmly and, once I saw her name, well, there I went.

"You must be a great person, Wendy. You have my sister's name!"

She smiled. "But of course! Where you in from?"

Well, that got me started and once she heard I was from Santa Monica and what I been doing, I was looking for the red carpet to be rolled out and the trumpets to blare. The incredulous look on her face gave it away. She was dumbfounded.

"Really? You have flown all that way in that little plane?"

"Yup! Just a series of short trips added one on top of another! Heading back now. Only thing really an issue has been experiencing a new kind of weather. We have none in Southern California."

"What do you mean?"

"Well, it does rain once in a blue moon, but mainly all we have is a marine layer, some low coastal clouds that move in and then burn off early in the day. Nearly all the time the sky is blue, and no clouds. I've had to deal with all the heat and moist Gulf air back east, the constant convective activity. It has been an interesting challenge!"

"I'd say!" she replied, her smile acknowledging this pilot for taking the ultimate adventure. "Help yourself to some snacks and water over there," she added, pointing to the back of the small lobby. This FBO wasn't as pretentious or huge as Signature and Atlantic Aviation.

"Rest rooms?" I asked.

"Past all those snacks at the end of the hall," Wendy advised.

I excused myself. I desperately needed to pee, wash the morning grime off, and wet my head and back of neck to cool down. It was hot and humid in the middle of the country, and I was depleted. I soaked a few paper towels and ran them under the cold water, then stuck them on my neck and on top of my head, to lower my body temperature. It was just plain hot.

I was parched and decided to drink more water than I normally would as I didn't want to be further dehydrated. The next leg would be the longest and most grueling of my day.

After taking a few bottles of water I sat down near the snacks and grabbed a couple of apples and a Snickers bar to give me some sugar.

Now, I was taking this break in no rush. I wanted to rest as best I could, to be ready for the last push. Like when I was heading into Dallas, again it seemed surreal that I was going to be right in the middle of this vast land again, flying Two Niner Lima all the way.

Friends wanted to know so I kept in touch with them as I went, now texting them, "Landed Peoria." The love and support of so many who were following along with me nourished me from afar, as so many others had done every stop of the way.

I finished my respite, paid Wendy for the fuel and thanked her so for her kind service and courtesy. "Hope you'll make it back someday!" she said as I shook her hand good-bye.

I smiled. "Me, too!"

Who knew when the next adventure would happen?

Two Niner Lima was parked right in front. I went out to her and did a cursory walk-around, making sure the fuel tanks were topped off, and seeing all was in order. No need, as one of my flying mentors, Capt. Bob Libman, had told me a long time ago to do a detailed one, like the one before the first flight of the day. He told me way back when that he'd learned such protocols and lessons when he was a first officer flying the Lockheed Constellations of Eastern Airlines. I had adopted his instruction into my pilot routine.

We would be flying on a heading of two hundred thirty degrees. I checked in with Ground Control after obtaining the ATIS, and requested flight following at forty-five hundred feet down to MKC, Kansas City Municipal Downtown Airport. My clearance came right back, and I was cleared to taxi out to Runway 4.

However, I did do my normal run-up before requesting takeoff clearance. Those extra few minutes were too important not to take and verify all was okay. It was one thing to be cursory on the walk-around. But it was another to be flippant on the full ground check and run-up procedures before departing. So, not this pilot.

All was looking fine and within normal parameters. I taxied up to the hold line for Runway 4, contacted the tower and was immediately cleared for a straight-out departure. Off we went, climbing up to forty-five hundred feet. The scenery below me was farmland as far as I could see. There are so many farms here in the USA—no wonder we could feed the world five times over.

The long day was catching up to me. Flying Two Niner Lima never gave me any kick- back moments of rest or a chance to turn on the autopilot, listen to Sirius or my own mix, and watch the scenery go by. That was possible in more modern, current day airplanes which are almost like a lush Lexus or BMW, or any other finely appointed automobile. There was no autopilot in Two Niner Lima. I was always flying the airplane, constantly tweaking her as she burned fuel, getting lighter, as the decreasing fuel load created an imbalance and one wing got heavier than the other. I developed a routine of changing fuel tanks regularly.

Flying meant also navigating and communicating. I was monitoring ATC to see how things were going, identifying planes on the same route as Two Niner Lima, or going to the same airport. I was watching my iPad and Garmin 530 GPS monitor my flight route over the ground as well as our speed and time to destination.

And, more is always going on. Unfortunately, the seats were worn and leaning further backward due to the years. It was not at all a joy to sit for long durations. It was not "soft Corinthian leather," but a cloth seat with vinyl edges. I could never alter the pitch of the seat from its fixed position, so it didn't offer me much back support. If only it could be moved electrically like our car seats or in those modern piston airplanes. The cushion was, as well, on its last bit of oomph. During this trip, I vowed I would refurbish Two Niner Lima in many ways.

After a few hours, I knew, my fatigue would begin. Constantly flying the aircraft is not the only chore, along with changing the fuel. I'm constantly scanning the sky for other aircraft, adjusting the throttle, changing the mixture when climbing or descending, monitoring the engine instruments frequently, watching for trouble. Is the oil pressure falling? Oil temperature rising? What about the hottest number three cylinder? Was the Exhaust Gas Temperature under thirteen hundred degrees? What about the other cylinders? And, how about the Cylinder Head Temperatures?

There were many signals that might indicate a problem. Religiously, I checked for them every fifteen minutes or so.

Doing all this means the hours spent in the left seat are arduous. Including altitude into the equation, with its change in air pressure as you climb and descend, will add to the fatigue. The sky was no place to be complacent and chill.

On this third leg, the day was catching up to me. My back ached in the usual place, toward the right side, under the shoulder blade. I adjusted my neck with a few semi-chiropractic moves. My knee throbbed and I stretched and released both legs on and off the rudder pedals. Parched from the heat, I sipped a bit of water every half hour.

The flight had been smooth and in a little over two hours, I was descending into Kansas City. It was exciting to see it—another place I'd heard about for way too long. As I got closer and saw downtown, noticeable as most with its glob of skyscrapers standing tall and proud on the edge of the Missouri River. I had the same sense of exhilaration as I did with other river cities I'd visited on this Journey, recalling the thrill of seeing Mobile, landing in New Orleans, and coming up to Wilmington on that long straight-in approach to Runway 06.

MKC was coming up soon, so said the Foreflight map on my iPad, but I still didn't see it. After advising the Approach Controller that I was unfamiliar, he made it easy for me.

"Grumman Two Niner Lima, Downtown Airport is 10 miles straight ahead. Descend to twenty-five hundred, follow the river, and contact Wheeler Tower at 123.3."

"Roger, Approach. Grumman Two Niner Lima, following the river down to twenty-five hundred feet, over to Tower 123.3."

I contacted the tower and pulled the throttle out to twenty-five hundred rpms. That should, if I recollected correctly from my instrument training, give me a five hundred fpm descent rate, my targeted standard rate.

"Wheeler Tower, Grumman Two Niner Lima, three thousand nine hundred feet, descending, with Foxtrot. Request left base, Runway 19."

Roger, Grumman Two Niner Lima, cleared as requested, Runway 19, cleared to land."

Just as I came parallel to the downtown skyscrapers, now off to my right, I saw Wheeler Downtown Municipal Airport almost straight ahead, sitting on the south side of the river, slightly to my left at eleven o'clock.

The view was spectacular.

I slowed down to my pattern speed of one hundred five knots and put out a notch of flaps. Now I was sitting up straighter, getting Two Niner Lima ready. We eased down to the pattern altitude and started to reduce our power on base, rolling out perfectly onto final, red over white, just right according to the VASI lights. We had a well-controlled, slow final approach right at ninety knots over the fence. I reduced power to idle as we settled over the runway numbers, bled off a bit of speed, and Two Niner Lima kissed the ground again.

Kansas City, Missouri!

I wasn't tired at all.

I taxied to Atlantic Aviation instead as their fuel prices were significantly lower than Signature Flight Service. The linesman scurried out and directed me to park just off the front of the FBO.

When I turned, lo and behold, there across the field was the TWA Kansas City Star Lockheed Constellation, sitting next to a Lockheed-1011, whose livery I did not recognize. Maybe I would stay another day to see her and the TWA Museum? Filled with energy, I shut Two Niner Lima down and scrambled out. I'd just had a long day and had another ahead of me if I was to get to Denver tomorrow.

The thought of staying another day vanished quickly as Get Home-itis showed its ugly face, taunting me. I had vowed to see as many air museums as I could. And here was one honoring a beloved legacy airline and its flagship, its Starliner in the 1950s. Flying back and forth to Florida aboard Eastern Airlines, I became hooked on the Lockheed Constellation.

"We shall see" I thought. One problem at a time. My new mantra ever since reading and seeing *The Martian*. I had made reservations at a downtown hotel and I wanted to secure Two Niner Lima and get to the downtown hotel where I'd made reservations. Then I would see how I felt, and what the weather was doing, so I could make an informed decision.

Getting closer to home was overpowering and it bothered me

that I wasn't leaping at the chance to see another air museum, one I'd very much wanted to see. My reaction was puzzling. I thought perhaps it was some caution I sensed from the unstable weather patterns I had been experiencing in Michigan making me want to seize this open window to get to Colorado.

But that didn't add up.

It stood in stark contrast to my mission statement set a few short months ago.

Get Home-itis was spewing its ugliness for me to ponder.

CHAPTER XXVI

————————————————————————————→✈

BACK TO SOCAL
LEG THREE
KANSAS CITY, MO

The approach and landing into Wheeler Downtown Municipal Airport right on the Missouri River in Kansas City had jazzed me. I didn't feel so tired as I unloaded my bags and secured Two Niner Lima. Rolling the baggage cart the linesman had brought me, I was excited by the possibility of going to the TWA Museum.

Atlantic Aviation was situated in a two-story office building attached to a cavernous hangar of almost four stories fronting the tarmac, with the cursive Signature trademark on a sign in the front. I noticed when I walked toward the front door that the flagpole was adorned with three flags flying briskly in the wind. One was the Star-Spangled Banner, another was the State of Missouri flag, and the last, on the bottom, was a TWA flag, embossed with its last livery.

Ah, of course—because the museum is here.

I took care of business with a nice young woman, Stephanie, ordering fuel for the journey tomorrow, or if I stayed, the next day.

Again, I requested a top-off of all four tanks. I attended to my personal needs, then went back into the lounge, sat down, and stared out at the tarmac and the TWA Constellation parked across the field.

Stephanie had told me I shouldn't miss it. I took a few bottles of water from the snacks offered and placed them in my cooler for the next leg of the journey—another long day to Colorado. I sat, slowing down, now in Kansas City. Again, I was halfway across the country and proud of myself, knowing I was also halfway home. After the next leg, I would be getting back into familiar territory, Santa Monica just around the Rockies, then into Arizona and home.

I arranged for an Uber to pick me up and it was a quick trip over the river and past downtown to the Quality Inn I'd found on Hotel Tonight, my new go-to app for last minute sleeping arrangements. I took a few pictures out the car window, absorbing the positive vibes of KC, a place I had heard about for so long. It seemed as charming as Pittsburgh.

I was more tired than I'd thought I would be, and I didn't talk much to the driver. In his mid-thirties or so, he was taking his cues from his passenger. I was leaning back in the rear right seat, not my usual gabbing self, just taking in the view.

We arrived at the Quality Inn Downtown Kansas City. It was an old brick building, and the reviews on Hotel Tonight spoke of its recent renovations. The driver, whose name was Omar, helped me in with my bags. I fished a five-dollar bill out of my wallet and handed it to him with my thanks.

The Hotel appeared quite old but Stacy, the young woman at the reception desk, allayed my doubts. She was bubbly, warm and welcoming, and I was smitten. When I told her what I had been up to, she was fascinated, especially when I told her I was from Los Angeles and on my way back home.

"I've never been there. Someday. It's my dream to swim in the Pacific Ocean!"

"Oh," I responded. "L.A. is a can't-miss like all of California and the entire Southwest. You won't believe the scenery and the big western sky. And Yosemite—well, you just got to get there!"

She was hooked, but not by me. Long before I trudged into this Quality Inn, she was addicted to the dream and the lure of California magic she hoped would change her life.

I asked Stacy if there was a good dinner place nearby and she recommend a rib joint "a few minutes away." Further interrogation revealed the walk was actually a "couple of city blocks" away, about ten minutes, and "wasn't a bad walk at all."

She was so solicitous in getting me checked in and settled. Learning she was born and raised in Kansas City, I chalked it up to good midwest upbringing. She helped me get my bags into the elevator, then up I went to my room on the seventh floor.

By the time I got all my stuff unpacked and plugged in, I was beat. I called Flight Service to see if I had good weather for the next few days, to decide if I would stay another night and visit the TWA Museum. Exhausted, I changed into my hanging-out, baseball batting practice shorts and t-shirt emblazoned with the Hawaii Stars logo and stretched out on the bed.

Flight Service made my decision for me. More bad weather was due in from Canada and the northwest, moving easterly and shifting more toward the central part of the country. It was due to arrive in two days, although the briefer stressed that the next morning things would be clear all the way from Kansas City to the Denver area.

Vowing I would come back some day to see the TWA museum, I turned my attention to my growling stomach.

When in Kansas City, I thought, I must do ribs. While I channel-surfed on the TV and read through my emails, I debated about getting dressed again and going to that rib joint Stacy recommended. The more I lay there, the more tired I became.

Eventually I decided there was no way I was leaving this room tonight. I called a local rib joint and had Door Dash deliver my ribs, beans, and coleslaw dinner in less than an hour.

Regrettably, they were awful—too dried out, not enough barbecue sauce, and the coleslaw not at all pleasing. *Oh well*, I thought, wolfing most of it down anyway, *at least my belly is full, and I'm safe and sound.*

Deciding to be airborne by nine a.m. I set the alarm for six. With the time change from Central to Mountain Daylight, I was getting an extra hour back upon arrival in Longmont. Foreflight was estimating just shy of five and a half hours flying time, but that would be updated in the morning when I knew the strength of the winds behind or against me. Because of the storms heading east, even though far north of me, I was anticipating some tail wind component from the counterclockwise flow of the bad weather.

Before the sun even set, I fell asleep watching TV. Awakened by the noise, I looked at my phone and saw it was not yet nine-thirty. I would get a good night's rest and be ready to make it to Longmont, then rest more there over the weekend.

SoCal was getting closer.

CHAPTER XXVII

————————————————————————————→

BACK TO SOCAL
LEG FOUR
MKC-OIN-LMO

September 11, 2019

Wheeler Municipal Downtown Airport, Kansas City, MO to Oberlin, KS, for fuel stop, to Longmont, CO.

MKC-OIN

Route: Direct Distance: 280 nm

OIN-LMO

Route: Direct Distance: 214 nm

Total Distance: 494 nm.

Start time (MKC): 7:41:34 a.m. Wheels up:

7:58:17 a.m. Wheels down: 10:45:35 a.m.

Shut-Down time (OIN): 10:49:19:20   p.m.

Log Entry: Time Logged: 3.2 hrs. Flight Time: 2.8 hrs.

Early a.m. departure. 4,500′ smooth. OIN cute little airport. Good ldg. Self-serve fuel difficult.

Start time (OIN): 12:16 p.m. Wheels up: 12:26 p.m.

Wheels down: 1:17:51 p.m. Shut-Down time (LMO): 1:22:40 p.m.

**Log Entry: Time Logged: 2.4 hrs. Flight Time: 2.1 hrs.
Refueled at OIN. Density Altitude Adjustment. 6,500' through
Kansas. Lt. chop. Climb to 8,500'. Front passing north. Clouds.
Good ldg.**

It didn't surprise me one bit when I opened my eyes shortly after four a.m. Somehow the body knew this pilot would be flying today. I lay back, thinking I might fall asleep again, but soon realized there was no chance that would be happening. The butterflies were starting to nervously flap their wings. I decided to get up, call Flight Service, and get to MKC by seven-thirty for an early morning departure. Since I would be landing in Mountain time where weather wasn't supposed to get bad until the evening (if at all), with thunderstorms possible, I had an hour to play with.

I called Flight Service and confirmed everything was status quo per their advice last evening. A preflight briefing on Foreflight confirmed the weather report. I was confident we would have a good flight westward.

The hotel served breakfast starting at six a.m., so I jumped into an early shower after reading my e-mails and checking Facebook. I wanted to get some nourishment before the five hours of flying ahead of me.

After breakfast, I went back to the room and got myself together, packing last minute things. I placed an order with Uber and went downstairs, dragging my bags rather than going down to get the hotel baggage cart. When Uber showed up less than ten minutes after I clicked the app, I was already waiting outside.

Dean, the driver, was a Vietnam vet who had returned from the war to his family here. Born and raised in Kansas City, he pointed out some highlights as we drove back to MKC. It was interesting that when I took time to listen, so many like Dean wanted to share their stories. Maybe my account of crossing the country in Two Niner Lima triggered their recollections. My revelation seemed to open others' desire to share their own adventures.

The story he told me in the few minutes our drive took tugged at me. Although it was early, Dean was talkative and I noted the cup of coffee in the console holder. He boasted he had been driving since five a.m. A big burly man with a full, long beard, he was wearing a wool cap, even though it was summer. It made him a distinctive persona.

He had been wounded during the war by some shrapnel in his back, and he still complained of intermittent pain to the VA. He confessed to loving his "fellow grunts" with whom he had "visited hell and back," many he had lost. Speaking of those comrades in arms, his voice trailed off and he got quiet.

Proud of his hometown, he perked up as he pointed out the sites—among them, the new Convention Center, named after "good old Mayor Bartle," and spanned across Interstate 670. Another was the Kauffman Center for the Performing Arts, whose ribbed shell design reminded me of the Hollywood Bowl.

Despite a snafu with his father, to which I volunteered my support with a "Been there, had that" response, he really opened up, telling me he took care of his mom and sister. I saw a pained but proud United States veteran and I enjoyed the profound intimacy we shared in the moment. Maybe it was easier to discuss such difficult things with a total stranger than someone close.

Vets, especially of the Vietnam war, had it rough. Used up and spat out, Uncle Sam never really took care of them after their bodies were broken and their spirits beaten. Lynn's Father, Berkley, who was a colonel in Vietnam and one of General Westmoreland's up-and-coming young staff leaders, told me horror stories of what he had witnessed, both on the battlefield and in the VA, along with the always present politics.

Funny how we never seem to have enough money for the right things, but a lot for the agendas of the few. We still ignore to our detriment President Eisenhower's admonition: "Beware the Military Industrial Complex."

Despite morning rush hour traffic, Dan got me to Signature at MKC in twenty minutes, going over many of the bridges spanning the Missouri River. After he took my bags out of the trunk and put them on the sidewalk for me, I gave him a big hug, surprising him. I thanked him and wished him well.

At reception, I settled my bill and then walked out to Two Niner Lima, trudging with my bags. Spotting TWA's Lockheed Constellation, I heaved a sigh of regret and vowed again to come back and visit the Museum.

I was stoked, as I knew I would soon be back in the west.

My route would take me to Oberlin in western Kansas and then on to Longmont, Colorado, twenty-three miles north of downtown Denver. Anticipating I would burn almost twenty-seven gallons of fuel, I planned to refuel in Oberlin. Flight Service was reporting wind shear and strong gusts below two thousand feet, up to eight a.m. so I could linger a little longer than usual and have breakfast before my departure. I hoped to be airborne nearer nine a.m. to give some cushion to that advisory. Anything to avoid turbulence.

Sadly, I took note of the date—September 11, 2019, the eighteenth anniversary of the first attack *ever* on the continental United States. We all remember vividly what we were doing the morning it unfolded on our TV screens. Like so many other tragedies to which a life can bear witness, all marked with the same details: where you were, what you were doing, how you felt.

"Wake up! Turn on the TV!" Leanne, my girlfriend at the time and who lived in Boston, bellowed over my phone. The ringing woke me at six a.m. that day.

"What? Lee? What's the matter?"

"Just turn on the TV. We're at war!"

"What?"

"Get up and turn on the damned TV. Call me back soon." Lee was a kick-ass, wonderful soul, almost five feet, ten inches tall and much younger than me, but we were having some great times hanging together.

I couldn't believe what I was seeing. The South Tower in flames. Then an airliner crashing into the North Tower. The news from the Pentagon, and another airliner down over Pennsylvania. The collapsing towers, one after another, and the tragic finale.

The Kennedy Assassination. Challenger. And now this horror added to the list. It is still hard to believe those landmarks are gone. More tragic was our response. The War on Terrorism. More weapons, more wars, more young boys lost, more dreams shattered.

Sometimes I think war is all part of the control the rich and powerful have over us as they use us up for their own gain. War is big business.

Terrorism still exists. It always will. But, one man's terrorist is another man's freedom fighter.

Having watched the Vietnam debacle unfold and learning what our government had perpetrated against so many there, I knew this was more of the same madness. Instead of leading a peaceful, prosperous engaged country, we have become the world's largest weapon supplier.

After my walk-around, I climbed aboard Two Niner Lima and secured the iPad, iPhone and Stratus 3. I buckled up the seat belt, and loosely adjusted the shoulder harness to feel comfortable. I would make it snug on takeoff and landing.

Two Niner Lima turned over on the first downward movement of her propeller. As I adjusted the throttle down to the idle speed of 1200 rpm, I thought she, too, was as eager to head west. On video, I checked in with my followers, saluted those lost souls from our tragedy of eighteen years ago, and then got down to the task at hand.

ATIS reported no wind shear and I contacted Ground control, requesting flight following to Oberlin. Cleared to taxi out to Runway 19 at taxiway K(ilo) for an intersection departure, I considered asking for a full-length departure. But realizing I had five thousand plus feet remaining on Kilo, I dismissed the thought. Two Niner Lima had done it before, with far less concrete available for us to get airborne.

After the engine run-up, I had a surprise when I set up my radios and put KOIN in the Garmin 530 GPS as my destination. Lo and behold, it now recognized the destination and told me it was two hundred eighty nautical miles away on a heading of 265 degrees direct.

Run-up complete, we were cleared for departure on a quiet and still sunny morning. Two Niner Lima hustled us down Runway 21 and we rose and climbed up and over the Missouri River. Downtown Kansas City was a thrilling sight, with skyscrapers and the urban scene off to our right. Kansas City Departure cleared us through the Class B(ravo) airspace and had us resume our own navigation on our direct course. Up we went to forty-five hundred feet, our cruising altitude to Oberlin.

We were up against a headwind of about fourteen knots, which was slowly dissipating as we moved west.

The scenery was very much like before, flying over Illinois and into Missouri, with farms and green fields as far as I could see. The population thinned out as we moved further away from Kansas City. Shadows on the fields created a pallet of varying hues of green interrupted now and then by a town on the prairie spread out over our heartland. Clay Center. Concordia. Mankato. Smith Center. Philipsburg. Each a bundle of buildings and usually an airport nearby, interrupting the flow of the plains and sparsely populated state.

Once past Philipsburg, the terrain began to rise. I was only a few thousand feet above ground level as I neared Oberlin. I wouldn't have to descend much and decided to plan a lengthy straight-in approach to Runway 35.

Denver Center advised they would not be able to stay with me and told me to pick them up after my fuel stop, once I got up to a higher altitude. I told the controller I would, after refueling, and tuned into the OIN AWOS to get the automated weather.

Oberlin did not have a control tower so I announced my intentions at ten miles out, where I and turned right, almost 90 degrees to a heading of 350 degrees to line up for Runway 35. There OIN sat, directly in front of me, and I started slowing Two Niner Lima down to descend to pattern altitude. There was no chatter on the Unicom channel as no other plane was in the pattern.

I had plenty of time. We settled down on the final approach, now five miles out at 105 knots, and I put out my one notch of approach flaps. I snapped a photo on final approach. I was trying to accumulate as many pictures at that position as I could—not the easiest thing to do at such a crucial time of flying, especially doing so one-handed.

Getting closer, as if I were on my base leg, I trimmed to nine-ty-five knots and put out full flaps, slowing to ninety knots to a smooth landing. I couldn't believe how utterly empty the airport was here in western Kansas. Just this runway. It was as if I landed in a big field, so little around it was noticeable to me after flying into so many bustling airports.

The only buildings I saw were off to my left so I exited Runway 35, at the only taxiway there, and headed to them.

It was the typical small general aviation airport I had read about but into which I rarely flew. Out in the middle of nowhere, a town's main link to the outside world. Oberlin, Alan had told me a few nights ago, was the Puppy Center of the USA, for what reasons he didn't know. I surmised he must have been right. What else could folks do here other than farm?

As I approached the cluster of buildings, I saw they were a bunch of hangars and a small, one-story house, no more than five hundred square feet, with a big sign on the outside:

"Welcome to Oberlin, KS. Elev 2703."

Another sign, adorned with a Next Tech logo, pronounced, "Free Wi-Fi."

The entire airport was eerily empty, seemingly deserted. Not a soul in sight.

Looking for the fuel pumps, I taxied past the office. I was anx-ious, unable to see where they were. Foreflight had said there were fuel pumps here, and I deliberately chose OIN because of the low price. Now I started to think, whatever will I do?

Finally, I saw them under a lean-to shelter roof. I swung Two Niner Lima beside the pumps and shut down.

I clambered out and went directly to the office, which had such a homey feel inside. Set up neatly in the clean but sparse space was a sofa with a small coffee table, a water cooler, a round, four-seat table, a small refrigerator, and a microwave on a table. I ducked into the men's room for a moment and afterwards took a few bottles of water out of the refrigerator. Then I went outside to refuel Two Niner Lima, planning to come back after and sit for a few more minutes and text my friends waiting in Longmont to announce my landing at OIN.

Refueling Two Niner Lima took some time and was a struggle. At first, I couldn't activate the machine. After many rejections of my attempts to input her full registration number and process my debit card, finally I got it done.

Then, for whatever reasons, the process became even more of its usual challenge. I was glad I had eaten some Cheerios that morning. Pulling out the hose was arduous; it did not want to stay put. Seems it wanted to withdraw back into the pump, forcing me to keep pulling on it while I filled up all four tanks. I fought with this on both sides.

Now, I really did need to relax a bit and sip some water on that office sofa.

I walked back into the office, texting my friends of my status and estimated arrival time in Longmont. If I left right away, I would be airborne around noon and be in Longmont by one, allowing for the change back to Mountain time. I would make it for the lunch I'd planned with Mary Anne and her daughters Jennifer and Lauren.

After a few more minutes resting and sipping water, I signed the guest book, confirming Two Niner Lima and I were here from Los Angeles, heading to Longmont, and based in SMO. It was interesting to see so many other pilots had passed through OIN. I wondered they might think on seeing Two Niner Lima and Capt. Bob so far from home.

During my hour or so on the ground, I saw no people nor any airplanes. After flying into so many airports over all my forty years of flying, this has never happened before. It was spooky. Out in the middle of nowhere, no human contact, no one to chat or share the adventure with, or talk about flying in the region and ask what to expect enroute to Colorado. It was unsettling.

It was a public airport facility, but I felt I'd landed in a ghost town. While the solitude and quiet were in some way enjoyable, when compared to the hubbub of other airports and facilities, I was not at all comfortable and I was anxious to get going. It seemed I was an unwanted interloper who had interrupted a fixed scene in a movie—and the only way out was to just go—go quickly, and leave it be—so it could be restored to silence and not do the inter-loper any harm.

After the cursory walk-around and perfunctory checklist, I got back into Two Niner Lima and started her up. I taxied out to Runway 35 after checking AWOS for the weather as well as taking notice of the density altitude, and the sweltering summer heat I'd encounter in the afternoon. I made a note to adjust for same at my run-up before departure.

I turned the wrong way on the runway, thinking it was a taxi-way. I had not pulled up the airport diagram which would have placed the little plane on its location on the airport, like it does on the sectional map when enroute. There were no directional signs, and I taxied all the way to the end of the runway, thinking it was Runway 35—but there was 17 painted on the concrete at its end.

Uh-oh.

Pulling up the diagram I realized my mistake and announced my dilemma on the Unicom frequency, which was still quiet, still with no planes in sight. I was concerned about this error, although no harm, no foul. The bones of this seventy-one year old pilot pur-suing his adventure were feeling this long, tiring day.

Announcing my intentions, I back-taxied down Runway 17. I wasn't so rattled but that mistake told me the long day was hitting me. I took a deep breath as I swung Two Niner Lima around to do a run-up. I completed it and got ready to go.

Runway 35 was only 3,501 feet, so I held Two Niner Lima back, brakes engaged, letting the power rise fully to the adjusted density altitude throttle setting, and off we went. Two Niner Lima quickly accelerated, and we lifted off half-way down the runway.

I climbed up to 6,500 feet, as the terrain was higher now. I would eventually have to get up to eighty-five hundred feet as I moved westward. The headwind had calmed down and we were traveling around 124 knots over the ground.

Now, I knew I was coming back west. The green fields were giving way to many more of beige and brown.

Back in the west. I grinned. So much land and space. I had the same feelings when driving across America. Whoa! Sure is big!

There was very little population in western Kansas and Colorado, and the towns were so far apart. Coming up upon them, a cluster of buildings usually marked their community.

Now on top of the weather, I could see the Rocky Mountains looming on the Continental Divide. There was something about that demarcation that energized me and made me smile.

Coming home. The West.

I parried with multiple Denver Center controllers, then Denver Approach, who had me come down below the broken ceiling as I entered the Denver Class B(ravo) airspace. Despite being at 8,500 feet indicated on the altimeter, because of the rising terrain as we moved westward, I was only a few thousand feet above ground level.

Approach asked me to advise when I had the airport in sight and sure enough, as I got about fifteen miles out, I saw LMO clearly, with the mountains its backdrop. The scenery was spectacular, with the city of Denver off to my left in the distance.

"Approach, Grumman Two Niner Lima has the airport in sight."

"Roger, Grumman Two Niner Lima, Radar services terminated, squawk VFR. Good day."

"Grumman Two Niner Lima, Roger. Good day."

I pulled the power back at ten miles out and began a slow descent onto the 45 for a left- turn pattern approach to land on Runway 11, the active runway per AWOS. Announcing my intentions over the Unicom frequency I heard a few other planes in the pattern. Slow and deliberate, even after the long day, I forced myself to be rigorous now.

I gradually reduced my power on each leg of the pattern, nailed the final approach, and gently touched down. Exiting Runway 11 at Taxiway A(lpha) 2 1 taxied straight on to the ramp to Fly Elite Aviation, the only FBO there.

As I taxied into a tie-down space, I saw Mary Anne, Jennifer and Lauren sitting on a bench in front of Fly Elite, waiting for me. It was a welcome sight, indeed. Mary Anne and Jennifer came out and we all hugged hello. It had been years since I had last seen them.

I unpacked Two Niner Lima and secured her for my stay, then trudged into the FBO. Right away, I noted the cool vibe. The receptionist was a young girl in her twenties, quite pretty, and wearing sunglasses. Other women behind the counter were just as young, all with good figures, in jeans (and another in sunglasses), and all seemingly hip. A few young men lingered there with them. I certainly didn't wonder why. Aviation aficionados, indeed.

They all were friendly and welcoming. I checked in, advised I would call for fuel the day before my departure, and then inquired about the rates for tie down each night.

"There is no charge," said Monica, whose name tag displayed her moniker.

"Really? Wow! Great!"

I was stunned. I couldn't believe it. But I had always heard wonderful things about Colorado. Progressive, hip, Rocky Mountain high.

And free tie-downs.

It was going to be a great weekend, for sure.

CHAPTER XXVIII

BACK TO SOCAL
LEG FOUR

COLORADO AND FRIENDS

Lauren had to leave before I got into the FBO office, but Mary Anne and Jennifer were there, explaining that Lauren had to pick up her daughter from school and couldn't make lunch. We loaded up Mary Anne's SUV and off we went, looking forward to catching up. I had made it a point to stop here after too many years of not seeing Jennifer and her mom.

I missed Jennifer, a friend with whom I'd shared a close relationship years ago. I wanted to find out why she had gone off the grid, so to speak. She was unreachable by cell and was never on Facebook, responding infrequently to private messages.

When Mary Anne fired up a joint and offered me a hit, I knew I was in Colorado. Wow! Here marijuana is legal. I took a hit and settled back in my seat as Mary Anne shared her experiences as a consumer in this new, legal market. In fact, before we made it to the restaurant, she stopped at a local dispensary to pick up some product.

Mary Anne is my age, a very cool, hip woman, who lives with her boyfriend an hour up in the mountains, west of Longmont, where we would stay through the weekend. Politically and civically, we were all on the same page so we were laughing and railing and raging at the current state of affairs in the USA. I learned a lot about Colorado politics, and the mix of red and blue in this progressive state. I had been here a few times, when first traveling cross-country by car and on some business trips to Boulder. But I didn't know much about life here and that's what I wanted to discover. Colorado was another possibility for a future residence.

I had met Jennifer years ago when she had just moved to Los Angeles. A beautiful, young woman of twenty-five, tall, blonde, and ever so sexy and attractive, she was an ingenue trying to break into movies and television. She was going out with one of my clients. Well, one thing led to another, and when she broke up with him, we started dating. We had a wonderfully intimate, close relationship, with lots of fun times. We dated on and off for a few years, and I was smitten. We never got close to marriage, but she always made me feel so special and the way I felt and doted with her always had me holding her in a very special place in my heart.

It had many years since we had seen each other. She had moved back to Denver to be near her mother and sister, and she took care of Lauren's kids while she battled frequent health maladies. At times, things were grim, and I heard from Jennifer once in a blue moon, when she wanted to discuss the legal issues of adoption in case the worst happened. Thank God, Lauren was getting through it all but every year brought more heartache and worries.

Mary Anne and Jennifer decided on a chic café and we settled down for lunch. I shared with them my status and my summer adventure with Two Niner Lima. It was good to be on the ground, relaxing with friends over a meal.

I was beat — the long day of flying had taken its toll. We finished up and went to Jennifer's and Lauren's house. Lauren had picked up the kids from school, so we all relaxed with a glass of wine, catching up on the years.

Mary Anne lived with an ex-Brit, Richard, a most interesting and intelligent man, warm and funny and ever so affable. The breadth of Richard's intellect fascinated me and we hit it off, especially since he had heart issues as well. He was dealing with his mortality as I was. We had a most enjoyable three days together.

They lived about an hour west of Longmont, in Drake, up at almost eight thousand feet on Storm Mountain in the Rockies. Mary Anne and Jennifer took good care of me, treating me royally.

Jennifer and I took some long walks in the cool mountain air. Walking over the hills, up at such altitude, was a bit strenuous and left me out of breath but it was by far the most pleasant stop. The view from Mary Anne and Richard's home was breathtaking. Mountains towered above the pristine valley, and the homes below were on large parcels of land. So much room between them conveyed a liberating sense of open space and freedom. The fresh air was noticeably invigorating. Besides the company, the utter silence and desolation of the mountain community enraptured me. The silence was deafening and so welcome to this city boy. The loudest noise I heard over that weekend were crickets chirping madly at night.

We each talked about our lives, our journeys, our gratitude to still be friends, our fondness for one another still evident. We rehashed events, things that happened, what was not said, and what needed to be said. I was puzzled by her sudden departure and for the first time in all the years we knew each other, I heard more of this woman, my friend, whom I discovered I hardly knew, despite our intimacy and friendship.

Jennifer, now nearing fifty, shared with me the horror and heartbreak she'd endured trying to make it in Hollywood. She shared the trauma of being raped twice on the casting couch, the degradation and rejection of auditions, and lastly, the all-too-many false promises made to her. Worse and most horrific, she told me of the treatment she was suffering from her boyfriend who, jealous and possessive, had made her life so miserable until she was able to get away and disappear.

Now I understood why she left Los Angeles and went off the grid so suddenly. I held her as she cried inconsolably, the pain still there, the fear still haunting her. All I could do was be a friend, listen to her and comfort her. Her honesty and disclosure stunned me. I could hardly believe the trauma she had endured.

I thought of my sister and many of my women friends. I read the newspapers and see the reports on TV but hearing firsthand from Jennifer about the pain it caused her—pain she will carry with her that will haunt her forever—angered me.

WTF is wrong with any man who could do such things. Harvey Weinstein? Jeffrey Epstein? Donald Trump? All of these pigs who would treat such vulnerable souls that way. Women are always so vulnerable. The tears rolling down Jennifer's cheeks as she shared with me things I could never imagine made me worry more about my dear friend.

Even though we shared no physical intimacy during my stay, we were never closer.

The weekend went quickly. Sunday, on our way down out of the mountains, we went to Estes Park and viewed the world-famous Hotel Stanley. We ate some lunch after strolling the grounds where Stanley Kubrick shot *The Shining*, and where *Dumb and Dumber* was also filmed. In the lobby sat an original Stanley Steamer automobile, a car first built in 1897 and manufactured from 1901 through 1924, propelled by steam, not gasoline. Approximately 10,500 were built during this time by the Stanley Motor Carriage Company.

High on a hill, overlooking Lake Estes, the hotel was a magnificent, stately edifice, surrounded by its own maze and many gardens. The familiar carpeting was a reminder of *The Shining* and Jennifer gave me a tour. Being in the biz, she regaled me reciting the different scenes at various spots in the hotel.

We arrived back in Longmont by mid-afternoon and decided, as I had to order fuel anyway, to take Lauren's kids to see Two Niner Lima. We all drove over and Lauren's son, Daniel, lit up when sitting in the left seat. I arranged for the fuel and, because I'd be leaving before the FBO would be open, I got the gate code that would get me onto the tarmac so Mary Anne could drive me right up to the plane to unload my bags.

I made sure to get a good night's sleep despite Jennifer's four cats. She gave up her bedroom for me, sleeping on a futon in the living room with the cats. I took a Benadryl to make sure I would have no asthma attack from my allergies, and to make sure I slept soundly. The next day would be a long one for me. It would be a flight of 820 nautical miles with two fuel stops. The first would be in Las Vegas, New Mexico, and the next in Demming, New Mexico, before getting over to Tucson. It was the way I had flown east, so I was going back to SoCal via familiar territory.

Depending on the weather, I would, if need be, stay north of the oncoming storm, cut across the mountains of Arizona and then refuel in either Safford, Arizona, or in Truth or Consequences, New Mexico, both of which would be my alternates. My destination was Tucson as I was intent to come full circle in my Journey, thus coming back to my first stop. I felt comfortable with my instrument rating proficiency and knowledge to understand what I might be able to do and how far I could go.

But the weather was having other ideas and I wasn't so sure I could make it. Storms were trekking northward up from Baja and I hoped I could beat them by making an early morning departure. I had my alternates, and would be back in familiar territory, even thinking I could overnight in El Paso or one of my alternates, depending on the weather.

Before I shut down for the night I called Flight Service. They were optimistic that I might beat the storms moving north. I crawled into bed, turned out the light, and slept soundly.

Tomorrow, I would be back in familiar southwest desert territory.

Almost home.

CHAPTER XXIX

———————————————————————————————→✈

BACK TO SOCAL
LEG FIVE
LMO – LVS – TCS

September 14, 2019

Longmont, CO, to Las Vegas, NM, for fuel stop, to Truth or Consequences, NM

LMO-LVS

Route: Direct Distance: 292 nm

LVS-TCS

Route: Direct Distance: 179 nm

Total Distance: 449 nm.

Start time (LMO): 7:29:15 a.m. Wheels up: 7:36:42 a.m.

Wheels down: 9:56:14 a.m.

Shut-Down time (LVS): 10:03:41 p.m.

Log Entry: Time Logged: 2.6 hrs. Flying Time: 2.3 hrs.

Early a.m. departure. Up to 9,500′. 10,500′. 12,500′. Smooth. Light chop. Good ldg except wrong runway. Advised on Unicom.

Start time (LVS): 11:02:20 p.m. Wheels up: 11:18:25 p.m.

Wheels down: 12:56:17 p.m. Shut-Down time (TCS): 12:58:35 p.m.

Log Entry: Time Logged: 1.9 hrs. Flight Time: 1.6 hrs.
Wx forced stop to AVQ/SAD. Dodging clouds and build-up.
Nice, long straight-in R-13.

I got a solid night of sleep with no hassles from the dislodged cats. I jumped into the shower around five-thirty a.m., aiming to be airborne by 8 a.m.

When I got dressed, Jennifer was already up and making breakfast. I had a bowl of cereal with fruit and a piece of toast. We gabbed a bit and I had my necessary cup of coffee to get the motor running. Before I knew it, Mary Anne had arisen, and it was time to go. I packed up my bags and loaded them into her car.

It was a short drive to Vance Brand Municipal Airport on the west side of Longmont. I really enjoyed this town. The vibe was so welcoming and friendly, or maybe it was just my dearest friends, who were nothing short of loving, hospitable, and gracious. Beside Two Niner Lima, after I unloaded all my bags, I hugged them both tightly and said goodbye. I told them I hoped so many years wouldn't go by before my next visit. Now I knew where to go for some real peace and quiet.

It was a cloudless, cool morning, a hint of another beautiful day. Of course, the prospect of traveling next to the Rockies, had me on high alert. I detected only a slight morning breeze—nothing significant, thus turbulence unlikely from the wind spilling over the Rockies. My energy was exploding. I knew with any luck I'd soon be back at the very first stop of this amazing adventure. The long day of flying would have me enjoying a visit with Paul and Carol again, in Tucson

Almost home.

Following my usual routine, I loaded up my bags, and preflight went smoothly. The only hiccup was that the iPhone holder had fallen off its perch from the right-side windshield window and my attempts to get the suction cup holder to grab were not taking. Rather than dawdle to fix it, I chose to get moving.

A check of the weather and the perfunctory call to Flight Service told me the storms from Baja were moving north more rapidly than anticipated. Tucson now looked in doubt. Taking a few minutes to brief myself on Foreflight and be familiar with my alternates (Truth or Consequences and Safford) I decided to go as far and for as long as I could. We were clear to Las Vegas and if I couldn't get to Demming, I'd see where things were when we refueled after this first leg.

I was disappointed but knew better than to think past this first leg. Mother Nature would be the boss today.

Two Niner Lima was as eager as I and she turned over promptly. The airport was quiet and peaceful, with no other traffic moving or going anywhere so early. Only right before I departed, as I waited after our run-up to depart on Runway 29, did another aircraft land in front of me. The AWOS was reporting the density altitude already at eighty-four hundred feet, over thirty-two hundred feet higher than the field elevation. I had adjusted the mixture setting when checking the engine at run-up. It was going to be a very hot day coming to Longmont.

Despite the increased density altitude, the air was smooth as we lifted off, and we flew straight out and climbed up to seventy-five hundred feet. I contacted Denver Departure, got our squawk code and now had flight following cleared through the Denver Class B(ravo) airspace direct south to Las Vegas. I then turned right heading south, onto our magnetic heading of one hundred seventy-nine degrees.

It was a crystal-clear morning and downtown Denver, and its skyscrapers were right in front of me. I snapped some pictures of Denver's urban sprawl hugging the Rocky Mountains for miles, the ribbons of freeways heading in all directions bounded by our continental backbone.

I gazed eastward from where I had just come a few days previous, appreciating the vast yellow and beige of the plains of Colorado, its eastern lands visible to the horizon.

Rising terrain had me soon request ninety-five hundred feet as our cruise altitude. The air remained smooth, but for some light, intermittent chop which I suspected was from the morning breeze off the mountain range and onto and over the higher terrain. I passed by Centennial Airport, formerly the principal airport for this great metropolitan area until the new Denver International Airport (DIA) opened in 1995. We flew past Colorado Springs and Pueblo.

I was in awe of the incredible vistas laid out before me. Off to my right, the Rocky Mountains rose, their jagged peaks growing further westward. The morning light from the rising sun in the east lit up the mountains. The view was spectacular. The brown foothills turned to beige then, and the mountain perched behind stood dark and green. I thought of Mother Nature forming these rugged peaks with the magma flowing from all the eruptions eons ago. The incredible forces. Whoa!

I love speculating about that awesome power of those eruptions. California has such interesting topography as well, with all its mountains and deserts that are always there. Now, from my perch inside this fishbowl of Two Niner Lima's cockpit and clear canopy, I was again in awe of God's creation.

How lucky I was to be able to do this thing called flying and see such sights. If only others could see and feel the special and magical views we pilots are afforded.

It sure does give one different insights. The topography reveals itself, with cities and towns laid out and about, the grids of roads and highways running along and perpendicular to them, or to the fields and farms. A pilot can see the development and growth of the area, or none at all in the remote areas. When water is nearby, be it a lake or a river, there will for sure be a town or a city on its banks, obvious for the survival of the settlers and a gateway to the outside world. While the view is not like Apollo 8 on Christmas Eve in 1968 or Voyager 1, peering back at our Earth from millions of miles away, the sights from Two Niner Lima's perch have been humbling.

The terrain continued to rise. I could see over a hundred miles south in the distance to where the plateaus of New Mexico began. The Rockies, off to my right in the distance, were snow-capped, adding to the exquisite picture. Only when we got a bump of turbulence was my peaceful, easy feeling interrupted, and thoughts of the weather and what lay ahead took over. There were a few more jolts, still an indication of the weather changes coming.

As I got further south and past the line of the Rockies, I passed into New Mexico where the rising terrain was almost at seven thousand feet. I had just been handed over to Albuquerque Center and requested climb to ten thousand five hundred feet to give myself more of a cushion over the land. Even though it was not the correct altitude for my direction of flight, the controller didn't hesitate to give his approval.

The sky was still clear in the morning sun but further southward it was growing hazier. In the distance, I could see puffs of clouds at my altitude—the beginning of the storm moving north, and it appeared to be lying smack on our heading. A wave of trepidation came upon me as I pondered how far I would be able to go. I would decide when I stopped for fuel, but from looking on my iPad at the weather developing, it appeared my only alternative was to climb and get south and cross the New Mexico and Arizona mountains before the storm closed my path to Tucson.

Las Vegas Municipal Airport was coming up soon.

The air was still quite smooth as I descended—hardly any upset or bumps coming down—and Two Niner Lima rewarded us with one of those landings that brought a smile after a slow, deliberate long final approach. We rolled out and right before Runway 02-20, we turned off and taxied to the terminal, a small house with a Phillips 66 sign next to it. I wheeled Two Niner Lima on the tarmac in front of the terminal, next to a glistening single-engine turboprop, a Daher TBM930, N900CX—another dream plane for this pilot.

As I got out and headed into the terminal to take a break, a linesman drove up in the fuel truck and inquired about my fuel status. I requested he top all four tanks and continued inside. I would have the snack I had prepared from Jennifer's kitchen—an apple and a piece of bread lathered with some peanut butter. With some water and a candy bar, that would be enough to recharge my batteries.

The terminal building was a small house, with a décor inside right out of the Sixties. On the wall behind the reception desk was a glass case of model airplanes, mainly WWII vintage aircraft. What really impressed me was the inlaid tile indicia on the floor proudly announcing *Las Vegas*.

I put my iPad on the oak coffee table between the two couches and plugged it in, along with the portable charger. When I checked the weather, I didn't like what I saw. More puffy cumulous clouds were forming in the direction we were heading. I decided, after I got my wits about me and rested for a few minutes on this reprieve, I would call Flight Service. I needed to speak with a briefer about the weather on my route to Demming, which seemed now verboten. If I took my alternate route to Safford I might beat the storm and make it to Tucson.

I munched on a Snickers bar but couldn't sit still, wondering and worrying about the next leg and which way I should go. My anxiety pushed me to call Flight Service instead of lollygagging as I ate. I could see the weather clearly on the iPad, and plan my route of flight on Foreflight, more easily than on my iPhone.

There it was. Clearly, I might not make it to Tucson. The green blob of the storm indicated precipitation, with yellow and red splotches of heavier, intense rain and thunderstorms, moving up into Arizona and starting to edge up near my alternate route to Safford. Demming was now clearly out. I could easily make Truth or Consequences, about two hundred miles south and east of this frontal activity, and then determine if the storm would beat me across when I had to head west.

The butterflies were flapping their wings fast and hard.

I decided it was best to get going so I paid the receptionist and headed out to Two Niner Lima. I noticed I didn't gab with her as much as usual and acknowledged my anxiety. After giving myself a pep talk I decided if there was any doubt, I'd stop at Truth or Consequences before turning west and across the mountains. No time for any apologies. I was alert and ready.

Two Niner Lima and I got ourselves settled and we taxied out, back to Runway 14. Run-up confirmed we were good to go, and as I taxied up to the hold lines of the Runway, I looked towards my continued heading of 179 degrees and further rightward to the next leg's direction to the Sorroco VOR and down to Truth or Consequences of 235 degrees. Those puffy cumulous clouds were denser but still broken.

I hesitated. Maybe I should stop here now? No, I reckoned. *Push on, you have flown above the clouds before. If it gets bad, do a 180-degree turn around and come back here,*

Okay. Fair enough. I had an out, a plan, so we would watch and see just how far we could go.

No, God, not funny, if you think you aren't going to get me home and put me in some sort of incident in this deteriorating weather in a small, piston airplane.

"Enough, Bob," I said out loud, announcing my intentions. "Let's do it!"

"Las Vegas Unicom, Grumman Two Niner Lima, taking Runway 14 for straight-out departure."

I lined Two Niner Lima up on the runway and stopped. I took a deep breath, let it out, and then took another deep breath and let it out with a sigh. My Life Spring training trick to calm myself came in handy.

"Okay! Here we go!"

I pushed the throttle in all the way, and, having made the adjustment for the density altitude at the higher elevation on a hot, summer day, and having over eight thousand feet of runway, I let Two Niner Lima accelerate on her own, building up the necessary airspeed and power, and started rotation, pulling back on the yoke at almost seventy-five knots, ten knots higher than normal at sea level. Two Niner Lima rose slowly this time, and I kept her nose slightly down as she accelerated and climbed into the hot, dense New Mexico air.

As we climbed past one thousand feet above ground level, I

turned on course, heading south to Truth or Consequences. As I turned, I saw clouds looming ahead of me at my altitude, and realized I would need to climb up to at least ninety-five hundred feet to clear them. I checked in with Albuquerque Center.

"Albuquerque Center, Grumman Two Niner Lima, over."
"Grumman Two Niner Lima, Albquerque Center."

"Albuquerque, Good morning. Grumman Niner Three Two Niner Lima just off Las Vegas, 8,200 climbing 9,500, enroute Safford, Arizona, direct Truth or Consequences, direct Safford. Request advisories, over.

"Roger, Grumman Two Niner Lima. Squawk 2655."

Besides wanting the Controller's extra set of eyes, I wanted to let him know my route of flight and I needed to get as much information about the weather as I could. Looking down at my iPad mounted in its cradle, I didn't think I could beat the weather in the two hours it would take me to get to Safford, then at least an hour and fifteen minutes to Truth or Consequences, and another hour or so across the mountains.

The butterflies were kicking up a storm.

"Albuquerque, Grumman Two Niner Lima has the weather and not sure if we will be able to make Safford so will divert to Truth or Consequences if the storm gets there before we do."

"Roger, Two Niner Lima. Keep me advised. Current weather at Safford is still VFR." "Roger."

Now, I was in line with my plan. But every time I looked down at my iPad, my doubt grew more. The air was smooth on top, but as the clouds continued their build up, I found myself requesting higher altitudes.

I climbed up to 11,500 feet. I would have to be at least 12,500 to give myself a few thousand feet above the New Mexico mountains when I turned direct Safford. The sky was getting greyer, and rain was surely coming this way.

I now needed to get over the clouds, which were above me. I climbed up to 13,000 feet. This altitude was the service ceiling of Two Niner Lima, about as far as she could go. She was still climbing when I leveled out, and showing no strain. She was just purring away.

Thinking Two Niner Lima could probably go higher if need be, I wasn't worried about the altitude. I looked at the storm's progress on my iPad. With any luck, we might beat it into Safford. We droned on south toward Truth or Consequences. About thirty miles north of there, I turned toward the mountains and headed direct to Safford, serenely pleased that Two Niner Lima was doing so well at an altitude it rarely flew. And, I was most pleased with myself in Two Niner Lima's left seat, navigating to avoid the weather, way up over the mountains to assure a smooth ride.

I was upbeat and almost giddy at how well we were doing, not realizing what was starting to overtake me.

After another ten minutes or so, as we approached the mountains, with the sky growing darker in the distance ahead of me, Albuquerque Center broke the silence.

"All aircraft, SIGMET TANGO now current."

SIGMET advises of weather that is potentially hazardous to all aircraft. Convective SIGMETs are issued if there may be lines of thunderstorms at least sixty miles long affecting forty percent of its length and exhibiting a strong radar reflectivity, with embedded or severe thunderstorms expected to occur for more than thirty minutes. Any such convective SIGMET implies severe or greater turbulence, severe icing, and low-level wind shear.

He outlined the location of "significant precipitation and embedded thunderstorms," which included "from Safford, Arizona to . . ."

I didn't need to hear the rest.

That did it for me. No way am I going that way. I would not dare tangle with that kind of weather so I would have to divert to Truth or Consequences. Two Niner Lima would be no match. I informed Control.

"Albuquerque, Grumman Two Niner Lima, over." "Grumman Two Niner Lima, Albuquerque."

"Albuquerque, Grumman Two Niner Lima will divert to Truth or Consequences because of the Sigmet and weather in Safford. Turning direct now."

"Roger, Grumman Two Niner Lima."

It was the only decision to be made. I was still at thirteen thousand feet, but now heading direct to Truth or Consequences after turning immediately upon hearing the SIGMET.

It's one thing for a light, single-engine piston plane to fly through some rain, but it's another for a small plane like Two Niner Lima to even think about wrestling with heavy precipitation and thunderstorms. My view on the iPad confirmed the weather moving north and up, soon to be blocking my route to Safford.

No, I wasn't going to be a hero. Thunderstorms, heavy precipitation and flying over mountains all added up to an easy choice. A thunderstorm can rip apart a small plane like mine, or any plane, so there was no other alternative but to accept this reality.

I had just enough money left for fuel and a few nights lodging, but I would have to adjust. My friend Cary had come through and loaned me a few dollars before I left Longmont, and I'd thought I was all set. But, I decided, I would worry about that later when I got settled in whatever lodging I could find.

I checked my iPad for the information on Truth or Consequences. Field elevation was lower, as the plateaus of New Mexico went down as we headed south, and it was situated at 4,862 feet above sea level. I was about forty miles away.

Visibility was hazy but I thought I could make the town out, all the way in the distance—a hash mark in the otherwise deserted New Mexico highlands. I didn't begin my descent until I was twenty miles out, trimming out for a pleasant five hundred feet per minute descent, after advising Albuquerque. Any faster and the ears can pop so I took my time.

"Albuquerque Center, Grumman Two Niner Lima, leaving One Three Thousand, beginning our descent."

"Roger, Grumman Two Niner Lima, advise when you have airport in sight."

"Roger, Grumman Two Niner Lima."

I hesitated to advise until I got a bit closer. I was feeling pretty darn good—content and happy as I lined up on final, descending slowly.

Fat, dumb and happy. That should have been my second warning sign.

I checked on my iPad and then tuned into the appropriate frequency. Truth or Consequences AWOS was reporting VFR, the winds light and variable.

I was feeling darn good about my decision. I was smiling. Ah, Truth or Consequences.

How unusual a place the Universe is bringing me. What will be my Truth? What will be my Consequences?

I chuckled at God's perverse sense of humor.

At ten miles out now, I began the long straight-in approach, continuing on my descent down to pattern altitude. Then I advised Center.

"Albuquerque Center, Grumman Two Niner Lima, has the airport in sight. Request frequency change."

"Roger, Grumman Two Niner Lima, Frequency change approved. Squawk VFR.

"Roger, Albuquerque. Grumman Two Niner Lima, VFR, over to Truth or Consequences. Thanks for your help today."

I clicked the microphone twice and then pushed Comm 2 on the Audio Panel. "Truth or Consequences radio, Grumman Niner Three Two Niner Lima, inbound for landing, landing Runway 13, straight in approach, descending seven thousand eight hundred."

I was surprised to hear a reply.

"Roger, Grumman Two Niner Lima. Winds light and variable."

We got down to six thousand feet, my target for the pattern altitude and at which I wanted to slow myself down to landing speed. I trimmed nose up to slow down, set the throttle at 2100 rpm, and put out one notch of flaps. Two Niner Lima slowed as we got her set now at 105 knots. I tweaked her some more, reducing the throttle to 1700 rpm to begin my landing descent, and put out full flaps, trimming for final approach speed at ninety knots. We were right on the money.

What happened next, I didn't expect, not at all. I thought I had everything set up perfectly. Maybe it was because I was feeling too good. As I crossed the threshold, I did as usual—or so I thought—looking down to the end of the runway, reducing power, holding my attitude, speed reducing. But instead of the wheels kissing the ground, I bounced—and not a small one at that—which got my attention.

I didn't immediately react. I let Two Niner Lima try to settle down, but we bounced again, harder, and now a surge of adrenalin spiked as I applied power. Power applied would break the descent and smooth out the rough bounces. I needed to avert any repeat bounces to avoid rapid porpoising, which would certainly demand an immediate full power go-around.

If the bounces continue and the increase in their speed accelerates, the condition worsens. Then, as is often the case when pilots touch down nose first, or hit too hard, the nose wheel could break off or the propeller could strike the ground. Either way, major damage might result.

The power I applied caused Two Niner Lima to stay airborne. As I leveled off, and then held the proper landing attitude, I reduced the power. I had plenty of runway left to work this out before initiating a go-around.

We touched down, with but another bounce—a small one, and acceptable. We rolled out, and I sighed with relief, retracting the flaps and dumping any remaining lift. I was puzzled by what had just happened, but happy to be down on the ground.

The airport was deserted. I taxied to the terminal, a small house of a building, and saw another Phillips 66 fuel sign standing tall. I figured this must be the place. I headed toward the transient parking spaces marked on the tarmac and spun Two Niner Lima into a parking space right in front of a sign attached to the chain link boundary fence:

"Welcome to Truth or Consequences Municipal Airport."

I shut Two Niner Lima down, took my iPad, unplugged my iPhone and noted my time, recording the shut down time and wheels down time. Sliding the canopy back I stepped out on the wing walk and reached back to get the gust lock from the seat pocket. The wind seemed to be blowing more than light and variable as was reported. The sky was darkening.

Rain was coming soon.

I walked into the terminal and a middle-aged man, in good shape and ruggedly handsome, was behind the counter.

"Hi! Restroom?

"Straight-back to the right."

"Thanks. Be back in a second."

I hustled back and washed off the grime and woke myself up with some cold water. I felt a bit sluggish and tired even though this leg was far shorter than I had anticipated. Our flying day was done. I would have to stay over somewhere.

I returned to the reception desk, exhausted. With two long legs, I'd had more flying than my usual day. I patted my head and neck and face with a lot of paper towels soaked in cold water. Now I was ready to deal with the logistics of lodging and exploring Truth or Consequences.

"Hi! Bob Young," I said, holding out my hand to the man behind the desk.

"Welcome. I'm Randy, the Airport Manager" he replied. Randy was in his forties and, as I would learn, just returned to his hometown after twenty years in the Coast Guard.

"What brings you to Truth or Consequences?" he asked.

And so began one of the most enjoyable receptions of my Journey. Randy was wowed by my adventure in Two Niner Lima and happy to hear I was almost home, even if I had to be stranded in his hometown.

"This is just a quiet, solid town. Some good things to see. I think you'll enjoy it!" He told me of some restaurants, where to stay, and what to do, sharing the don't-miss sights.

"Let me see what I can do to get you the pilot's discount at the Travelodge, where we send our visiting pilots. What's your cell? You relax—I'll have them call you."

What a nice gesture, I thought, and gave him my number and he pointed to the conference room. I took out a couple of water bottles out of the refrigerator (Randy had offered) and sat down to take the Tylenol he also gave me for my headache. I checked my phone messages, then texted my friends that I'd diverted to Truth or Consequences due to deteriorating weather and was now unable to make Tucson. Then I called Paul and Carol and told them I wouldn't be there until later.

Randy came into the conference room.

"Everything is taken care of, Bob. I gave them your cell number. They'll call you in a few minutes to get your credit card information."

"How much will it cost, Randy?" I asked, a bit anxious about my dwindling reserve.

"Oh, I think with the discount, it's sixty-five dollars a night. With what I saw about the weather, you may be here a few days."

Just then my cell phone rang.

I didn't recognize the number, but the screen said New Mexico so I thought it must be the Travelodge®. My hunch was correct, and I excused myself. Randy went back to the front desk as I made the final arrangements with the hotel, reserving two nights.

I hung up and went to thank Randy.

"Do you have Uber in town? I'm wondering how to get to the hotel." Town was a good fifteen-minute ride away.

"No worries, Bob. I'll give you our courtesy car. You can use it for however long you're here."

"Well, I'm on a tight budget. How much a day?"

"Nothing. It's free. It's a courtesy car."

"Oh, wow. . . is everyone always so nice? You know, in all my travels across the country , I keep discovering how wonderful everyone is. Thank you so much, Randy."

"My pleasure. Just doing my job. And, yes, I'd like to think we're pretty special here in New Mexico. So, where have you been on your journey?"

I told him what I had been up to for the past few months, and after I enthusiastically shared my time in Roswell, we started discussing UFOs, both of us convinced the government is hiding the truth.

"They sure are! Hell, I even saw one myself one night on duty. Scared the bejeezus out of me. But with the equipment we're using now, I am also a believer."

Randy described his encounter and the weaponry the Coast Guard was using, and what the Navy is doing with its weaponry, electro-magnetic impulse, power for aircraft and other gizmos. He finished with, "I can't say any more because of my security clearance, but we all know it is true."

I didn't argue, but it sure was interesting hearing from someone who was in the military and had a UFO encounter. Oh, my. . .

After taking care of my calls and texts, I looked at the weather on my iPad and saw the storm had now moved northward, blocking the way I had planned. Now it was coming up toward TCS. I thought I'd best unload my bags from Two Niner Lima and get her fully secured for the duration.

I went outside. Rain was obviously coming. The wind was blowing, the first of the counterclockwise rotations before the storm's arrival far stronger than when I landed. A few drops of rain hit me, and I hurried to Two Niner Lima so I could do my thing and avoid the coming deluge.

I did my usual, got my bags and did the walk-around. Now it was raining steadily. I put on my AYSO Soccer jacket, the one with *Coach Bob* stitched on the front. The moniker earned me instant respect, or so I thought, when so many addressed me so, during my coaching of youth soccer. Other than flying and a good woman, well, that was my passion. How I loved teaching those kids and making a difference.

As I put my jacket on, Randy came back, driving the courtesy car through the adjacent security gate onto the tarmac.

"Let me help you!" he said as he jumped out of the car and grabbed some of my bags.

I took the others and we dumped them into the cavernous trunk of this old, beige Lincoln Continental Town Car. I always loved this car. My dad had a few over the years and I always enjoyed driving his, as well as those I rented while on business trips when I needed a big car.

Randy helped me secure Two Niner Lima's cover. I got the chocks out and using my tie-down ropes, also pilfered from dear John at Troy/Oakland, we got Two Niner Lima ready for the bad weather. It was time to head out.

"Have fun while you're here, Bob. If you need anything, here's my card. Just call me."

I gave him a big hug.

"Thank you for your kindness and help. It is so appreciated."

"When you come back, look for me. I'll be here. Good luck!"

Relieved, I jumped into the car. I had a place to stay, I had wheels and a new place to explore. I would enjoy the few days here, resting for the last leg home. Randy's kindness after my plans went astray had just knocked me out. People were so basically decent and loving . Again I felt so loved, but I was still far from home.

I wasn't feeling so alone now. This Journey had clearly brought me needed nourishment, sustaining me far more than I had ever imagined.

It made me feel so very good about Me again. It had been a long time.

Best yet, only one more day of flying and I would be home, completing my transcontinental and back sojourn with Two Niner Lima. Unreal. Regardless of this diversion, I was pleased and happy.

Ah, yes, Truth or Consequences. I put the beat-up now-lumbering Town car into gear and headed out the gate down the gravel road Randy had pointed out, smiling at the Universe's plan bringing me here.

I passed an old Lockheed Jet Star, one of the USA's first jet fighters, high on a pylon at the end of the road, a salute to nearby Holloman Air Force Base and the New Mexico high desert airport's place in our aviation history.

Despite the grey sky, the New Mexico mountains formed an impressive backdrop to the high desert laid out before me.

It was going to be an interesting visit, for sure.

CHAPTER XXX

———————————————————————————————✈

BACK TO SOCAL
LEG FIVE
TRUTH OR
CONSEQUENCES, NEW MEXICO

I followed the road to the Interstate, the signs to Truth or Consequences showing me the way. The highway was empty—very few cars out this way in the New Mexico desert. As I turned and looped around the interchange entering the freeway, there ahead of me was the huge Elephant Butte Lake. Set against the mountains behind it, it's part of the largest state park in New Mexico.

With me leaning back in the front bench-type seat, the car lumbered along, its suspension suspect. I didn't push her too fast, doing only fifty-five miles per hour. I couldn't help but lean back, as the car was so old, and the automatic seat adjustment for the upper portion was inoperative. It was one of those big old classic cars that needed a driver smoking a cigar, leaning back, and cruising down the highway with the radio blaring. I couldn't tune in KLOS but I was deliriously happy despite the setback and diversion. Notwithstanding the onset of a headache, I was excited to see why the Universe had brought me here.

It was a short drive to the exit for Truth or Consequences. On Waze, I had punched in the address for the Travelodge® and there it was, right off the exit, next to a gas station and a restaurant. Across the way was another gas station and a Denny's. The main part of town appeared to be a short drive down the street from the motel. It appeared I was centrally located and wouldn't have to order Door Dash delivery in order to eat.

I checked in under the all too familiar *porte cochere* and met the nice young lady who had called me when Randy made my arrangements. Emily was of Indian or Pakistani descent, and when I saw an older woman come out to help her, I thought it was her mom. They were Hindu. Their kind hospitality was delightful, and I wondered how they had come here and were now managing a motel all the way out in pretty much nowhere.

I didn't start poking my nose into their business but knowing we had such diversity made me proud to be an American. Diversity is what brings strength to our country, creating a powerful coalition of people and cultures. I wondered if they felt comfortable, and it reminded me of my conversation with Mohammed in Roswell. The attitudes emanating from the White House from 2016 through 2020 had sadly disappointed me, making me even more conscious of another's plight.

Both sides of my family were from old Russia. My mother's father left Minsk as a child in the late 19th century, when it was part of Russia (now it's in Belarus). My father's family was all from Ukraine. His grandfather, after whom I was named, was from Odessa, and he arrived in the United States in 1881. His grandmother was from Kiev, and his mother was from Poland. Because of that, my parents always reminded me of where we came from and why.

When arriving on our shores our family had all seen Lady Liberty as their first glimpse of America. Their hopes and dreams were all they had left, and they broke down in tears of joy at the sight. I learned the inscription on the Statue of Liberty, visible from my dad's Court Street office in Brooklyn, from my brother and sisters:

"Give me your tired, your poor,
Your huddled masses yearning to breathe free,
The wretched refuse of your teeming shore.
Send these, the homeless, tempest-tossed to me,
I lift my lamp beside the golden door!"

My Mother would always tell me what her father, a newly arrived Russian immigrant, would say to his four children when they sought his advice:

"Do what you want. This is your America!"

So, empathy for immigrants was instilled in me, in all of us seeking the American dream.

And, here I was, in a small New Mexico desert town, in our America, where another family was finding a better life and a way to be part of something bigger than any of us. Yes, that was the America I knew and grew up in—exceptional because of our moral character standing up for freedom and leading all the world.

Now, sadly, what morals are left? Only money is important? I wanted to scream because all I saw for these past months was the kindness and love and decency from so many Americans, black or white, yellow or brown. It didn't matter where I was, or who I met, decent people helped me along the way.

I just don't get this hatred and disavowal of the America I knew.

I thanked Emily, told her I would see her tomorrow for breakfast, and took my room card key. Then I drove to the parking space in front of my room where I steered the big old Lincoln to a stop.

The motel was old, a one-story brick relic of the 1960s, and the room showed its age. Still, it was clean and adequate for a few nights, and the price was right. I unloaded my bags and plugged in all my devices to recharge—and it hit me how tired I was. I unpacked the rest of my belongings and got in bed, where I fiddled with the TV, checked my e-mails and messages and made some calls. I thought it would be good to rest, even nap a bit, and then walk across the street to Denny's for an early dinner.

Finally, I closed my eyes to rest, putting my glasses on the night table beside me. I yawned a few times and thought I might fall asleep soon, but my mind was racing. I was reliving my day, coming back to the botched landing which had taken me by surprise.

I thought I did the right thing, diverting when weather blocked my route of flight, but I couldn't understand what happened when I landed. I had been landing Two Niner Lima all summer long and that was the worst landing, other than my struggle with the advancing storm at VLL.

I was perfectly set up and descending at the right speed on a long final approach. What had happened? When I got established and saw the runway in front of me, about twenty miles out, I was so happy, almost giddy. There I was, sitting fat, dumb and happy, feeling pretty darn good despite the diversion.

I was reminded of that feeling, and the one Bill Beecher taught me so long ago:

"If you're feeling that when flying an airplane, then you really are fat and dumb, so you better do something because you ain't gonna be happy for too long."

On that long final approach, I continued on, preparing for the landing, thinking it would be piece of cake. Then I got it loud and clear: It must have been the onset of hypoxia.

Hypoxia is a word of Greek origin that means a lower-than-normal amount of oxygen. I realized the gravity of not thinking through my climb up and over the mountains to thirteen thousand feet to avoid the weather. FAA regulations require that if you are at or over twelve thousand five hundred feet for more than half an hour, you must use supplemental oxygen. I had been at thirteen thousand feet for almost forty-five minutes.

This requirement didn't even enter into my thinking as I pulled up Two Niner Lima's nose. I was concentrating on the climb, worrying about the mountains and the weather, and listening for any strain on the engine. I recalled how startled I was by how easy she kept on going right up there. It never even dawned on me that I needed supplemental oxygen. This discovery upset me greatly.

As one climbs higher into the atmosphere, the partial pressure of oxygen decreases. This means that the number of oxygen molecules in each volume of breath decreases and many of the hemoglobin molecules that normally deliver oxygen to the cells travel empty. Gradually, as I did, one will experience increasing levels of hypoxia.

The first symptoms are subtle, and I realized that must have been what happened to me. I hadn't recognized the first crucial signs of hypoxia—a slight headache or pressure behind the eyes. Had I not heard that Sigmet warning and still had enough of my wits about me to grasp its implications, it could have severely impaired my judgment. Loss of judgment, the inability to make calculations, euphoria and diminished vision are some of the onset symptoms.

I was lucky. Very, very lucky. Someone up there was definitely watching over me. Had I not heard the warning at that very moment in time, when I was still aware enough of what was going on, I don't like to think what would have happened. I would have flown smack into severe weather and instrument meteorological conditions, my oxygen-starved brain not realizing the significance of that moving green blob tinged with red and yellow on my iPad. The threat was far in excess of Two Niner Lima's capabilities, and my own.

I must have been affected by the altitude. Even though my descent was a long one, the lack of oxygen had taken its toll and I bounced when I landed. Bounces like that are usually caused when coming in too fast, or flaring at too high above the ground, or even hitting nose first. I couldn't put my finger on it as I played the last portion of the trip over and over in my mind, thinking I'd had it all together.

A wave of dread and fear come over me as I realized what could have happened. I blurted out loud, "Thank you, God. Thank you, for seeing me through."

My rush to get home may also have been a factor. I was so intent on getting to Tucson that it didn't occur to me to consider the risks associated with crossing the mountains at thirteen thousand feet. I thought back to when I had the change in plans and realized I hadn't planned at all. I had just looked at the map, never diving into any detail.

I shivered, to think I'd come so close to being another pilot lost in a private airplane incident. The NTSB report would have said, "Pilot continued flying into IMC conditions. The aircraft broke up in flight and was destroyed. One fatality."

I smiled, a sense of gratitude and extreme relief flowing over me. Yes, it must be—the Universe was taking care of me. Still smiling, I fell asleep for a few hours.

When I awoke, it was almost seven p.m. After a hot shower I went across the street to Denny's for something decent to eat. I still was thinking about the close call I had flying that afternoon and landing as the storm hit Tucson.

For dinner, I splurged on some broiled salmon and a salad. Andrew, the young waiter, wasn't a day over sixteen. A little unsure, he confessed to me he was new on the job, and this was his first day. I told him he was doing just fine and like school, he would learn more every day and would certainly get the hang of it. The healthy meal at Denny's gave me some much-needed nourishment.

The quaint town and pleasant downhome service had me feeling good as I walked back to the motel.

I awoke after a deep sleep and when I turned on my phone, I saw it was coming up to 10 a.m. so I had missed the complimentary breakfast. Good thing there was a coffee maker in the room. Despite the weak, coffee-flavored hot water I made, it got my motor running. It was a nasty day with gray, dark skies, and heavy rain on and off. A perfect day to relax, I thought, to see the town, then write a bit and rest. I checked the weather on my iPad and My Radar and learned the rain would abate for my departure the next morning.

Eventually I got through my e-mails, Facebook and all the newspapers to which I still subscribed—the *L.A. Times*, *Washington Post*, and the *New York Times*. After getting my fill of news I needed some food in the tummy. After a quick shower I went back to Denny's for the Grand Slam breakfast. It would hold me until dinner.

Truth or Consequences was the county seat of Sierra County, New Mexico, with a small population of less than six thousand year-round residents. Founded in the late 1800s, it was a popular vacation resort because of its hot springs, for which it was originally named. However, it didn't grow dramatically until the construction of the Elephant Butte Dam and Reservoir, part of an early large-scale irrigation effort made in the early twentieth century.

The city of Hot Springs had changed its name to Truth or Consequences, the title of a popular NBC radio and TV program. In March, 1950, the host, Ralph Edwards, announced it would air the tenth anniversary show from the first town that renamed itself after the program. City officials jumped at the chance of such great publicity, as the popularity of the natural hot springs had faded with the advent of pharmaceuticals.

My tour of the city showed me its Main Street was divided into two one-ways in opposite directions, and the stores and buildings on that street were painted in various pastel colors.

First I went to the Spaceport America Center and snuck in a few minutes before closing time. Dolores, a lady I guessed to be in her seventies, said she would stick around and close after I left. There was no one else in the Center and I quickly reviewed the exhibits and promotions for the FAA-licensed spaceport. It's located on eighteen thousand acres in the New Mexico desert adjacent to the White Sands Missile Range, about twenty miles southeast of Truth or Consequences. I enjoyed how the exhibits were geared to educate visitors about space. Most were aimed at the children, although this adult was enthralled. Various photos and paintings of Virgin Galactic's coming efforts to take paying customers into space hung in full view. I could only imagine what it would be like to experience weightlessness and appreciate the sight of this big blue marble from such a distance. Although delayed due to an accident, it appeared that they would soon be flying, and I made a note to come back. Maybe someday I'd buy a ticket and make that ride, I mused. Then I laughed out loud, thinking I'd have to win the Lotto to afford it.

I left the Center and came back to Main Street, parking the big old boat of a car in an empty space. It was quiet, as you would expect on a Sunday afternoon. I walked down and back, past the post office, reading signs posted along the way, and learned more about this quaint town in the middle of nowhere. I strolled by the Hot Springs Bathhouse and saw a billboard about the Healing Waters Trail. A map of the city showed it sitting along the Rio Grande. At Las Palomas Plaza, adjacent to the Geronimo Springs Museum, I read that I was standing on "an historic spot where people came to relieve their aches and pains by soaking in the healing hot waters."

I went into the Museum and read the entire story of the city's benefactor, Ralph Edwards. I learned more about the man who hosted the famous radio and tv show for which the city was named.

Geronimo and his exploits and encounters were a big part of the history of this area. Fascinated, I saw exhibits of the history of the Apache tribes here in New Mexico. I read *The Legend of the Apache Tear*. When Indian warriors leapt to their death rather letting the Spanish invaders capture them and turn them into slaves, the tears of their wives turned into stone. The stones were meant to be carried by young lovers for good luck.

I kept moving on through the museum, appreciating exhibits exploring the cowboy in the west. Various displays of hats, branding irons, saddles, and tools were in one room, and samples of distinctive pottery, arrow heads and arrows filled glass cases. There was even a replica of a bank teller's window circa 1917. It had bars, like those you see in a western movie. Antique typewriters from Underwood and Remington sat nearby.

It was a fascinating, moving display, especially the history of the Native Americans and the white man now claiming the land as their own. The Apaches hadn't stood a chance.

One of my pet peeves these days is about how we write and glorify our history to make this country seem so wonderful and exceptional. As a child studying the American west, I learned that reaching for our Manifest Destiny was paramount. This visit, however, taught me more truth about the horrors our ancestors perpetrated.

Like any soul who has lost its way, I yearn for the day when, in the United States of America, we can have these discussions and acknowledge how wrong we were. Or, at the very least, begin to take responsibility for our ancestors' errors. From the extinction of Native Americans, to enslaving an entire race. That continues even today in various forms of racism, disguised within the law.

I walked back to the car and drove back to the motel, stopping by Ralph Edwards Park for a quick tour. Deep in thought, I was disturbed and upset by what I'd read, and seen in the Museum.

The sky was lightening now, the rain abating, and it was almost dinner time. I went back into my room and checked on the weather. Flight Service confirmed all was go and it was clear to Santa Monica. My only issue would be thunderstorms heading southward from the Arizona mountains to Phoenix in the early afternoon. The briefer made it clear I'd need an early departure for smooth flying. I was planning to fly direct to Demming, then on to Tuscon and into Goodyear Airport in Phoenix where I would refuel.

Depending on the winds, I might be able to make Santa Monica nonstop from there. I would have enough choices enroute to refuel either in Palm Springs or Riverside when entering the L.A. basin, if I was running low on petrol.

I hung up and decided to eat an early dinner next door at Johnny B's, a local haunt, where I had a delicious dinner of home-made fried chicken, mashed potatoes and salad. The service was delightful. Everyone was friendly and warm, noticing my Santa Monica AYSO *Coach Bob* jacket and asking about me and what I was doing here. It made for a pleasant meal and cemented the good vibes and feelings I had about this town. Someday I would return.

Back in my room, I watched TV until I was tired enough to turn out the light before nine p.m. I wanted to get to the airport by seven the next morning for an early start. It would be another long day of flying — and then I would finally be back home, completing my Journey.

I would make sure to talk with Two Niner Lima bright and early before departure to make sure we did.

CHAPTER XXXI

——————————————→✈

BACK TO SOCAL
LEG SIX
TCS – GYR – SMO

September 16, 2019

Truth or Consequences, NM, to Phoenix Goodyear Airport, Goodyear, AZ, to refuel, then to Santa Monica Airport, Santa Monica, CA

TCS-GYR

Route: TCS Direct DMN (Demming) Direct AVQ (Marana Regional Airport, Tuscon, AZ) Direct GYR

Distance: 332 nm GYR-SMO

Route: GYR Direct PSP Direct SMO

Distance: 324 nm

Total Distance: 656 nm

Start time (TCS): 7:22:27 a.m. Wheels up: 7:38:15 a.m.

Wheels down: 9:24:20 a.m.

Shut-Down time (GYR): 9:26:25 a.m.

Log Entry: Time Logged: 3.1 hrs. FlightTime: 2.6 hrs.
Early a.m. departure. Smooth Air. @6,500′ up to 10,500′ @ TUC.
Nice landing R-3.
Start time (GYR): 10:11:23 a.m. Wheels up: 10:16:25 a.m.
Wheels down: 1:02:44 p.m. Shut-Down time (SMO): 1:05:29 p.m.

Log Entry: Time Logged: 2.9 hrs. Flight Time: 2.7 hrs.
Quick re-fuel to avoid thunderstorms. Climb to 6,500′ then to
8,500′ @ PSP. Almost 3 gals. reserve. Issue: Class B airspace with
LAX Approach.

Before I shut the lights off to get some sleep, I realized that if all went well tomorrow, I would be back in Santa Monica, back to where the Journey began. I was stoked and, wouldn't you know it? Sleep took forever, as my mind raced and wandered, thinking about flying back to familiar scenery and locations, and finally getting home. I felt rejuvenated by the Journey. My confidence was back, and my spirit was soaring.

I awoke early and confirmed with Flight Service the good weather awaiting me. It was clear all the way, except for some thunderstorms drifting southward from the northern Arizona mountains. If I left the Phoenix area by noon, I should have no problems. I would need an early morning departure—no later than eight a.m.

As usual, I was up early enough to make it so. After taking another look at my iPad and confirming with Flight Service and Foreflight that we were good to go, I quickly showered. I was at the complimentary breakfast by 5:50 a.m. where I greeted Emily and her Mom a hearty good morning. A bowl of cereal, some fruit, and a cup of coffee was enough to get me started.

Back in my room, I packed up, then loaded my bags in the Town Car. I departed the Travelodge® at 6:30 a.m. on the dot, all business-like and prepared. The sun, just starting to come up, was lighting up the New Mexico mountains. In this crystal-clear morning there wasn't a cloud in the sky.

There was no rush hour traffic—really no traffic at all, so early out on the Interstate, and I pulled up to Two Niner Lima a few minutes before seven a.m. Randy had given me the gate code, and I drove onto the tarmac, parked near Two Niner Lima and unloaded my bags.

Before I unbuckled her cover, I looked around, taking a deep breath, relaxing myself before I began the day in earnest. I looked out at the airport, still as it was. No one was in sight. How I loved these mornings, whether getting ready to fly, or even sipping coffee on my couch at home before anyone is up, the world my own.

Today I was reveling in the peaceful quiet and my pending (assuming all goes well) completion of this amazing Journey.

There were wisps of cirrus clouds high in the sky, reportedly at twenty-five thousand feet. The morning air was cool but there was a hot summer day coming. From the slowly increasing daylight I could see the ball of sun ready to pop up and over the horizon, right behind the mountains. I took a picture, as the peaceful solitude captured my final moment of return so well.

I patted Two Niner Lima on her red snout and proclaimed, "Going home today, girl! You ready?" I could have sworn I heard her let out a chuckle and a gleeful, "All right!" We both knew it was time and we were ready to go.

I unsnapped the cover tabs and took off her cover, folding it up for stowaway. Unlocking the canopy, I slid it back. Then I undid the gust lock, and took my iPhone, iPad, and Stratus 3 from my small duffel bag and put them on the glare shield.

Randy had filled up all four tanks and my walk-around was perfunctory and methodical. I was a tad low on oil and made a note to add some at GYR, then went through my preflight chores. Despite my excitement to be getting home, I was still making sure to stay disciplined and focused as I discharged my duties.

I quickly scribbled a note to Randy, hopped out of Two Niner Lima, and slid the note under the door. I was grateful for his kindness and wanted him to know the difference he'd made to this stranger. A bit smitten by the vibe I'd experienced in this out-of-the-way place, I wanted to come back and do some more exploring.

I walked around the left side of the small terminal building, which was still locked in the early morning hours, back to the outdoor Porta Johnny to go to the bathroom one last time before departing to GYR. It would be almost 3 hours of flying time and, as my friend Charlie always advised, "Never pass up a bathroom."

I smiled with thoughts of my very best friend back in New York, and all my friends who loved and nourished me this summer on my Journey.

Now ready, I climbed into Two Niner Lima, buckled in, fitted my headset, and got ready to start her up. I set up the iPad in its cradle on the yoke and placed the Stratus 3 in its holder on the dash but couldn't get the iPhone holder to stick to the cold window. After a few tries, I decided to hand-hold my phone for pictures and videos.

Before I started going through the check list, I paused to take one last look at the New Mexico mountains. That ball of sun was now just peeking over them and the western sky was beginning to glow as big as ever.

"Lord, dear God, get us home now" I prayed aloud. "We're ready. I ask for your courage and strength to guide us safely this last day of flying. Amen."

I felt so connected to everything and everyone now. I'm still not sure what it was all about, but I knew my Journey had brought me back to Me again. I was renewed and felt my strength and belief in Me again restored. I felt a sense of peace and calm, unusual for this pilot disciplined to be on his toes.

"Just get us home safely. Okay, Two Niner Lima, you ready to go?"

I went through the checklist. Slowly and surely, despite the budding excitement, I was on top of my game today. Two Niner Lima turned over on the very first downward swing of her prop.

She, too, was ready.

I taxied away from the terminal and out to Runway 31. AWOS was reporting the winds relatively calm.

Our run-up went smoothly and Two Niner Lima seemed perkier than usual, or perhaps it was just my few days away from the left seat. Maybe I was projecting my eagerness to get home onto her. Our attachment symbiotic, a pilot and his airplane.

I adjusted the mixture for the density altitude. We had a runway of over seventy-two hundred feet, and we had done this before. I had no doubts this day returning home.

Over the Unicom I announced my intentions, with no other aircraft in sight. We took Runway 31 and off we went, accelerating smoothly. I kept Two Niner Lima down, and when I was at seventy-five knots (ten knots greater than my normal rotation speed) I pulled back ever so slightly on the yoke. Two Niner Lima leaped off the concrete and gathered speed, climbing rapidly in the cool, morning air.

We turned on course, heading south to Demming, and settled down at eighty-five hundred feet as our cruise altitude, in contact with Albuquerque Center for Flight Following advisories. It was a beautiful morning, the air was like glass, and Two Niner Lima and I were enjoying the sights. We were showing a ground speed of 120+ knots which would give us almost four gallons in reserve for landing at GYR, just within my limit. Three or less is time for worry but the Garmin 530 and Foreflight were both indicating we would be fine. I made a note to worry about that and keep checking the headwinds and the reserve projection, or otherwise, a stop in Demming might be in order.

As we flew away from TCS I got a much better view of Elephant Butte Lake. Nestled up against the mountains, it stretched out almost forty miles long, sitting five miles north of the town. It was one of the largest man-made lakes in the United States and afforded much summer relief to many in the arid desert region of New Mexico.

We droned on with no issues, passing Demming off our left-hand side. I thought back to my first stop there when I saw the airport on the west side of town. I was able to pick out those three huge hangars on the south side of the airport boundary line, now being used in all sorts of, dare I say, nefarious and horrific ways.

We were now on a heading of 266 degrees, heading almost directly west when a band of puffy cumulus clouds confronted us. With the mountains of Tucson in the distance, I held us at eighty-five hundred feet as we passed over them. The air remained smooth with hardly a ripple.

Albuquerque Center handed us over to Tucson Approach.

We were proceeding direct to AVQ (Tucson Marana Regional Airport). Then we would head up to GYR on the western side of greater metropolitan Phoenix, or the Valley of the Sun as the locals call it. It's a cavernous valley lying in the Sonoran Desert. Re- fueling at GYR on the west side of the Valley instead of CHD far on the east side of the Valley would give us a true shot at a non-stop flight from GYR to SMO. Yes, the Valley was that big.

In front of us was the Rincon Mountain range and I aimed Two Niner Lima to pass between Rincon Peak and Mount Lemmon through the Reddington Pass. The terrain was rising so I requested and was granted climb up to ten thousand, five hundred feet.

As we went through the mountain pass, we passed by Davis Monthan Air Force Base. Adjacent was Tucson International and the view was spectacular from up high. The runways were laid out in intersecting symmetry, the many jets in storage also there, standing by, hoping for a chance again to be up in the sky.

Approach queried my destination and had me turn right fifteen degrees to stay away from the protected airspace for those two facilities. Foreflight on my iPad showed me well out of the control zone by a good distance, but there are so many aircraft are coming and going, and the controller can see them all. Without hesitation, I immediately complied, and skimmed the western edge of the mountains I had just come through. I was heading northwest now.

As we passed AVQ off to our left my thoughts went back to my first leg on our Journey. I looked far north and through the morning haze I could make out Phoenix in the distance, less than seventy miles away. When Tucson Approach handed us off to Phoenix, I began planning my approach.

I tuned in the ATIS for Goodyear Tower and got the current weather. Then I punched up Phoenix Approach to advise that I got the information with my first call after the hand-off. Controllers want to know you have the weather information for your destination. Most importantly, it reveals you're no rookie. Rookies, or other non-professionals, can get treated like second-class citizens over the airways. Getting low on fuel, I couldn't afford any delays getting into GYR.

"Phoenix Approach, Grumman Two Niner Lima, ten thousand, five hundred with Yankee."

"Good morning, Grumman Two Niner Lima. Phoenix Approach. Descend and maintain forty-five hundred at your discretion. How do you intend to transit Class Bravo airspace?"

"Roger, Phoenix. Grumman Two Niner Lima, leaving ten thousand five hundred for forty-five hundred. Will transit to GYR from the west."

GYR sat right on the edge of the Terminal Control area, and I would have to go way down to get under the altitude restrictions by coming from the west.

We were all set now. I pegged Two Niner Lima at a leisurely descent rate of five hundred feet per minute and got us down to forty-five hundred feet. GYR was now coming up, sitting just behind some jagged small mountains a few thousand feet high. I debated how to get around or over them.

The Controller interrupted my hesitation. "Grumman Two Niner Lima, descend to three thousand and contact Goodyear Tower at 120.1."

"Roger, Grumman Two Niner Lima, over to Goodyear, 120.1."

With that instruction, I chose to head towards the west as they were landing on Runway 3. By going that way, I would clear those small mountains and make a right base entry.

As I lined up on my base entry, I saw them right in front of me—huge cumulus clouds, boiling upwards, but still far away. Not far enough away to kick up some winds as they slowly moved southward, but enough to keep me on my toes as I turned final. We were right on the money. I slowed Two Niner Lima down now, to ninety-five knots as we rolled out on our final approach, facing into the wind. I deployed full flaps, trimming Two Niner Lima nose up to our target final approach speed of ninety knots.

The wind was no problem for us. We were too close to home now to mess it up and, as I flared Two Niner Lima, slightly raising her nose, I kicked out right rudder to straighten out. I lowered my left wing, slipping Two Niner Lima with the opposite rudder slightly pushed down and into the wind — and we touched down with a perfect landing. That was one of my most challenging pilot chores: flying into a crosswind, slipping, then aiming to touch down on the windward main wheel first. And yes, our landing was that sweet, confirmed when we got that kiss of the wheels as we rolled out.

I retracted the flaps as we exited Runway 3 at taxiway A(lpha) 4 and then approved on to A(lpha) after advising Ground Control I wanted to go to Lux Air Jet Center for fuel.

Lux Air must have heard my communication with Ground Control. As I approached the beige southwest-themed building, I saw the familiar linesman poised in front of a transient parking spot directing us to him. I proceeded down the tarmac and swung around facing him as he brought his arms up and crossed, signaling me to stop. As I shut down Two Niner Lima, a fuel truck drove up and the driver got out and asked if I needed fuel.

"Yes, sir. Top off all four tanks, please."

"Where you in from?" asked the young man. He seemed more like a teenager than a seasoned veteran experienced in handling this work.

"Oh, this morning? From Truth or Consequences, New Mexico. Just completing my round-trip across the country for the summer. Heading back to Santa Monica now."

"Wow! You flew this?" It was always the same perplexed inquiry. I wondered how Two Niner Lima felt by the temerity of those who dared question her abilities, never mind her stamina.

"Yes, sir, I sure did. Just a bunch of small cross-country trips, back-to-back." He was in his early twenties, tops, so I decided to ask more. "You a pilot?"

"Not yet, sir. Learning now. Almost ready for my private checkride. What kind of plane is this?"

"It's a Grumman Yankee, the trainer version of the Grummans. Have you ever flown a Grumman Tiger?"

"No. All we have here are Diamonds."

"Well, if you get the chance, take it. I learned in a Tiger. They really put Cessnas and Pipers to shame. Great handling, and this puppy, well, I put in a bigger engine and it's my little rocket ship." As I talked with him, I shut down all my equipment, took my iPhone and iPad with me, and clambered down. I was looking back at the thunderstorms approaching and didn't like what I saw.

"Bad weather's coming, huh?" I inquired.

"Yeah—looks like in a few hours we should get some serious rain." The youngster had already affixed the grounding cable attachment to the muffler and was pulling out the hose to get the refueling done. I always loved that attachment. It had serious jagged clamps with teeth, always reminding me of some predator looking for a meal.

"What's your name?" I asked, holding out my hand.

"Leo," he said as we shook. "Nice to meet you."

"Bob Young. Pleasure is mine, sir. Thanks for your help. Better get myself moving here if I want to beat the weather."

He waved as I trundled off. He had just begun fueling the first tank on the right wing. When I was younger I had thought, as I still do today, what fun it would be to work at the airport, guiding the planes in and refueling them. Ah, anything to be around airplanes. I smiled. Leo was doing just that and learning to fly.

The terminal had a western motif entry, almost like a western saloon, with a covered front porch and big sign above it that announced, *Phoenix Goodyear Airport*. It was not as rich and luxurious looking as others I had visited but it had more than enough leather couches and chairs.

I made my way to the men's room where I washed the morning heat off my face and neck. It was getting hot, and I had almost three hours of flying time across the California desert before me. Despite the clouds coming, I decided to pause and refresh with some complimentary water, a candy bar and an apple I had taken from my morning breakfast at the Travelodge®.

My thoughts now were about the last and final leg of our Journey. I was feeling nostalgic about the summer and the entire adventure, almost done. I was also excited that I would be completing the round-trip, getting back to where it all started a few months before. I felt extremely proud to have accomplished the mission, Two Niner Lima handled it with such aplomb and, to tell you the truth, I am simply blown away that I had flown so far and back, all in Two Niner Lima, without a hiccup.

We were now on the verge of making it so. Jean Luc is smiling.

Now back in familiar territory, I reviewed my flight plan from GYR to SMO. I knew this desert. The beige, almost white sand and light brown mountains always comforted me.

I would fly direct to Blythe at sixty-five hundred feet then direct to Palm Springs. Rising terrain there would make us go up to eighty-five hundred feet. We would stop for fuel at PSP or in Riverside once through the Banning Pass, if necessary.

Piece of pie—we had done this before, a few times over my flying years.

In fact, I knew we would be just fine when I realized GYR had the same runways and same tower frequency as SMO. Runway 3-21. 120.1. Talk about a coincidence? No, that was a good sign for sure.

The Universe was with us today.

Leo came in with the fuel information and gave it to Alice, the receptionist at the front desk. She also asked about Two Niner Lima and where I had been. As I waited for her to tell me how much I owed Lux Air, I shared my Journey. She must have appreciated the smile I was wearing. I was grinning from ear to ear.

"Well, young man, that's quite the adventure you've had."

"It was the dream of a lifetime," I replied. "Ever since I bought my plane, I've wanted to do it. Can't believe I'm almost home."

"You should be awfully proud. Sounds like it was a terrific summer."

"It sure was, Miss Alice. It sure was."

I signed the credit card slip, still smiling, then walked out the door onto the tarmac and over to Two Niner Lima.

In a few more hours, I would be home, and I was excited as one could be after being away for so long. It was, in fact, the longest time I'd been away from SoCal since I moved to Los Angeles in 1973. Now back in familiar territory, and seeing the desert, it hit me that I had missed my home very much.

I cautioned myself against feeling too giddy at this moment.

"Last leg. Pay attention!"

When I got to Two Niner Lima, I reminded her as well. "Okay, girl. Last leg. Let's make it so!" I patted her on the nose and did a walk-around, the second one of the day. Then I removed the chocks Leo had put out and slid into the left seat.

As I went through the check list I realized I was moving too fast, doing things almost by rote. The words were not registering, but my instinct from many years' habit was moving me through my tasks. I took a deep breath.

"Slow down, Bozo!" I admonished myself. Careful not to let my enthusiasm overtake me, I did a slower, more meticulous reading of each item.

Two Niner Lima didn't hesitate when I engaged the starter, promptly turning over as the first blade on the prop moved downward. She was ready.

I flipped on all the radios, got the ATIS information, checked in with Ground for taxi instructions and further requested Flight Following back to Santa Monica. I was cleared to taxi via Taxiway A(l-pha) to Taxiway A(lpha) 7 for a Runway 3 intersection departure.

As I taxied out and down Taxiway A(lpha), I passed United Airlines' 737 Max fleet parked in the infield. Some twenty were grounded there until the FAA and politics would grant them a new lease. While Boeing did shortcut the certification process, it was curious that no USA pilot flying this equipment for multiple carriers had any problems, but foreign carriers and their pilots did. The contention that it came down to flight training was a valid argument. However, that didn't excuse the manufacturer from not disclosing to pilots who would fly the newly certificated aircraft about the automated system they built had caused fatal crashes.

Ground Control broke into my thoughts. "Grumman Two Niner Lima, Ground. We have your clearance. Ready to copy?"

"Ground, Grumman Two Niner Lima, stand by."

I wanted to get down to the intersection and in position to do my run-up before writing down my clearance. Another few seconds and I was there, positioned, brakes on.

"Ground, Grumman Two Niner Lima ready to copy clearance."

"Roger, Grumman Two Niner Lima is cleared out of the Class B(ravo) airspace. After departure, maintain VFR. Altitude at your discretion. Contact Phoenix Departure on 120.7. Squawk 2648."

I repeated the clearance back to the Ground Controller.

As I was doing our run-up making sure Two Niner Lima was all set to go again, I noticed clouds off to my left, moving closer now. We would be making a left downwind departure, heading out on a course of 267 degrees to SMO, scooting fifty or so miles away from them. The wind was now at twelve knots, gusting to eighteen, with the storm coming closer. I made a note to adjust for that on takeoff.

Run-up complete, we were ready.

Tower cleared us for immediate takeoff, and we were up quickly with lots of runway to spare. I flew straight out, crabbing into the wind as we climbed on the runway heading until I reached one thousand feet above ground level, turned crosswind and then onto the downwind, still climbing. As I reached mid-field and began my right turn to my course to SMO, Tower advised me to contact Phoenix departure.

I did as instructed and we continued west, climbing to sixty-five hundred feet. I was happy but also worried that maybe I was too happy. I was getting more excited as familiar territory passed by. *Keep breathing*, I reminded myself. The sky, the ground, the beige desert colors, all said *home*. I was also very curious about how I would feel when got near SMO in the L.A. basin.

The good news was that we had a bit of a tail wind now. We were getting far away enough from those thunderstorms marching south to Phoenix so that the counterclockwise rotation of the low-pressure area moving southward was giving us a push westward. I was reading on the Garmin 530 and Foreflight via the Stratus 3 a groundspeed of 136 knots. The JPI Fuel Monitor showed an estimated reserve of almost four-plus gallons into SMO. I made a note to confirm that reserve when we were coming up to Palm Springs and then decide go or no-go all the way to Santa Monica.

When we leveled off at our cruising altitude, Phoenix Departure handed us off to Albuquerque Center. We made it through Arizona and as we entered California airspace, Albuquerque directed us to contact L.A. Center.

We passed Blythe and then I saw the green fields of the Imperial Valley. In the distance to the south, the Salton Sea stretched for its length of thirty miles. These familiar sights were comforting and I took plenty of pictures as we cruised by, then entered the Coachella Valley.

L.A. Center handed us over to Palm Springs Approach who cautioned me about rising terrain. I requested climb up to eighty-five hundred feet, which was granted.

It was a joy to see the desert and, as I had many times before, I picked out Bermuda Dunes Airport (UDD) We droned westward. Rancho Mirage sat nestled against the Santa Rosa Mountains, and Palm Springs was smack up against Mount San Jacinto, with its airport (PSP) reposing on the west side of town.

My reserve was showing almost 4.6 gallons remaining on arrival at SMO. Realizing I would make it home with enough fuel, I decided not to stop anywhere for refueling. I knew I had "get-home- itis" but I was following the book, meeting my required fuel reserve of half an hour flying time for VFR (Visual Flight Rules), so no further concern now.

Palm Springs Approach had its hands full and was calling out conflicting traffic coming through the Banning Pass. As I entered the pass, Approach instructed me for about ten minutes to stay north of the freeway. Inbound traffic was directed to stay on the south side of the freeway. I was busy looking for traffic, which I never saw, but bounced about by the winds in the pass, I felt those butterflies kick up again. The turbulence was giving us some good moderate jolts (moderate defined as rapid bumps without appreciable changes in the aircraft's altitude or attitude).

Palm Springs bid us farewell as we neared the end of the Pass and we contacted L.A. Approach. As we exited the Banning Pass, the air smoothed. There, in the distance, almost one hundred miles away, I saw the faint outline of the Los Angeles skyline.

Before, in front of me, was the entire LA Basin. I was stunned. I was here. We did it!

I took out my iPhone and made a video for my followers:

"Well, kids, you're not going to believe it! I am in the L.A. Basin! I can't believe it myself. I flew back to the east coast and now I'm coming into the Basin. Right now, thirty-three minutes from Santa Monica. We will not need a fuel stop. We'll have a full reserve of almost twenty-five minutes. And, I'm just grinning from ear to ear. I really can't believe it. I'm so happy—what can I say! L.A., baby— here you go!"

For the video I scanned the Basin so everyone could see what I was seeing.

Trying to keep my calm I focused on the task at hand. But as I peered through the L.A. haze, I felt such pride of accomplishment that I persevered.

I felt so good about Me—that I had shown an indominable spirit of strength and courage, lifting myself out of my doldrums and flying Two Niner Lima to Connecticut and back.

Despite what the Universe dumped on me, I am not going to be stopped. And home was now but half an hour away.

I passed by Riverside Airport, one of the very first airports I had visited when learning to fly. Then I headed to the north side of the basin, where I flew over Ontario Airport and direct to the Pomona VOR. I would enter the L.A. Class B(ravo) airspace as I always had coming from the east when flying VFR. When I got to Dodger Stadium, I would request to either get down to twenty-five hundred feet or proceed along the Santa Monica Mountains at forty-five hundred feet. The stadium was a waypoint at which I'd need to contact Santa Monica tower. It had served as a demarcation point for me since I learned how to fly in air-traffic congested Los Angeles.

Time to get us ready for descent and landing. I tuned in the SMO ATIS. Off to my right and ahead, I could see through the Cahuenga Pass into the San Fernando Valley. Time to get down.

"L.A. Approach, Grumman Two Niner Lima. Leaving eighty-five hundred feet for forty-five hundred, with Tango. Request clearance into Class B(ravo)."

"Grumman Two Niner Lima, clearance denied."

I didn't understand. I'd never heard that before and was taken aback. I would be more accurate with my request.

"Approach, Grumman Two Niner Lima inbound Santa Monica with Tango. Request clearance and descent to twenty-five hundred, direct."

"Grumman Two Niner Lima, clearance denied."

Now I was really confused. This never, ever, happened before. I stared at the Sectional Map on my iPad, trying to see if I was missing something. Did anything change in the four months I'd been gone? I saw nothing different than I'd seen in all the years I had been flying.

By this time, I was about ten miles from Dodger Stadium, which I could see clearly, and I could see downtown L.A. It looked as it had when I departed, and I could make out all the buildings succinctly defined. How the skyline had grown since I'd first arrived here fresh out of law school in 1973.

I didn't know what to do. Obviously, the Controller had a reason for refusing my clearance but I had no idea why he was so adamant and gave no explanation. It made me think I'd made some error in my request but I drew a blank as to what it could have been.

He must want me to proceed along the mountains at forty-five hundred feet and duck under the ceiling of that section once I passed the observatory. That would set me up for a straight-in approach to Runway 21.

I turned Two Niner Lima slightly to the right and proceeded at the correct altitude. When I passed Griffith Observatory and saw my path to SMO laid out, I tried again.

"Approach, Grumman Two Niner Lima. Request entry into Class B(ravo) direct Santa Monica."

"Grumman Two Niner Lima, clearance denied."

The JPI fuel analyzer was flashing. I now had just three point three gallons for my reserve. I could not fly out to the coastline and back, as fuel was now becoming a concern.

A serious concern.

I was befuddled and fear rose in my gut. Those damn butterflies were flapping again!

Real hard.

Then I realized what I must do. The pilot is the Pilot in Command, in charge of his aircraft and what's needed to maintain flight safety. If an emergency exists, he has the full authority of Federal Aviation regulations to override a controller's instructions.

"Approach, Grumman Two Niner Lima declaring an emergency. We are low on fuel. Turning direct to Santa Monica and descending."

Without giving him a chance to reply, I punched up Santa Monica Tower, set up in COMM 2 as previously prepared for our descent and landing.

"Santa Monica Tower, Grumman Two Niner Lima, inbound for landing with Tango. Just passing the observatory, leaving four thousand five hundred, descending. Request straight in Runway 21. We are low on fuel and declaring an emergency. Request priority."

"Grumman Two Niner Lima, Roger. Cleared to land, Runway 21, straight-in approved.

Do you need any help?"

"No—I think we have just enough fuel to make it, but I have to get us down now."

"Roger, Grumman Two Niner Lima. You are number one. Wind 240 at 8. Runway 21, cleared to land."

"Grumman Two Niner Lima, roger." I clicked the microphone twice. Tower understood. One of its own was almost home.

I pulled the power back to the approach setting I normally use in the pattern and started to get Two Niner Lima slowed down and ready for landing. I trimmed nose up to begin bleeding off the excess airspeed, and as we slowed, I dropped out the first notch of flaps, getting Two Niner Lima set up at one hundred five knots.

We were coming up to L.A.'s Twin Towers of Century City.

It was then I saw Runway 21. By now, the City of Santa Monica had chopped off seven hundred fifty feet from each end of the runway, reducing it down to thirty-five hundred feet from its original five thousand foot strip. The city had done this dirty deed to reduce, if not eliminate, most of the jet traffic into this historic airport.

Surprised, I cringed when I saw the shortened runway. Part of what was once runway was now dirt. I clicked on the microphone transmit button.

"What the hell did they do to the runway?" I asked, not trying to hide my disgust.

Silence ensued as I continued on the approach. I deployed full flaps as I passed Century City, now less than a mile from touchdown. More nose trim and power down to 1700 rpm, five hundred feet per minute descent rate.

"Last transmission unreadable," came from control. "Somebody say something?"

"Roger, Grumman Two Niner Lima. Just a bit shocked by seeing what they did to the runway. Returning after four months away."

"Understand, Grumman Two Niner Lima. We all are as well."

I clicked the transmit button twice again. We both understood and seemed to agree. It was a shame what the City of Santa Monica had done to its historic jewel of an airport.

We were all set up now. As I passed over the airport boundary and then the dirt where the full length of Runway 21 had been, I concentrated on my landing point and my airspeed.

Two Niner Lima slowly settled down and, as I passed over the numbers, we gently touched down. It was a good landing. I'd remembered to look to the end of the runway when flaring.

Two Niner Lima rolled out all the way down Runway 21. I was in no rush to exit quickly at Taxiway A(lpha) 3, which would have meant hitting the brakes hard. Besides, I was enjoying the scenery of the airport again, looking around at the familiar sights, finally back home. I retracted the flaps, slid the canopy back to get some fresh, SoCal air, and took it all in, even down to peering all the way out to the Pacific Ocean. From where, high on this plateau of the Santa Monica Airport, one hundred seventy-five feet above sea level, it was visible from the left seat of Two Niner Lima.

We exited at Taxiway A(lpha) 4, which was right in front of Proteus Aviation at the west end of the field.

"Ground, Grumman Two Niner Lima, off Runway 21 at Alpha, taxi Proteus."

"Roger, Grumman Two Niner Lima, taxi Proteus. Welcome home."

"Taxi Proteus. Good to be back. Two Niner Lima."

We slowly taxied until we passed the fuel pumps, then made a left turn into the tie-down spaces adjacent to Proteus. Our home space was Space 821 and I pulled into it, taxied back toward the edge of the pavement, then swung Two Niner Lima around to face the mountains, right on the painted T on the pavement, the wings right above each tie-down chain. I couldn't stop smiling.

We were home.

I shut down Two Niner Lima, shut off the iPad, shut off the Stratus 3, taking each out of their respective holder. Pulling the canopy further back, I took a deep breath, appreciating the warmth of the sunshine.

I got out and took pictures of Two Niner Lima back home. My favorite was my arm around her nose. I could swear we both looked damn proud of ourselves.

Phyllis had invited me to stay at her home for a while and was taking an Uber over to greet me. Bruce and Dolly had their son and his girlfriend with them, so Camarillo was out. I had texted her of my estimated time of touch down. Sure enough, she arrived just a few minutes after I shut down.

We waved to one another as she walked slowly out to me; she had been battling a recent flareup of her psoriatic arthritis and was encountering some difficulty walking. I had promised to stay with her and help her out for a while.

Phyllis had tried to start my car a few weeks before but had no luck so I knew the battery was not good and I would have to call Triple A for a re-charge. I took my bags out of Two Niner Lima and put them in the back seat of the car. After the jump start, I went home with Phyllis, unloaded my bags (without shutting off the car), then drove it back to my mechanic, V & S Auto Services, right across the street from the airport. I took an Uber back to my new digs.

Capt. Bob and Two Niner Lima were back in SoCal.

Home.

EPILOGUE DEBRIEFING

A good pilot always needs to debrief after a flight, to recognize where he might have messed up, where he needs improvement, and what he might have learned.

Bill Beecher ingrained a fundamental premise of flying in his student:

"As a pilot, you are always a student and always are learning. It never stops. You never stop."

Each and every flight would be a test of my proficiency, currency and flying skills, he said. "And then you'll review your strengths and weaknesses, what you could have done better or not done at all, and how you'll become as much a part of every flight as the airplane itself."

This summer our Journey was no different.

The Trip
May 28, 2019 – September 16, 2019
Eastbound:
May 28, 2019 – July 9, 2019
SMO-AVQ-CHD-DMN-ROW-ABI-ADS-SGR-
NEW-ABY-MYR-ILM- FFA-ORF-CDW-DXR
29.9 hrs. - 3,052 nm

Westbound:

August 28, 2019 – September 16, 2019

**DXR-AGC-VLL-SBN-PIAI-MKC-OIN-LMO-LVS-TCS-GYR-
SMO**

28.5 hrs.

2,713 nm

Totals:

58.4 hrs.

5,765 nm

**26 Airports. 26 different locations. Across the continent and back.
Almost 6,000 miles flown.**

I was, and still am, so very proud of Me.

I was, and still am, amazed that I did all this in Two Niner Lima. She is certainly not your typical cross-country airplane, built to be a trainer, not a cross-country machine. But Two Niner Lima performed so well and carried me to new horizons in my discoveries and renewal, without hesitation or breakdown.

On the trip, I encountered new weather experiences. Flying out west as I have done until this Journey was a snap. Weather was hardly ever an issue. But, once we got past the desert southwest and into New Mexico and Texas (going there and back) being on my toes about the weather was a must.

The constant convective activity imposed new flight experiences—flying over and between the building clouds. I was thankful for my preparation and ForeFlight. With the on-board weather from the Stratus 3 on my iPad, it was a game-changer. Learning this new digital program made me a better, safer pilot, and my choice to fly VFR easier and safer.

I went through my logbook and reviewed entries and photos,

remembering each leg. I was pleased with my decisions, handling the instrument approach into ADS without issue, and acknowledged I'd done a good job avoiding the clouds and threading my way through them as needed.

I was particularly pleased about the day I diverted from Charleston, besieged by the Mother of all Thunderstorms stretched out and off my right wing. After threading my way amongst the build-up of clouds and breaking through the line as I descended into Myrtle Beach—lo and behold, there it was. The Atlantic Ocean. Even as I write those words, the same thrill and intensity of accomplishment of my aviation experience that day remains with me.

I dealt with the deadly beast of Get Home-itis reasonably well, except for the near fatal mistake trying to beat the weather into Tucson by flying over the New Mexico mountains. I am still upset that I had not recognized the symptoms of hypoxia sooner.

My only excuse—or rationalization—was that I rarely flew so high, but even that failed to assuage my disappointment as Pilot in Command.

However, I was, and am, one lucky guy. Someone up there is watching over me!

An angel, for sure.

And, as with any lesson, it is hopefully one I have learned and will not make the same mistake again.

Landing back at SMO was ecstasy. Coming back into the L.A. Basin, seeing the skyline and familiar sites, as well as being back on final for Runway 21, I was complete. I had-achieved my dream, coming full circle back home to SoCal, on final approach to Runway 21.

And how about Runway 3-21 at my home airport having the same Runway layout as First Flight America? Runway 3-21 at SMO where I learned to fly was in synchronicity with Devil's Hill, where flying all began.

As my friend Scott told me over a celebratory dinner after arriving home, "You belong in the air, Captain!"

I agree.

The Plane

It had been almost two months since I landed back at SMO. I was getting antsy, missing the traveling and adventures and being in the left seat of Two Niner Lima. I decided to head over and see her, give her a bath, long promised after her run-in with those nasty green mosquitos at NEW. Maybe I would even do a few touch-and-go's while I was at it.

It was a warm mid-November day, a SoCal end of summer kind of day in L.A. when you can feel winter is on the way. The chilly morning was giving way to the warm L.A. sun, and I was excited to get going. I packed a bucket with a bunch of rags and sponges, some Palmolive dishwashing detergent, and Windex and was out of the house by eleven a.m.

There is nothing like seeing your best buddy after far too long, and as I drove up to where she was sitting outside of Proteus in tiedown space 821, I was thrilled to see her.

"My Girl!" I exclaimed as I pulled up and parked, as always, deep into the space toward the rear. "How's my girl?"

Patting her warmly on her snout I could swear I caught her sheepish grin. I removed the chocks and tie-down chains, unlocked her, and grabbed the fuel sampler for my walk-around. It was good to be back. At the airport. With my fellow warrior.

Walk-around done, headphones on, seat belt secured, I ran through the checklist. I wasn't sure she had enough battery power left after so long, but when I turned on the Master, the gyros whirred loudly, the fuel pump worked fine, and all seemed ready to go.

Ignition switch was turned on.

I pressed the starter.

Engaged.

With a slight hesitation, her prop moved ever so slowly, then bingo! Only two downward turns and she fired up!

I sat there for about then minutes and let her idle, to get her juices flowing. I was taking in the scenery, looking north toward the Santa Monica Mountains. The sky, with all its high, western blue, showed not a cloud in sight.

I was where I needed to be.

Although I was a bit rusty going through the start-up, like I was at Danbury getting ready for the trip back to SoCal, the familiar comfort of the left seat was badly needed. And is still needed for nourishment. My spirits lifted. I understood me even better, the feeling of being where I belonged evident in my smile and the joy flowing through me.

The plane I had seen at the wash pit had gone, so I called Ground, got taxi permission to taxi over so I could give the girl a well-needed and warranted bath.

Here I was, in November, in shorts, washing my girl. I could swear she was laughing with delight. Like the little girl playing in the bathtub, Two Niner Lima was enjoying my efforts to make her sparkle. When I scrubbed those green mosquitoes off her, I was sure I heard, "Thank you. Much better now."

I had called Bill's Air to arrange for her annual inspection and we made an appointment for late December.

With Two Niner Lima bright and beaming in the afternoon sun, we taxied back to Tie-down Space 821. Worn out by the arduous scrubbing, I decided to forego flying.

As I locked her up and secured the tied-down chains and chocks under her wheels, I gave her probiscis a big hug and loving pats to let her know how much she meant to me and what a superb flying machine she had been on our Journey. Simply flawless.

Somehow, when I said good-bye, all I saw was her smile, acknowledging she knew and had done what she was supposed to do.

I couldn't have asked for anything more.

The Pilot

"Maybe the Journey isn't so much about becoming anything. Maybe it's about un-becoming everything that isn't really you So you can be who you were meant to be in the first place."

—Mark Okano on Instagram

I had come across this quotation of one of my former players, Mark Okano, who was on the Orange County Flyers and Na Koa Ikaika Maui teams. A native Hawaiian, Mark could stick and was a team leader in home runs. I knew him a bit better than most other players and found this sensitive soul aware and evolved, with a spiritual side deeper than most. So, coming across this advice after a bit of time back home, struck me as an accurate assessment of my experience.

I have had much time to contemplate the impact. After my ecstatic arrival, I am settled in at Phyllis' home and have slowly unwound from the excitement of my trip. I let my friends know I was back, although most saw from my post of Facebook that I had returned triumphantly. I talked to a few clients about work and explored prospects, taking on some things to generate a few pennies. My spirits were soaring, and I went balls out to take advantage of opportunities. To continue my recovery and resuscitation I had to create income and make a living.

But as is with any high, one comes down. It wasn't long before I experienced the let-down, and now the boredom of the daily routine gnawed at me. I did some legal work here and there, got some movie projects going with some clients, got back into my walking and lifting weights routine, and settled back into life in L.A.

The breadth and expanse of our country was as intense as it was expansive. It's there for all to see. It is a must see, whether by car or plane.

I was astonished by what I saw and so proud to be a citizen of this great land, but sad to see on returning to the ground, that we are losing our way. The noise and clatter increases.

Not at all like seeing the USA from the left seat, the quiet muffle of the engine in my headset droning steadily—the place where I'm at peace, in control, steering my magic carpet to where I needed to go. From the left seat, I could not see the divisions evident nor hear the cacophony of ranting sides. Just beautiful vistas of promise and bounty, the accomplishment of Manifest Destiny painted before me by our creations.

But now, back on the ground, I'm not so sure where any of us might go with the rancor and bitterness growing and our divisions widening like the San Andreas Fault, upset by the constant strains and rumbles. We are filled with so much noise, and the painful cries of anguish and dismay continue the unrest.

Choose, they say. Us or them.

What? Us or Them? We are all one. I saw it. Vast and expansive. Flourishing.

Skyscrapers abounding, stretching to the heavens. The countless communities. The endless farms. So many joined together under one flag.

E Pluribus Unum. Out of many, One.

Two Niner Lima and I encountered none of that personal vitriol and enmity I have experienced back on the ground.

The city noise and traffic were immediately off-putting. I yearned for the peace and solitude of the Rocky Mountains and realized that city life is a bit too much. My Journey had shown me so many tranquil spots like Longmont, New Mexico, and out in the country in Ventura and Central California, that appealed to my quest for a slower, quieter pace of life.

I realize more about Me. When I left, I was beaten, down on my luck, having lost my home and my savings. I was disgruntled and angry, not happy with myself or very many others, a misanthrope cursing the world and his circumstance. The challenge of crossing America and coming back changed all that, rewarding me with new-found spirit and confidence. Hell, I can do anything now. I flew this small, two-seat aircraft across the USA and back, over mountains, through and over clouds and storms, landing and taking off from twenty-six different airports, successfully transiting this broad land.

I have my confidence back. That much I know.

And I think I'm loving my Self again. I am no longer so angry at others. My disappointment in my failure and circumstances was overcome from what I experienced and felt with all my friends and the wonderful people I met along the way. From the hugs of Gia in Phoenix, to the love of Ronnie in Dallas making sure I was fine, to the warmth of Zeke and Martha and their home on Henry Clay Street in NOLA, to Andre's warm embrace on the tarmac at ILM, to Lynn and Sal in Pittsburgh and Alan and Mer and Joey in the Motor City, along with so many others. Every one sustained and nourished me.

Now, I was feeling fine, thank you. I realize how much love all the dear friends in these pages had shared with me, and I with them. Yes, they welcomed me into their homes and fed me, not only with meals, but most importantly and poignantly, from hearts filled with love for this wayward vagabond.

I was truly at peace, enjoying a tranquil heart and nourished soul, the love exchanged bursting within me.

But now, I'm feeling like a fish out of water. I'm missing the left seat and Two Niner Lima. Truth be said, the adventure and visits were all so invigorating that now, back to the city, buckling down to work and dealing with business to generate money, pales in comparison. Two Niner Lima had always interrupted that tiring routine and managed to dispel my doldrums.

I know it's natural to feel some deflation after such prolonged excitement and the novelty of the adventure. Mark Twain put it perfectly by his account of an epic journey I had long ago read.

At the end of twenty days by stagecoach from Missouri to the territory of Nevada, Twain wrote:

"It had been a fine pleasure trip; we had fed fat on wonders every day; we were now well accustomed to stage life, and very fond of it; so the idea of coming to a stand-still in a village was not agreeable, but on the contrary depressing."

So, it has become clear to me that yes, the Journey was about letting go of all that which had held me, truly "unbecoming" everything that had been me. And, touching every one of my dear friends, who touched me back, heart to heart, I have begun anew to be Me. I found Me and my heart, still so big, filled with love, and no longer poisoned by the disappointment and anger of my loss and circumstance, now behind me.

Capt. Bob. In the left seat. With that adventure in my heart. Open to discovery and new adventures. Filled with love and being loved. Touching others. Being touched.

After all, what else is there?

The Beatles are so right. Love is all you need.

So, yes, The Journey continues. Other adventures await.

Although life still has its travails, and I am facing the adversity of rebuilding my life and world, I know there will be days that won't be so good, and I will be tested again and again.

But, today, despite anything the Universe might throw at me, I will face those tests excitedly and joyfully to the end of my life Journey.

On to other Journeys.

With love.

With compassion.

With gratitude.

And every day, with the excitement of that little boy who, in an Eastern Airlines Constellation cockpit for the first time, was in awe of all that awaited.

ACKNOWLEDGEMENTS

This book and my writing could not have happened without a lot of teammates assisting me along the way.

First and foremost, to my editor, Charlene Keel, and publisher, Micky Hyman and Red Sky Presents: Your affirmation and direction tells my story and is testimony to your kind patience and support, without which I would have never crossed the finish line.

To Terri Cheney, New York Times' bestselling author of "Manic": For years you taught me well, and shared your guidance and counsel in getting a first book together.

To Enid Kries Morrone: You manage so well to keep me grounded, all the while supportive and encouraging to help me soar and keep my smile beaming.

To Phyllis Henrici: Without your devotion and honesty, being a best friend, I would never have prevailed.

To my sister, Wendy: I would be an orphan without any family to laugh at it all without your unflinching love and support.

To all those who shared their hearts and love for this wayward traveler along this Journey: Words are inadequate to express my deepest gratitude and eternal love for being there for me when all seemed lost and when I needed you the most.

To America: You are a grand and expansive land filled with so many wonderful people, united by our common history and shared values. Don't ever forget that and what it means to be a part of the greatest and most noble experiment man has ever launched. E Pluribus Unum.

And, lastly, to each of you who spent some time reading these pages and traveling along with Captain Bob and Two Niner Lima: Love yourselves and each other. And, of course, keep getting to tomorrow. That judge really could die!

Robert J. Young
Los Angeles, CA

Made in United States
North Haven, CT
09 December 2022

28387211R00222